# D. H. LAWRENCE
## New Worlds

# D. H. LAWRENCE

## New Worlds

Edited by
## Keith Cushman and
## Earl G. Ingersoll

Madison • Teaneck
Fairleigh Dickinson University Press
London: Associated University Presses

Associated University Presses
2010 Eastpark Boulevard
Cranbury, NJ 08512

Associated University Presses
Unit 304
The Chandlery
50 Westminster Bridge Road
London SE1 7QY, England

Associated University Presses
P.O. Box 338, Port Credit
Mississauga, Ontario
Canada L5G 4L8

The paper used in this publication meets the requirements of the American National Standard for Permanence of Paper for Printed Library Materials Z39.48-1984.

Library of Congress Cataloging-in-Publication Data

D.H. Lawrence : new worlds / edited by Keith Cushman and Earl G. Ingersoll.
    p.   cm.
Includes bibliographical references and index.
  ISBN 0-8386-3981-X (alk. paper)
  1. Lawrence, D. H. (David Herbert), 1885–1930—Criticism and interpretation.   2. Lawrence, D. H. (David Herbert), 1885–1930—Settings.   I. Cushman, Keith.   II. Ingersoll, Earl G., 1938–
  PR6023.A93Z623397   2003
  823'.912—dc21                                              2002154972

PRINTED IN THE UNITED STATES OF AMERICA

Ah no, I cannot tell you what it is, the new world.
I cannot tell you the mad, astounded rapture of its discovery.
—D. H. Lawrence, "New Heaven and Earth"

# Contents

8 CONTENTS

# Acknowledgments

ONE OF THE GREAT PLEASURES OF D. H. LAWRENCE STUDIES IS BEING part of the international community of D. H. Lawrence scholars. For excellent counsel and sustaining comradeship over the years we offer thanks to Art Bachrach, James C. Cowan, Gerald Doherty, David Ellis, Betsy Fox, Jill Franks, Lou Greiff, Takeo Iida, Dennis Jackson, Mark Kinkead-Weekes, Sheila Lahiri Choudhury, and Carol Siegel.

We appreciate the many hours Earl Yarington III spent in helping to prepare the manuscript. Thanks to Tim Barkley and the staff of Creative Services at the University of North Carolina at Greensboro. We also thank our wives, Deb and Mary, for their loving support—and patience—during the long process of transforming this book from an idea to a reality.

We thank Laurence Pollinger Limited as representatives of the Estate of Frieda Lawrence Ravagli for permission to quote passages from the Cambridge University Press editions of Lawrence's works and letters. In addition, we thank the following publishers for permission to quote passages from the following contemporary novels: From *Regeneration* by Pat Barker (copyright 1991 by Pat Barker), used by permission of Dutton Signet, a division of Penguin Putnam Inc. and by permission of Penguin UK Ltd.; from *Babel Tower* / *The Shadow of the Sun* / *Still Life* / *The Virgin in the Garden* by A. S. Byatt, published by Chatto & Windus, reprinted by permission of The Random House Group, Ltd.; from *Zennor in Darkness* by Helen Dunmore, published by Penguin UK Ltd. and A. P. Watt Ltd. We thank Steve Turner Gallery, Beverly Hills, for permission to reproduce paintings and drawings by Knud Merrild, including the dust jacket image.

The essays by Laurie McCollum and Peter Preston appeared in radically different versions in *Etudes lawrenciennes*. The essay by John Worthen appeared in a radically different version in *The Journal of the D. H. Lawrence Society* (Eastwood). We thank the editors of these journals for permission to publish these essays in revised form.

# Abbreviations for
# Works of D. H. Lawrence

Note: *DHLR* refers to the *D. H. Lawrence Review* (1968–  ).

| | |
|---|---|
| *A* | *Apocalypse and the Writings on Revelation.* Edited by Mara Kalnins. Cambridge: Cambridge University Press, 1979. |
| *Amores* | *Amores.* London: Duckworth, 1916. |
| *AR* | *Aaron's Rod.* Edited by Mara Kalnins. Cambridge: Cambridge University Press, 1988. |
| *BB* | *The Boy in the Bush.* With M. L. Skinner. Edited by Paul Eggert. Cambridge: Cambridge University Press, 1990. |
| *EmyE* | *England, My England and Other Stories.* Edited by Bruce Steele. Cambridge: Cambridge University Press, 1990. |
| *Fox* | *The Fox, The Captain's Doll, The Ladybird.* Edited by Dieter Mehl. Cambridge: Cambridge University Press, 1992. |
| *FSLC* | *The First and Second Lady Chatterley Novels.* Edited by Dieter Mehl and Christa Jansohn. Cambridge: Cambridge University Press, 1999. |
| *FU* | *Fantasia of the Unconscious* and *Psychoanalysis and the Unconscious.* New York: Viking, 1960. |
| *FWL* | *The First "Women in Love."* Edited by John Worthen and Lindeth Vasey. Cambridge: Cambridge University Press, 1998. |
| *Hardy* | *Study of Thomas Hardy and Other Essays.* Edited by Bruce Steele. Cambridge: Cambridge University Press, 1985. |
| *K* | *Kangaroo.* Edited by Bruce Steele. Cambridge: Cambridge University Press, 1994. |
| *L* i. | *The Letters of D. H. Lawrence: Volume 1: Septem-* |

|  |  |
|---|---|
| | *ber 1901–May 1913.* Edited by James T. Boulton. Cambridge: Cambridge University Press, 1979. |
| *L* ii. | *The Letters of D. H. Lawrence: Volume 2: June 1913–October 1916.* Edited by George J. Zytaruk and James T. Boulton. Cambridge: Cambridge University Press, 1981. |
| *L* iii. | *The Letters of D. H. Lawrence: Volume 3: October 1916–June 1921.* Edited by James T. Boulton. and Andrew Robertson. Cambridge: Cambridge University Press, 1984. |
| *L* iv. | *The Letters of D. H. Lawrence: Volume 4: June 1921–March 1924.* Edited by Warren Roberts, James T. Boulton, and Elizabeth Mansfield. Cambridge: Cambridge University Press, 1987. |
| *L* v. | *The Letters of D. H. Lawrence: Volume 5: March 1924–March 1927.* Edited by James T. Boulton and Lindeth Vasey. Cambridge: Cambridge University Press, 1989. |
| *L* vi. | *The Letters of D. H. Lawrence: Volume 6: March 1927–November 1928.* Edited by James T. Boulton and Margaret H. Boulton with Gerald Lacy. Cambridge: Cambridge University Press, 1991. |
| *L* vii. | *The Letters of D. H. Lawrence: Volume 7: November 1928–February 1930.* Edited by Keith Sagar and James T. Boulton. Cambridge: Cambridge University Press, 1993. |
| *LCL* | *Lady Chatterley's Lover* and *A Propos of "Lady Chatterley's Lover."* Edited by Michael Squires. Cambridge: Cambridge University Press, 1993. |
| *MEH* | *Movements in European History.* Edited by Philip Crumpton. Cambridge: Cambridge University Press, 1989. |
| *MM* | *Mornings in Mexico.* London: Secker, 1927. |
| *MMM* | *D. H. Lawrence: Memoir of Maurice Magnus.* Edited by Keith Cushman. Santa Rosa, Calif.: Black Sparrow Press, 1987. |
| *MN* | *Mr Noon.* Edited by Lindeth Vasey. Cambridge: Cambridge University Press, 1984. |
| *New Mexico* | *D. H. Lawrence and New Mexico.* Edited by Keith Sagar. Salt Lake City: Peregrine Smith, 1982. |
| *P* | *Phoenix: The Posthumous Papers of D. H. Law-* |

*rence.* Edited by Edward D. McDonald. London: Heinemann, 1936.

*P II*  *Phoenix II: Uncollected, Unpublished, and Other Prose Works by D. H. Lawrence.* Edited by Warren Roberts and Harry T. Moore. New York: Viking Press, 1968.

*Plays*  *Plays.* Edited by Hans-Wilhelm Schwarze and John Worthen. Cambridge: Cambridge University Press, 1999.

*PO*  *The Prussian Officer and Other Stories.* Edited by John Worthen. Cambridge: Cambridge University Press, 1983.

*Poems*  *The Complete Poems of D. H. Lawrence.* Edited by Vivian de Sola Pinto and F. Warren Roberts. New York: Penguin Books, 1977.

*PS*  *The Plumed Serpent.* Edited by L. D. Clark. Cambridge: Cambridge University Press, 1987.

*Q*  *Quetzalcoatl: The Early Version of "The Plumed Serpent."* Edited by Louis L. Martz. Redding Ridge, Conn.: Black Swan Books, 1995.

*R*  *The Rainbow.* Edited by Mark Kinkead-Weekes. Cambridge: Cambridge University Press, 1989.

*RDP*  *Reflections on the Death of a Porcupine and Other Essays.* Edited by Michael Herbert. Cambridge: Cambridge University Press, 1988.

*SCAL*  *Studies in Classic American Literature.* New York: Viking, 1964.

*SEP*  *Sketches of Etruscan Places and Other Italian Essays.* Edited by Simonetta de Filippis. Cambridge: Cambridge University Press, 1992.

*SL*  *Sons and Lovers.* Edited by Helen Baron and Carl Baron. Cambridge: Cambridge University Press, 1992.

*SL* fac.  *Sons and Lovers: A Facsimile of the Manuscript.* Edited by Mark Schorer. Berkeley: University of California Press, 1977.

*SS*  *Sea and Sardinia.* Edited by Mara Kalnins. Cambridge: Cambridge University Press, 1997.

*TI*  *Twilight in Italy and Other Essays.* Edited by Paul Eggert. Cambridge: Cambridge University Press, 1994.

TSM     *The Symbolic Meaning: The Uncollected Versions of "Studies in Classic American Literature."* Edited by Armin Arnold. Arundel, U.K.: Centaur, 1962.

VG      *The Virgin and the Gipsy.* New York: Vintage, 1992.

WL      *Women in Love.* Edited by David Farmer, Lindeth Vasey, and John Worthen. Cambridge: Cambridge University Press, 1987.

WP      *The White Peacock.* Edited by Andrew Robertson. Cambridge: Cambridge University Press, 1983.

WWRA    *The Woman Who Rode Away and Other Stories.* Edited by Dieter Mehl and Christa Jansohn. Cambridge: Cambridge University Press, 1995.

# Introduction

## Keith Cushman and Earl G. Ingersoll

In DECEMBER 1924 THE ITALIAN CRITIC CARLO LINATI PUBLISHED AN essay on D. H. Lawrence entitled "Un esploratore di uomini" ["An explorer of men"] in *Corriere della Sera*, the newspaper that Lawrence once considered "about the best . . . in Europe" (*L* v. 90). In his essay Linati sees Lawrence as a writer whose works combine great imaginative intensity with insufficiently controlled theme and structure. The issue of *Corriere della Sera* with Linati's essay "wandered in" (*L*. v. 200) to Lawrence in Oaxaca on 22 January 1925. The vigorous, colorful—and little-known—letter that Lawrence immediately wrote Linati is one of Lawrence's most fascinating and appealing descriptions of his own art.

Lawrence found Linati's article extremely stimulating, all the more so because it criticized his writings for precisely those qualities that Lawrence believed were their most distinctive and important. Linati was curiously perceptive. He had somehow grasped the essence of Lawrence's art without knowing what to make of it. The formalist assumptions Linati brought to bear were not useful. He was eager to "tidy [Lawrence] up" in "a world so anxious for outside tidiness." But in Lawrence's opinion, books were not "toys, nicely built up of observations and sensations, all finished and complete." He didn't "care a button for neat works of art." He couldn't "bear art that you can walk round and admire" (*L* v. 200–201). Books that are too neat and tidy run the risk of lifelessness.

Lawrence responded to Linati's further criticism that he was too intensely engaged in his writings by insisting that the author should *not* be like someone in a theater audience, sitting high above the stage and "benignly look[ing] down on the foibles, follies, and frenzies of so-called fellow-men." Novels are not "little theatres where the reader sits aloft and watches . . . and sighs, commiserates, condones and smiles." Linati should "stick to

15

Synge, Anatole France, Sophocles'' if he wants to read that sort of detached writer. But if you are looking for Lawrence, you will find him ''in among the crowd, kicking their shins or cheering them on to some mischief or merriment.'' Lawrence ringingly concludes that ''whoever reads me will be in the thick of the scrimmage, and if he doesn't like it – if he wants a safe seat in the audience – let him read somebody else'' (*L* v. 201). The artist must passionately engage his audience and rouse it out of the safety of aesthetic detachment. The artist's goal is to involve his reader, to shake him out of his assumptions, even if it means kicking him in the shins. Literature must be challenging, exciting, even dangerous. Don't read Lawrence unless you want to be ''in the thick of the scrimmage.''

It's now well over a century since Lawrence's birth in 1885, almost 75 years since his early death in 1930. In an era that is wary of literary canons, he remains part of the big parade of ''major British authors,'' safely a historical figure. He has his 47 pages in the latest edition of the *Norton Anthology of English Literature* (two stories, nine poems, and an essay). The 1996 *Oxford Companion to Twentieth-Century Literature in English* devotes more space to Lawrence than to any other writer (Stringer 379–81). Lawrence would be pleased that his writings have survived (what ever happened to the Nobel Laureate John Galsworthy?—or for that matter, the other Nobel Laureate Anatole France?). Lawrence's many books are all in print, and he is read. There is vindication in that.

But surely this great outsider, nay-sayer, and shin-kicker would also be somewhat amused if he could know what an important cultural figure he remains, even in these increasingly post-literary times. He would have mixed feelings about being part of that big parade, even if he spent part of his lifetime striving to join it. From 1915, the time of *The Rainbow,* onward, he was not accustomed to being accepted. What would Lawrence make of the thriving D. H. Lawrence Societies in the United States, England, Australia, Japan, and Korea and the Lawrence conferences that attract scholars and Lawrence fans from all over the world? In his native Eastwood, Lawrence plays a significant, even lucrative role in the British ''heritage industry.'' As an adolescent he told his girlfriend Jessie Chambers (the prototype of Miriam in *Sons and Lovers*) that people would call him ''a fool'' for wanting to become a poet: "A collier's son a poet!" (Chambers 57). The letters and writings of the collier's son are now enshrined in the imposing, grandly scholarly 35 volumes (with more to come) of the Cambridge Edition of the Letters and Works of D. H. Lawrence. The Cambridge Edition collects and annotates over 5,600 of Lawrence's letters (while Lawrence threw out the thousands of letters he received, among them his letters from Linati). The Cambridge Edition even includes early, unpublished versions of both *Women in Love* and *Lady Chatterley's Lover*, and an early version of *Sons and Lovers* will also appear.

Although Lawrence would be struck by the worldly success he has enjoyed after his death, his pleasure in the fact that he is still read would be rivaled by the fact that he has remained controversial. He recognized that a serious, often confrontational writer could not expect to be too successful in his own lifetime, for most readers would prefer not to be "in the thick of the scrimmage," putting their shins at risk. It's not an entirely bad thing that to many readers in the past quarter of a century, Lawrence, the one-time healer and priest of love, became Lawrence the misogynist and imperialist, a somewhat suspect figure within the politically correct academy. And as Peter Preston demonstrates in his essay on Lawrence in recent fiction that leads off the collection, Lawrence has remained—despite the shifts in his reputation over the years—a crucial presence in the fiction of contemporary British novelists. He seems to be especially present in the novels of female writers (notably Pat Barker and A. S. Byatt).

But a serious writer who was too widely accepted would somehow not be doing his job. Lawrence knew all along that the forceful, challenging response to life articulated in his novels, stories, poems, and other writings would be unsettling to his readers. And after all, if a reader disagreed with him, so much the better. As he explained in his *Memoir of Maurice Magnus*, "it is terrible to be agreed with. . . . All that one says, and means, turns to nothing" (*MMM* 54).

The contributors to *D. H. Lawrence: New Worlds*—whose books form a basic library of contemporary interpretations of Lawrence—join a growing critical consensus that the beginning of the twenty-first century offers an opportunity for reappraisal of the major modernist writers. Such a reconsideration is especially pertinent for Lawrence, for in recent years, as noted above, political voices within the academy have called his achievement into question. The diversity of approaches in the fourteen essays of *D. H. Lawrence: New Worlds* demonstrates how Lawrence studies have profited from the new methodologies of the last two decades. The collection also underscores the internationalization of Lawrence studies, for it includes essays by scholars from the United States, Canada, Britain, France, Israel, and Japan.

*D. H. Lawrence: New Worlds* is not a survey. But after the first three strikingly diverse essays that open the collection and Michael Squires's unusual overview of Lawrence's fiction, the book moves chronologically across the arc of Lawrence's career. Along the way, *D. H. Lawrence: New Worlds* includes studies of four of the major novels: *Sons and Lovers*, *Women in Love*, *The Plumed Serpent*, and *Lady Chatterley's Lover*. It also features essays on *Kangaroo* (the "Australian" novel) and *Quetzalcoatl* (the earlier version of *The Plumed Serpent*, published for the first time only in 1995). Other essays engage with Lawrence's poetry, plays, and travel writing. John Worthen, for example, offers a stunning new perspective on the rhapsodic, pseudo-biblical play *David*, locating the play among Lawrence's other Southwestern writings. Judith Ruderman's essay draws on the methodology of cultural studies to explore Lawrence's place in the debates regarding "Englishness" and "Jewishness" in his time. (Lawrence's attitude toward the Jews, though culture-bound, won't win him new admirers.) Keith Cushman's essay on Lawrence's relationship with the Danish painter Knud Merrild features photographs—and interpretations—of a number of Merrild's portrait sketches of Lawrence that have never before been reproduced. (Both Peter Preston and Cushman analyze representations of Lawrence.) The book does not aim for comprehensiveness, but it nevertheless does justice to Lawrence's prolific, multifarious career.

The title of the collection focuses attention on the new worlds Lawrence explored in Australia, Mexico, and New Mexico as a self-imposed exile from Europe and Euro-centered culture. The Lawrence texts in this cluster include *Kangaroo*, "The Woman Who Rode Away," *Quetzalcoatl*, *The Plumed Serpent*, *David*, and "Altitude" (an unfinished play). Essays on this segment of Lawrence's literary career are particularly valuable because of the customary emphasis on the works of the first half of his career and because several of these texts have been highly contested sites in Lawrence studies.

Keith Cushman and John Worthen offer fresh biographical perspectives on Lawrence's sojourns in Taos, New Mexico. Laurie McCollum's new reading of "The Woman Who Rode Away" (the most controversial of Lawrence's stories) draws on the theories of anthropologist René Girard to recuperate the narrative as an expression of sacrifice. The collection also offers two essays on *The Plumed Serpent*, a novel too often dismissed as misogynist or proto-fascist. One is by Virginia Hyde, a well-established Lawrence scholar, and the other is by Carrie Rohman, a scholar new to Lawrence studies. Hyde presents a new reading of *The Plumed Serpent* in the context of post-colonialism and multiculturalism. Making use of *Quetzalcoatl*, she rereads *The Plumed Serpent* as a product of a writer unique in his time for being able to "imagine under the skin" of colonized and post-colonial cultures. Hyde also demonstrates some surprising affinities between *The Plumed Serpent* and *Etruscan Places*. Rohman, in her decontructive approach to the same novel, focuses on the human/animal binary as a central feature of the contemporary discourse on primitivism, produced by theorists such as Jacques Derrida and Marianna Torgovnick. Subverting the traditional notion of the human as different from the animal/other, Rohman sees the novel as "troubling the distinction between human and animal consciousness" in ways which earlier readings have ignored.

Two essays in the collection reflect the fact that Lawrence's worlds were inner as well as geographical. In his psychoanalytic approach, Gavriel Reisner breaks new ground by struggling against almost a century of Freudian readings of *Sons and Lovers* to demonstrate how a Lacanian perspective opens up new insights into the relationship between Paul Morel and his mother. Holly Laird reads *Amores* (1916), Lawrence's second book of poetry, as a record of his inner life as he "fought . . . with the several faces of death in life: with deadening conventionality, with exhausting passion, with wasting sickness, with wearying financial impecunity, and with depleting love fights." In the bargain Laird recovers the rarely discussed *Amores* as an important work in the Lawrence canon.

The mention of such names as Girard, Derrida, and Lacan and of such methodologies as cultural studies and post-colonialism

suggests yet another way that *D. H. Lawrence: New Worlds* high-
lights what is "new" in the study of Lawrence. Unlike the fiction
of his contemporaries James Joyce and Virginia Woolf, Lawrence's writing has been slow to benefit from the new critical
methodologies that have revitalized literary scholarship. But the
essays collected here demonstrate that even though "theory"
may have come late to Lawrence studies, it is here to stay, illumi-
nating texts both familiar and unfamiliar.

Michael Squires's essay on the "calculus of change" in Lawrence constructs a challenging new theoretical paradigm for understanding Lawrence's evolution as a novelist and short story
writer. Drawing on an extensive variety of published and unpublished texts, from early short stories through *Lady Chatterley's
Lover*, Squires offers an original, comprehensive reading of the
phases of Lawrence's career as a fiction writer. Holly Laird's
essay on *Amores* draws on the ideas of French theorist and fiction
writer Georges Bataille. The theorizing in tropology of Roman Jakobson, Jacques Lacan, and Paul Ricoeur allows Kyoko Kay
Kondo to read *Women in Love* as a lesson in the empowering
agency of metaphor for Rupert Birkin, the central character, and
by implication for the reader as well. Jack Stewart, who shares
Kondo's interest in tropology, focuses on metonymy as the principle of contingency to provide an insightful entry into Lawrence's
travel writings. Like Stewart, Neil Roberts is interested in contingency, which he reads as an element of the travel writing that
Lawrence translated into such novels as *Kangaroo*, especially as
that novel again moves Lawrence studies into a post-colonial context. Ginette Katz-Roy's deconstruction of the mythological underpinnings of *Lady Chatterley's Lover* further reveals the value
of applying "theory" to Lawrence texts.

The essays of *D. H. Lawrence: New Worlds* present a vital, complex, multi-faceted, original, provocative Lawrence. Unfortunately, as Thomas L. Jeffers has put it, "the fog of sex wars has
obscured [Lawrence's] candescent many-sidedness" (204). That
many-sidedness is on vivid display in this collection. Here is Lawrence the problematic Englishman, the expressive poet, the psy-
chologically tangled son, the brilliant travel writer. Here is
Lawrence the creative anthropologist, the multiculturalist before
his time, the mythmaker, the friend and inspiration of painters.
These essays place Lawrence where he belongs: in the thick of the

scrimmage. And they invite the student of modernism to join the exhilarating fray.

## WORKS CITED

Chambers, Jessie. *D. H. Lawrence: A Personal Record by E. T.* London: Jonathan Cape, 1935.

Jeffers, Thomas L. "Lawrence, *Sons and Lovers*, and the End of Sex." *Hudson Review* 52 (1999): 191–204.

Stringer, Jenny, ed. *The Oxford Companion to Twentieth-Century Literature in English.* New York: Oxford University Press, 1996.

# D. H. LAWRENCE
New Worlds

# "I am in a Novel": Lawrence in Recent British Fiction

Peter Preston

## I

ON 28 OCTOBER 1928, LAWRENCE WROTE TO ALDOUS HUXLEY ABOUT his new novel, *Point Counter Point*, published earlier that year:

> I do think you've shown the truth, perhaps the last truth, about you and your generation, with really fine courage. It seems to me it would take ten times the courage to write *P. Counter P.* than it took to write *Lady C. . . . .* I do think that art has to reveal the palpitating moment or the state of man as it is. And I think you do that, terribly. (*L* vi. 600)

Although he admired the truthful picture the novel drew of Huxley's generation, Lawrence despaired at the book's message, and its drive towards "inertia and final atrophy of the feelings" (*L* vi. 600). He also objected to some of the characters, in particular Rampion, whom he describes as "the most boring character in the book – a gas-bag" (*L* vi. 601). Rampion, of course, is a portrait of Lawrence himself, as he both acknowledged and denied in a letter to William Gerhardie on 14 November: "No, I refused to be Rampioned. I am not responsible" (*L* vi. 617).

His best-known reaction to Huxley's novel, however, can be found in one of the *Pansies* poems, entitled "I am in a Novel"; it is part of a group written in the early days of December 1928:

> I read a novel by a friend of mine
> in which one of the characters was me,
> the novel it sure was mighty fine
> but the funniest thing that could be
>
> was me, or what was supposed for me,
> for I had to recognise

25

a few of the touches, like a low-born jake,
but the rest was a real surprise.

. . . . . . . . . . .

My Lord! a man's friends' ideas of him
would stock a menagerie
with a marvelous outfit! How did Archie see
such a funny pup in me?

*Poems* 489

In spite of Lawrence's objections, his friends frequently "Rampioned" him and managed to create many beasts for the Lawrence menagerie. He is "in" *Point Counter Point* in the same sense as he is "in" Gilbert Cannan's *Mendel* (1916), Helen Corke's *Neutral Ground* (1933), or H. D.'s *Bid Me to Live* (drafted in 1927 but only published, in a heavily revised version, in 1960).[1] In these novels he appears not under his real name, but in thinly fictionalized versions, although it could be argued that the density of the fictionalization varies according to who is reading the novels.[2] Members of those circles in which Lawrence and Cannan, Helen Corke, H. D., and Huxley moved would presumably have no difficulty in identifying these fictional Lawrences; others on the periphery of these circles might also be able to make the identification, as might the well-informed general reader, who could at least recognize a Lawrentian type. Nonetheless, these are in effect *romans à clef*, whose full resonances may only be appreciated by those in possession of the key. They have some characteristics in common with what Jeffrey Meyers calls a literary genre of the 1930s—the Lawrence memoir—which constructs a version of Lawrence and the memoirist's relationship with him which presents the author in a chosen light: as essential support or confidante, as a victorious antagonist, as a putative lover.[3] "Lawrence" becomes an infinitely variable and vigorously contested figure, as the memoirists strive to claim a deeper understanding, a fuller intimacy, or a more incontrovertible superiority.[4] And no doubt the memoirists' anxiety to state their case led them to include passages which are as fictive, if not as fictional, as anything to be found in *Mendel, Point Counter Point*, or *Bid Me to Live*. This essay, however, is about how Lawrence is "in" recent fiction in rather different ways.

## II

Consider the following quotations from recent novels:

It gave Ravelstein the greatest satisfaction to have the inside dope. Like the child in the Lawrence poem sitting under a "great black piano appassionato," "in the boom of the tingling strings," while the child's mother plays. (Bellow 58)

"Hywl, you may find this fig *confiture* especially apt with that brioche. Best use for figs, in my view, especially since D. H. Lawrence's embarrassing comparison with female genitalia—though you honeymooners won't want to hear all this smutty talk from an old codger such as myself. . . ." (Lanchester 188)

A blue light that was warm, rather than clear, with a special frequency. *Pass me a gentian. Give me a torch.* Gamini wished to be bathed in it. (Ondaatje 119)

The first of these quotations is taken from Saul Bellow's *Ravelstein*, published in 2000. Ravelstein is a teacher of political science who revels in the fact that his former pupils are in positions of power and influence in government and can thus give him "the inside dope." The poem's sense of closeness and intimacy, of being one with the piano (and therefore with the mother) is thus evoked to define Ravelstein's love of being an insider in politics. Bellow (or Chick, his narrator) misremembers Lawrence's poem, however, and thus confuses its time scales. The poet as child certainly experiences "the boom of the tingling strings" while sitting under his mother's piano, but "the great black piano appassionato" is the instrument he hears in the poem's present, whose sound takes him "back down the vista of years" to the earlier memory. In spite of this misremembering, however, the allusion is used very naturally, as if readers will have little difficulty in understanding its application to Ravelstein's situation.

The second quotation, from John Lanchester's novel *The Debt to Pleasure*, published in 1996, is apparently more straightforward. The narrator, Tarquin, is entertaining his brother Hywl and his new wife on their honeymoon. These comments on Lawrence's poem "Figs" are entirely in character with mischievous and sly Tarquin, and the sexual element he refers to is certainly present in Lawrence's poem: "it stands for the female part; the fig-fruit: / The fissure, the yoni, / The wonderful moist conductivity towards the centre" (*Poems* 282). But if we think about the ways in which Lawrence has been culturally transmitted over the past thirty years, Tarquin's "reading" of "Figs" may have as much to do with Alan Bates's virtuoso rendering of the poem, as a speech by Birkin, in Ken Russell's 1970 film of *Women in Love*. Furthermore, Tarquin himself, although something of a voyeur and gourmand of the emotions, is ambivalent about sex, so his reference to Lawrence's "embarrassing comparison" is a means of both confessing and distancing himself from his prurient interest in the honeymooners.

The final quotation is from Michael Ondaatje's novel *Anil's Ghost*, also published in 2000. It is a clear reference to Lawrence's late poem "Bavarian Gentians": "Reach me a gentian, give me a torch" (*Poems* 697), a torch whose blue flame will light the poet on his journey to the underworld. Lawrence's words are appropriate to the novel's strong motif of death, and especially applicable to Gamini, who has gone beyond any wish to preserve his own life in his determination to care for the victims of political atrocities in the hell of Sri Lanka, where Ondaatje's book is set. What is striking here is that although Ondaatje, by printing them in italics, makes it clear that these words are a quotation, he makes no attempt to identify their source. He uses many other quotations and identifies them either in context or on his acknowledgments page at the end of the novel, from which Lawrence is absent. "Bavarian Gentians" is a frequently anthologized poem, but it lacks the kind of currency enjoyed by, say, "Snake" or "Piano": Ondaatje here relies on readers having a quite extensive knowledge of Lawrence's work, and being able both to recognize the quotation and to locate it in a poem written by someone anticipating his own death.

These may seem like quite small examples—passing mentions of Lawrence, which, although they are used to define or intensify significant local moments, are not germane to the overall structure and themes of the novels in which they appear. But even such passing allusions can tell us a good deal about the assumed cultural scope of readers and the kinds of associations authors may hope to evoke. Or to put it another way, we need to consider the kinds of meanings readers may construct from such allusions. Over the past few years I have become very conscious of the frequency with which Lawrence is mentioned or referred to in recent British fiction. My current list of such references since 1960 runs to seventy-five titles, including books by such well-known writers as Martin Amis, Malcolm Bradbury, Angela Carter, Lawrence Durrell, John Fowles, Doris Lessing, David Lodge, Ian McEwan, Alan Sillitoe, David Storey, and Jeanette Winterson. Many of the references are as brief as those I have already quoted and may be used simply as period "color," as Philip Larkin does in his poem "Annus Mirabilis": "Sexual intercourse began / In nineteen sixty-three / (Which was rather late for me)— / Between the end of the *Chatterley* ban / And the Beatles' first LP" (Larkin 34). Phrases like a "Lawrentian woman" or a "Lawrentian man" may be produced, like cultural counters, as indicators of unconventionality or sensuality. Reading Lawrence may be seen either as part of a standard literary education or as a step towards liberation from that education. In A. Alvarez's introduction to his ground-breaking 1962 anthology, *The New Poetry*, Lawrence is seen as a writer who took British poetry "Beyond the Gentility Principle."[5] He may be evoked in regional, class, or occupational contexts as offering some kind of example for writing about the Midlands, the working class, or the mining industry. His life and literary career may be used as paradigms of class and educational mobility, of the exiled artist, of sexual freedom, or the healing of the division between mind and body, or of proto-Fascism, misogyny, and male supremacism.

These uses of Lawrence are inseparable from the larger story of the fluctuations in his reputation since 1960, both in the academy and among a wider readership.[6] The upholder of true "healthy" values, constructed and celebrated by Leavis, paved the way for the working-class hero of the 1950s and 1960s, who was succeeded by the putative liberation guru and the priest of love of the 1970s, who was in turn rapidly toppled by a feminist and left-wing backlash.[7] In the last three decades, although Lawrence has continued to be taught in both schools and universities in Britain, his dominant position in the canon has been fundamentally challenged, as that canon has been both extended and reshaped, so that, say, Virginia Woolf and James Joyce are more likely to be discussed as exemplary writers. In America, he has been even more vigorously anathematized.

In a recent article in *TriQuarterly* Gary Adelman published the results of his survey of a group of English and American writers on what Lawrence means to them. He decided to undertake this survey after teaching Lawrence to an undergraduate group who became increasingly antagonistic as the course went on. Adelman already knew that none of his colleagues taught Lawrence, apart from the occasional short story, regarding him at best as "a crude historical curiosity" (Adelman 509). Nonetheless, he was taken aback by the vehemence of his students' attacks on Lawrence and sent a selection of their comments to 110 writers, mostly novelists, of whom forty-four responded. In his accompanying letter Adelman wrote that for some time "I have felt in my bones that [Lawrence] has 'disappeared' as a point of reference for writers" (513–14). Most of his respondents confirm this impression and cite a number of reasons for Lawrence's disappearance. Terry Eagleton sees him as "pathologically sexist" (524), while A. S. Byatt regards him as having suffered from the effects of literary gender politics and a loss of the ability to read subtly and within a historical context. Many wish to separate Lawrence's "message" from his qualities as an artist, while others see him as the wrong writer for his time: as Martin Amis puts it, he is "simply too grandiose for the modern era" (516). Margaret Drabble makes a similar point in arguing that "the mood of the 80s and 90s has been so hard-edged, so determinist-defeatist in some ways, so merciless in other and above all cynical—a world in which DHL does not fit" (528). Helen Dunmore, attempting to explain why Lawrence's reputation has gone into such a decline among the younger generation, remarks that he is "too complex, too contradictory, too ambitious for current student taste" (530).

In spite of this response to Adelman's survey, which appears to confirm Lawrence's unpopularity with both readers and writers, Lawrence continues, as I have already suggested, to have an impact on contemporary British fiction. This is not simply a matter of "influence." I am not talking about a "school of Lawrence"; if I were to do so I could certainly extend my reading list considerably. This essay is largely about "Lawrence" as—and I use the term advisedly—a signifier, one whose relationship to its referent is extraordinarily arbitrary and labile, because that referent is under constant construction and reconstruction, resulting in versions of Lawrence which are all true—and all false. As Lawrence says in his 1925 essay, "Morality and the Novel," "Everything is true in its own time, place, circumstance, and untrue outside of its own place, time, circumstance" (*Hardy* 172).

One final general point. The kinds of passing allusions to Lawrence that I have quoted are much more likely to be employed by men than women writers: when he is present in the work of the latter it is usually as part of a much more sustained engagement with his work.[8] Given the extent to which the attack on his reputation in the academy has been led by feminist scholars, this may seem surprising, and I shall return to the question in my conclusion. It is, however, because of the presence of this sustained engagement with Lawrence—a kind of debate with his literary practice, his imagined personality, or the dangerous allure of his presumed "beliefs"—that I have chosen in this essay to concentrate on novels by women authors. These books illustrate some of the range and variety of possible engagements: in Pat Barker, an appropriation and reworking of ideas and even passages from *Sons and Lovers*; in Helen Dunmore, the appearance of Lawrence as a major character; and in A. S. Byatt, his presence as a constant narrative antagonist, alternately admired and rejected.

## III

Lawrence is almost never mentioned in Pat Barker's novels, and she alludes only once to one of his characters, yet he has a strong presence in her work.[9] Michael Ross has discussed the relationship between the two writers in terms of creative intertextuality. Barker's own view of Lawrence appears to be unequivocally hostile, and she claims that she found Lawrence's representations of working-class life unhelpful: "I felt that the experience of the women was so minimized in [his] work, and to some extent distorted, that to me there was no way into it" (quoted by Ross 52). Nonetheless, Lawrence had, in Ross's words, "insidiously found his way into Barker's novels," to such an extent that the echoes of his work betray a "well-nigh obsessive preoccupation" with Lawrence and suggest "a profound yet incompletely realized engagement with him" (52, 53, 58). The verbal, situational, and thematic echoes of Lawrence are obviously there, and the ways in which Barker *uses* them exemplify what Carol Siegel calls a "revisionary response which is friendly to the precursor and enabling to the inheritor" (Siegel 165). Yet, as Ross points out, such re-visioning is not straightforward; intertextuality is a two-way relationship, and the changed emphases or reconfigurations of the more recent text may highlight in a new way elements of its precursor. Paradoxically, if the overt relationship is hostile, the later text may remind us of what is actually present in its intertext. Thus, Barker may unconsciously be reacting to what Ross describes as "a more nuanced sensitivity to feminist issues than [Lawrence] is popularly given credit for" (Ross 58).

Most of Ross's examples are taken from Barker's earlier novels, but I will focus on an episode in *Regeneration* (1991), the first novel in a trilogy about the 1914–18 war completed by *The Eye in the Door* (1993) and *The Ghost Road* (1995). In all three novels, *Sons and Lovers* is the Lawrence novel most often alluded to. The allusions cluster around the fictional Billy Prior, a battle-traumatized working-class officer in the care of the psychologist W. H. Rivers, a historical figure who pioneered the study and treatment of war neuroses. Class is a major issue in the trilogy, its codes, constraints, and distinctions affecting the characters at every level—social, sexual, and medical—and Prior is set against Rivers, a member of the intellectual elite. Billy Prior's parents visit him in hospital and, separately, ask to speak to Rivers. Mr. Prior and Rivers discuss Billy's pre-War job as a clerk:

> "Twenty years wearing the arse of your breeches out and then, if you're a good boy and lick all the right places, you get to be supervisor and then you sit on a bigger stool and watch other people wear their breeches out. Didn't suit our Billy. He's ambitious, you know. . . . His mam drilled that into him. Schooled him in it. She was *determined* he was going to get on."
>
> Rather unexpectedly, Rivers found himself wanting to leap to Billy Prior's defence. "She seems to have succeeded."
>
> Mr Prior snorted. "She's made a stool-arsed jack on him, if that's what you mean."
>
> "You make it sound as if you had no say."
>
> "I didn't. . . ." (*Regeneration* 56)

This is strongly reminiscent of Morel's reaction to the news that his son William has a job as a Co-op clerk: " 'What dost want ter ma'e a stool-harsed Jack on 'im for?' said Morel. 'All he'll do is to wear his britches behind out an' earn nowt' "; to which Mrs. Morel replies, " 'He is *not* going in the pit . . . and there's an end of it' " (*SL* 70). The echoes are audible enough, but Lawrence dramatizes a conflict between husband and wife which in Barker is reported and can at this stage be seen entirely from the husband's point of view. Mr. Prior is less concerned than Morel that

Billy's job has distanced him from his father, and Barker's re-visioning of the scene brings into focus Morel's anxiety on this score: he twice uses the phrase "i' th' pit wi' me" and also says "It wor good enough for me, but it's non good enough for 'im" (70). This is emphasized by Mrs. Morel's response, echoed in Barker, stressing the primary role of mothers in determining their sons' social fate. Nonetheless, in spite of his sense of powerlessness in determining Billy's future, Mr. Prior is given the opportunity to offer his own uninterrupted narrative of events. He does so in near standard English (he uses two or three dialect words, but the narrative is silent about his accent) and he is articulate about Billy's character and his own role in the family. In the Lawrence scene, as is so often true, the difference in articulation between Mr. and Mrs. Morel is very marked, while the point at which the conversation breaks off leaves Mrs. Morel with the last word in the argument.

The fact that Rivers hears Mr. Prior's account *before* he sees Billy's mother may be a conscious re-visioning of the situation in *Sons and Lovers*, in which many readers have noted a privileging of the mother's viewpoint. That reading of *Sons and Lovers* can be challenged, of course: Mr. Morel's articulateness is different from his wife's, but Lawrence's sensitivity to the power of dialect gives it its own force. Furthermore, the sheer frequency of Mrs. Morel's "victories" (and their clear endorsement by the narrative voice), and the way in which the family's concerted hostility demonizes and isolates Mr. Morel, become the means by which the novel offers the material for another way of seeing him. Barker takes this process further, allowing Mr. Prior articulation on the same terms as his wife, and giving him a kind of poise and dignity that many readers believe is progressively denied to Morel.

On first meeting Mrs. Prior, Rivers notes her "carefully genteel voice," a comment which makes more telling the text's silence on Mr. Prior's mode of speech. Her account of Billy's career and his relationship with his father shows a similar if differently stressed understanding of the ambivalent situation in which Billy finds himself:

> "He's never been able to accept that Billy was different. And I think there might have been a bit of jealousy as well, because he has, he's had a hard life. I don't deny that. A lot harder than it need have been, because *his* mother sent him to work when he was *ten*. . . ."

"Would you say Billy and his father were close?"

"*No!* And yet, you see, the funny thing is our Billy's . . ." She sought for a way of erasing the tell-tale "our" from the sentence and, not finding one, gave a little deprecatory laugh. "All for 'the common people,' as he calls them. I said, 'You mean your father?' She laughed again. 'Oh, no, he didn't mean his father.' I said, 'But you know nothing about the common people. You've had nothing to do with them.' Do you know what he turned around and said? 'Whose fault is that'" (58)

This passage conflates allusions to three scenes in *Sons and Lovers*. The first, already cited, is Mr. and Mrs. Morel's argument about William's job as a clerk; the second is Gertrude Coppard's first meeting with Walter Morel, recounted in the opening chapter of Lawrence's novel; and the third occurs much later in the book, when Paul is beginning to make his way in the middle-class world (*SL* 18, 298–99).

There are a number of notable contrasts between these passages and their "originals" in *Sons and Lovers*. Again it is striking that scenes that are dramatized in *Sons and Lovers* are reported in *Regeneration*: we hear about the conflicts between the Priors from the protagonists themselves. In Lawrence's novel Paul sets out a philosophical and ethical position about the common people—"the difference between people isn't in their class, but in themselves.—Only from the middle classes, one gets ideas, and from the common people—life itself, warmth. You feel their hates and loves"—which is quickly undercut by his mother's question, "whom do you mix with now, among the common people?" (298). In his mother's account of the corresponding conversation in *Regeneration*, Billy Prior gets no opportunity to state his ideas about the common people, the reported conversation ending with Mrs. Prior's outraged sense of hurt at his suggestion that she has played a part in his alienation from his own class. Some of the ideas attributed to Mr. Morel in Lawrence's novel are here voiced by Mrs. Prior: it is she who speaks about earnings and the father's possible jealousy and sense of distance from his son. She shows sympathy for her husband's hard life and an understanding of his feelings, suggesting that what Mrs. Morel felt for her husband only in their early days together has survived longer in this marriage. She is, however, notably less confident and fluent than her husband in the immediately preceding scene: that "carefully genteel voice" delivers a speech that is punctuated with questions, silences, and unfinished sentences: and when she uses the giveaway dialect form "our Billy," it almost breaks down as she struggles to correct her mistake, only increasing the irony of the situation with her comments on the common people. Furthermore, she reveals that in respect of class she is less conscious than her husband of the real nature of her relationship with Billy. But the point is not to deliver "victory" to Mr. Prior where it is denied to Mr. Morel; it is rather to extend equal sympathy to both husband and wife, and to re-vision scenes in such a way as to suggest that both have a more complex understanding of relationships and tensions within the family than seems to be allowed in Lawrence.

## IV

Lawrence appears as a character in Helen Dunmore's *Zennor in Darkness* (1993), which is set in Cornwall in 1917 and culminates in the Lawrences' expulsion from the area in October of that year. When the novel opens, the experiment in communal living with the Murrys having ended in June 1916, Lawrence is tending his garden, keeping house, helping on the Hockings' farm, and working on the revision of his "Reality of Peace" articles, published that summer in the *English Review*. Helen Dunmore thus provides the reader with an accurate biographical framework of situations and events: this version of Lawrence has not been "Rampioned." For Dunmore, however, the challenge is not simply one of accuracy. She is creating a work of fiction, and the Lawrences must play their part effectively in the drama of the novel. Nonetheless, the "Lawrence" of this novel is also D. H. Lawrence, an extremely well-known and controversial figure, a circumstance of which other characters are well aware. Dunmore sets Lawrence against a fictional character, Clare Coyne, a young woman whose father married his Cornish servant, and on being widowed brought his daughter to live near his in-laws. Clare thus moves between two worlds: her father's middle-class dilettante scholarship and the working-class lives of her mother's family, a doubleness which, in this novel, echoes Lawrence's own.

Lawrence is seen as a representative yet special consciousness suffering the horror of the war. He thinks with pain of the souls

of the dead soldiers "released every evening into the low grey
skies above the Flanders plains, hungry for the lives they had
been torn from, wanting to tell someone" (*Zennor* 187). He tells
Clare that soldiers are no longer free to act as men, but are "part
of a machine of colossal stupidity" which robs them of the ability
to take responsibility for their own souls: "The war has fooled
England's soul out of her" (262–63). For him the war has brought
not only national suffering but personal harassment—the prosecution of *The Rainbow*, the humiliating medical examinations,
the suspicions aroused by being married to a German wife. "The
war wants to crush him," he reflects, and he knows that he could
be crushed "as easily as a snail is battered to bits by a thrush
which does not even want to eat it" (124). In his retreat to Cornwall he finds it wonderful to "have your back to the land, to the
whole of England . . . to this madness which finds a reason for
everything" (65). To some extent he can set against his sense of
nightmare and frenzy his love for the land and his delight in nature, but at the same time he realizes that the system of state
control is closing in on him: "it's not enough any more to have
few wants and try to hide away from the war in the hollow of an
empty landscape. There aren't any empty landscapes. . . . Ordinary things are dangerous" (126). Helen Dunmore creates a Lawrence who, although deeply pained by the war, is not brought to
the depths of nightmarish despair or the pitch of anti-democratic
anger that are sometimes emphasized in accounts of Lawrence in
these years.[10]

Dunmore also dramatizes Lawrence as a man involved in a
complex, absorbing, and stormy marriage, which is seen very
much from Frieda's point of view. Although Frieda resents the
way in which Lawrence allows other people to attach themselves
to him and distract him from his real work, she is not threatened
by those "who want Lorenzo and what he can give to them. . . . I
have lived with him for five years and I know they cannot capture
it" (86). Yet she *is* vulnerable, conscious of her status as the
"Hunwife," an object of suspicion and the victim of spying and
gossip. Where Lawrence is willing to hide, Frieda is discontented
and restless. She is uneasy about his developing relationship with
Clare and ambivalent about his anxiety that they should meet
and become friends: "Is he offering her Clare so that he can have
William Henry [Hocking]," she wonders (130).[11] In fact Frieda,
correctly surmising that Clare already has a lover, immediately

realizes that she is "no moth sucked to the flame of Lorenzo's vitality" (201).

Yet Clare needs and receives something from Lawrence, whose primary role in the narrative is one perhaps more characteristic of a 1960s or 1970s view of him, as a liberator of both Clare and her cousin-lover, John William. It is to Lawrence that John William reveals his feelings about his experiences at the front, even undergoing a post-traumatic episode in his presence. Clare herself is drawn to Lawrence by what makes him a threat to her family and neighbors: his red beard, his German wife, his otherness, the sense of expanded possibility that he carries with him. The Lawrences represent a new way of being that both challenges and attracts her. At first, she finds Lawrence a puzzle: his bearing is that of a gentleman, yet his face can seem "common, even mongrelish" (61). Above all, however, he seems to be a person "who does what he chooses," who exudes a "sense of freedom" and "doesn't look as if he knows or cares what people think of him" (54, 58). Lawrence responds to a similar kind of doubleness in Clare, attracted by the idea of "a lady who skins rabbits" (68).

What Lawrence offers Clare is symbolized by his response to her drawings, which are detailed botanical sketches to assist her father's work. Lawrence is "quick and intent" when he looks at them, regarding them with a kind of attentiveness they have never before received, and she is glad that he is "prepared to criticize and challenge her" (58, 61). He encourages Clare to allow another side of her artistic nature to emerge, freer, bolder, more full of "life." A similar sense of freedom is evident when Clare first visits the Lawrences. Lawrence and Frieda's cottage is "quite unlike any she has seen before," and the intimacy of their conversation is "both exciting and embarrassing"; she realizes that she has "swung far out of the orbit of home" and feels "so alive" (199–200, 212). Like Lawrence, she identifies with the carving of a mermaid in the local church—an object of fear and hatred for many local people—and relishes her double nature, for she can both swim and breathe, can exist both in the sea and on land.

In the last part of the novel, after John William's death and Clare's discovery that she is pregnant, the Lawrences' example steadies her determination to stay in Cornwall and keep the child: "They do what no one approves of, but they survive. They have made a life for themselves" (283). Ironically, it is Clare's father, believing Lawrence to be his daughter's lover, who betrays him to the authorities and precipitates the Lawrences' expulsion from Cornwall. But Clare has learned the important lessons: the courage to live in her own self, in spite of public disapproval, and the confidence to express that self in her own way. In her farewell letter to Lawrence, in which she tells him about her pregnancy, she writes, "I am hoping to make my living as you do, by my own work. . . . My own drawings, not flowers any more. . . . Perhaps I should not write and tell you this. But I had never met anyone like you before" (310). Dunmore thus emphasizes the Lawrence of whom Lady Cynthia Asquith wrote in May 1915, that he was "a Pentecost to one, and has the gift of intimacy and such perceptiveness that he introduces one to oneself" (Asquith 19). This is the Lawrence, as Helen Dunmore points out to Gary Adelman, who existed "before he was greatly changed by the disillusionments of the First World War" (Adelman 530).

# V

A. S. Byatt has published eight full-length works of fiction, and Lawrence plays a significant part in all but three of them. The exceptions are *Possession* (1990), *Angels and Insects* (1992), and *The Biographer's Tale* (2000), all of which are set wholly or partly in periods other than the second half of the twentieth century. The remaining five cover the full span of Byatt's career, from her first two novels, *The Shadow of the Sun* (1964) and *The Game* (1967), and including the first three volumes of a planned quartet about the life, family, and friends of Frederica Potter—*The Virgin in the Garden* (1978), *Still Life* (1985), and *Babel Tower* (1996). The sequence and dating of these novels are of some significance, for although they are all set at times between 1953 and the late 1960s, they were written and published over more than thirty years, so that the author and her readers have access to events, including the fluctuations in Lawrence's reputation, of which her characters are unaware—a point which is emphasized by occasional narrative interventions.

My comments here are confined to the first three novels of the Frederica Potter quartet, in which Frederica's engagement with Lawrence, as reader, student, teacher, and author affects her relationships with her father, her friends, her lovers, and her husband, and plays a crucial role in defining the scope of action open to her as an educated woman. In *The Virgin in the Garden*, for instance, the debate over Lawrence is a focus of conflict between Frederica and her father Bill Potter. For Potter, a left-wing school teacher who has broken out of a stifling non-conformist background and who devotes his spare time to adult education and community activities, Lawrence's work represents sane and liberating values. Frederica, however, who believes that the Leavisite Bill encourages her to read *Women in Love* because it offers a potential behavioral model, rejects what Lawrence says in that novel: "If I thought I'd really got to live the sort of life that book holds up for my admiration I'd drown myself . . . *now*. I don't want the immemorial magnificence of palpable real otherness. . . . I hope to God Lawrence is lying" (34). Frederica does not reject all of Lawrence's work, however. When her older sister, Stephanie, announces her forthcoming marriage, Frederica reflects that "[i]t had its secret attractions . . . as one recognised from a reading of . . . *The Rainbow*, to be enclosed with a transfigured man and transfigured possessions in a private place" (189). Nonetheless, during her own first full sexual encounter, she compares her feelings with Lady Chatterley's, thinking "with a moment of nausea . . . of Constance Chatterley's florid spreading circles of satisfaction" (420).

*Lady Chatterley's Lover* is central to Frederica's quarrel with her father. Complaining that Lawrence's characters "hector and gabble but they don't talk" and that Lawrence himself "lied in a way when he indicated all those values 'beyond' or 'under' [language]," she compares him unfavorably with Racine, whose characters "love in language . . . [and] . . . speak the unspeakable." Both authors, she thinks, "indicate forms of what isn't speech, and yet one is as clear and precise and formal about what it isn't as the other is yelping and muttering" (349–50). Bill Potter dislikes Racine, who is among both Frederica and Clifford Chatterley's favorite writers. "'After all,' [Sir Clifford] said, in a declamatory voice, 'one gets all one wants out of Racine. Emotions that are ordered and given shape are more important than disorderly emotions'" (*LCL* 139). Frederica does not want her emotions quite so comprehensively ordered as this passage suggests, but she is still a teenager who is struggling to find her footing in the world. And while Constance Chatterley is happy for her relationship with Mellors to happen in a place beyond words, Frederica cannot live without them.

*Still Life* continues Frederica's quarrel with her father about Lawrence. At Cambridge she develops a "sceptical mistrust of her father's undue respect for Leavisite 'values' and the 'life' located and propounded so easily in D. H. Lawrence. These things, values and life, seemed in certain lights to be morals and God without name or authority" (*Still Life* 182). Lawrence's "authority" and the way it is accepted by her father and many of her Cambridge contemporaries are progressively challenged as the novel goes on. Frederica's left-wing fellow-student, Tony Watson, speaks "approvingly of D. H. Lawrence's decency, intelligence . . . and vision. It was a habit of mind and morals she associated with her father" (113). Raphael Faber, the fastidious, highly intellectual don with whom Frederica falls in love, dislikes Lawrence's hectoring tone, finds his characters incredible, and believes that his whole approach to art—"inventing people and giving them names and social backgrounds" (215)—is out of date. Her ambivalent feelings about Lawrence become dramatized in Frederica's relationship with Nigel Reiver, an ex-soldier, businessman, and landowner, a person outside her previous experience. When they become lovers, he seems at once to extinguish her Cambridge life—a warning which, at this stage, she fails to heed: "After a time, Nigel shut everything else, S. T. Coleridge . . . John Milton . . . the shimmer of Cambridge, the puzzle of the undissociated sensibility, out of her busy mind" (324). By doing so, it could be argued, Nigel brings Frederica closer to Connie Chatterley's "florid spreading circles of satisfaction" and temporarily detaches her from her commitment to verbal articulation. Their relationship also represents an irony resonating from a passage in *The Virgin in the Garden*, when Frederica resists a possible identification of her family with the Brangwens, because if Stephanie is Ursula then Frederica must be Gudrun, "and I don't want to have to be her" (*Garden* 348). Just as the artistic Gudrun is attracted to but eventually feels stifled by the industrial magnate Gerald, so Frederica enters into a potentially destructive relationship with Nigel. In both cases what is involved is that central concern of Lawrence's fiction, the search for otherness in the pursuit of wholeness and the resulting conflict, as the characters, in their desire to achieve oneness and yet retain singleness, struggle to achieve star equilibrium.

The Lawrentian aspect of Frederica's marriage to Nigel becomes a central issue in *Babel Tower*. The novel is set in the mid

1960s, and Frederica's desire for independence is seen in the context of women's changing expectations in those years. Immured in Nigel's house in the country, Frederica feels intellectually unfulfilled and escapes with her young son to establish a new life as a teacher and writer in London. A parallel plot concerns the composition, publication, and prosecution for obscenity of a fantasy novel called *Babbletower*, which, as the substantial passages from its text demonstrate, combines J. R. R. Tolkien and the Marquis de Sade. The trial of this book, which inevitably carries echoes of the 1960 English trial of *Lady Chatterley*, forms one part of the novel's double climax. The other climactic episode is Frederica and Nigel's divorce hearing, and Lawrence is equally present in this courtroom.

Much of Frederica's interest in *Women in Love*, the novel she teaches and to which she most frequently refers, concerns its use of the language of desire, singleness, and otherness. These issues are of more than academic interest to Frederica because she applies them to her own marriage and that of her dead sister Stephanie. She sees Stephanie—also a brilliant student—as having left the Cambridge circle of words and ideas, choosing instead marriage and a life of "sensuous happiness," like Lady Chatterley "walking into the woods to be annihilated"; Frederica reflects that this "was our myth . . . that the body is truth" (*Babel* 125–26)—a Lawrentian myth of the 1950s and 1960s. But the obverse of this myth is that language is unimportant, and Frederica comes to believe that Nigel shares with Lady Chatterley a hatred of words. The extravagantly logocentric Frederica, however, cannot survive without them, so that it becomes impossible for her to live out her version of the myth with Nigel. She notes that Birkin, who for much of the novel scorns "love" and "connection," ends "in a mystical vision of oneness and connectedness, beyond language" (306). Frederica realizes that she was attracted to Nigel precisely because of his otherness and out of desire for connection. "Sexual love for Lawrence," she reflects, "confuses and abolishes grammatical categories, no I and you, no subject, but my and her in a paradisal One where everything is silent, where language is unnecessary and defeated" (311). Frederica has come increasingly to resist this oneness, feeling that it has destroyed in her "a separateness that was a strength" (311) and replaced it with a kind of fusion that she finds distasteful; for her, Forster's "only connect" and the Lawrentian "oneness" are ultimately

"myths of desire" and "ambiguous words of power" (312, 385).
The irony of Frederica's situation emerges at her divorce hearing,
when Nigel's counsel asks her about her reasons for marrying
him. Frederica herself introduces Lawrence, "who says we should
listen to our passions, to our bodies"; and when in response the
counsel suggests that Nigel's attraction for her might be summed
up in those hated words, "the immemorial magnificence of palpable, real otherness," Frederica, despite routinely and characteristically noting that "the prose is dreadful," can only agree (491).

# VI

In Dennis Hopper's *Easy Rider* (1969), Jack Nicholson's laconic toast, "Here's to good ol' D. H. Lawrence," appears to con-
fer on Lawrence iconic status, as if he were the presiding spirit of
the film's bike-powered, coke-fueled search for America. Thirty
years later such an unambiguous invocation is impossible, and
Frederica Potter's anguished cry may be a more fitting summing-
up of subsequent engagements with his work: "I love Lawrence
and I hate him, I believe him and I reject him totally, all at the
same time. It's wearing" (*Garden* 348). These sentiments appear
to be close to Byatt's own feelings about Lawrence. In her introduction to a recent reissue of her first published novel, *The
Shadow of the Sun*, Byatt comments on her relationship with
Lawrence, "whom I cannot escape and cannot love." Although
she learned from Lawrence "that you can stop the action of a
novel and move it into another dimension with the vision of a
place, or an event, or a ceremony," she cannot "love the man who
wrote the *Plumed Serpent*" (*xii*). Comparing him to Proust (another favorite of Clifford Chatterley's) she concludes that "altogether Proust has more to teach on every page, but is not close to
my blood, as Lawrence is. I choose the words advisedly" (xii).

Byatt's words may help us to understand why Lawrence, in
spite of the overall decline in his reputation, particularly in the
academy, since the 1970s continues to inhabit British fiction. One
reason would certainly be that, in Britain at least, Lawrence's
reputation with the reading public has usually existed quite separately from that in our schools and universities. He continues to
exert a powerful regional fascination, and his work is valued for
the ways in which it dramatizes the social and economic transfor-

mations wrought by the English Industrial Revolution. Similarly, in his fiction and plays up to about 1920, it is possible to find in his work a vivid dramatization of the effects on individuals, families, and communities of widening educational opportunities, especially for the working classes. Thus the experiences of William and Paul Morel (not to speak of Lawrence himself) can be seen as part of a tradition in English fiction which also encompasses Dickens's *Great Expectations* or Hardy's *Jude the Obscure*. Furthermore, among non-specialist readers—and I write with the experience of thirty years as a teacher in Continuing Education–he continues to offer a challenge, to ask questions about relationships and individual identity that remain relevant to contemporary readers.

Explaining his striking presence in fiction by women is less straightforward. One simple answer is that he writes a good deal *about* women, that in his dramas of change and self-discovery the protagonists are often female. "Odour of Chrysanthemums," "Daughters of the Vicar," *The Rainbow, Women in Love, The Lost Girl*, "The Woman Who Rode Away," *The Virgin and the Gypsy*: in all these texts women are the chief protagonists. And where the male voice threatens to disturb the balance or to attempt to reduce the woman to "the Other," as with Birkin in *Women in Love*, the female voice functions in the text to undercut the hectoring or tendentious male. In both cases, it is hardly surprising that women writers should wish to engage with the structures, themes, and narrative voices in Lawrence's work. Furthermore, as Carol Siegel has brilliantly demonstrated, Lawrence participates in a tradition of women's fiction, in that his writing "developed in his reaction to his reading of Victorian women authors" and that his need "to reinterpret women's texts . . . can be seen to be the general structuring force behind his fiction" (Siegel 186). Siegel also points out that as women writers have rejected Lawrence's attempts to appropriate the female voice, they have been brought closer to those Victorian models against whom he was reacting. He thus acts as a bridge between Victorian and modern literature, who, by arousing such a strong reaction in many female readers and writers, enables them to connect more securely to the traditions in which they belong. In this respect Lawrence's example is, perhaps paradoxically, wholly enabling, for it is by arguing with Lawrence that writers like

Byatt and Barker are better able to define or sharpen their own ideas.

It is also worth reminding ourselves that literary allusions function in Lawrence's fiction in very similar ways. In the second part of *Mr Noon*, for instance, the narrator's engagement with Tolstoy—a novelist whom Lawrence once very much admired— helps to define the ways in which Noon's relationship with Johanna is different from hers with her husband. A character's preferences for particular authors are also used, positively or negatively, to reveal elements of their selves that they may not be able to express in other ways. As I have already suggested, Clifford Chatterley's liking for Racine, whom Constance dislikes, is related to Frederica's arguments about the balance between words and feelings, separateness and oneness.[12] If Byatt and Barker wrestle with Lawrence, so he struggles with George Eliot, Tolstoy, Dostoevsky, and (comprehensively) with Hardy. At one time all these writers seemed, as Lawrence does for Byatt, close to his blood, but they had to be confronted and rejected. Even as he admitted them to his imagination, these influences made him anxious.

Byatt's acknowledgment that Lawrence is close to her blood in a way Proust could never be expresses both affinity and anxiety. Her concern with language, relationships, and the role of women brings her inevitably to Lawrence, and just as inevitably to a rejection, through Frederica, of what she reads in his work, his "myths of desire" (*Babel* 312). Pat Barker, seeking models for writing about working-class women, turns to and rejects Lawrence, but in order to do so must go through the process of revisioning of specific scenes in *Sons and Lovers* as a means of confronting issues of class, the experience of women, and the articulation of feeling. Helen Dunmore's novel seems the least conflicted of the three. She creates a vibrant yet curiously gentle figure suffering the war, faithful to a particular kind of marriage, and above all enabling others to live out their full human potential. Yet her "Lawrence," who carries great conviction within her beautiful and moving novel, presents some problems if we try to identify her image of the novelist with the man who, during 1917 and after, created the apocalyptic *Women in Love*.

My final point, however, concerns not the detail of how Lawrence is used in these books or the tussles with his ideas that his presence usually implies. It is more to do with the fact that it is

*Lawrence* who is used in this way. What other twentieth-century writer is so frequently named, alluded to, argued with in the fiction of the past thirty years? The authors may wish to defend, re-vision, challenge, or dismiss their constructions of Lawrence's ideas. To knowledgeable Lawrentians it may seem that they create a parodic version of Lawrence in order to knock it down. They—or, their characters—may be atoning for a youthful enthusiasm for his work. The fact remains that in spite of all the accusations of bad artistry, misogyny, sexual and political fascism, Lawrence is still *there*, still "in" our novels, still to be reckoned with, still our contemporary. As Doris Lessing demands in her characteristically trenchant response to Gary Adelman, "Who has said D. H. Lawrence is no longer important?" (Adelman 519).

## NOTES

1. Helen McNeil's introduction to the Virago edition of *Bid Me to Live* (1984). John Worthen tells me that it is possible that H. D. may have been working on material that found its way into the novel as early as 1921, much closer to the Mecklenburgh Square period that it recreates.

2. See Maurice Beebe, "Lawrence as Fictional Character," in *The Spirit of D. H. Lawrence: Centenary Studies*, ed. Gamini Salgado and G. K. Das (Macmillan, 1988), 295–310.

3. Jeffrey Meyers, "Memoirs of D. H. Lawrence: A Genre of the Thirties," *DHLR* 14 (1981): 1–32.

4. The controversy between Catherine Carswell and John Middleton Murry following the publication of the first edition of Carswell's *The Savage Pilgrimage* in 1932 is an obvious example of this kind of tussle for the possession of Lawrence's soul.

5. *The New Poetry*, ed. A. Alvarez (Harmondsworth: Penguin, 1962; revised edition, 1966). Alvarez's introduction is called "The New Poetry, *or* Beyond the Gentility Principle," and includes the following: "In the seriousness of what I have called the new depth poetry, the openness to experience, the psychological insight and integrity of D. H. Lawrence would, ideally, combine with the technical skill and formal intelligence of T. S. Eliot" (32).

6. See Peter Preston, "Lawrence in Britain: An Annotated Chronology: 1930–1998," in *The Reception of D. H. Lawrence Around the World*, ed. Takeo Iida (Fukuoka: Kyushu University Press, 1999), 1–43. The present essay extends some brief comments in this chapter, which sought to consider Lawrence's reception across a wide front, on which such matters as productions of Lawrence's plays, cinema and television adaptations of his fiction, his publication and presentation in paperback, and his more recent incorporation into the heritage industry, are given equal consideration with published academic criticism as indicators of his place in the culture.

7. F. R. Leavis's *D. H. Lawrence: Novelist*, first published as a hardback, was given much wider currency by its publication in a Penguin paperback in 1964.

Harry T. Moore's biography, *The Intelligent Heart*, was published in 1954, issued as a Penguin in the 1960s, and reissued in a revised form as *The Priest of Love* in 1974. Kate Millett's feminist attack on Lawrence appeared in 1968 and was issued by Virago in 1977.

8. Carol Clewlow's *A Woman's Guide to Adultery* (1989), Maureen Moore's *The Illumination of Alice Mallory* (1991), and Philippa Gregory's *Perfectly Correct* (1996) are other examples of this kind of sustained engagement in novels by women.

9. In Barker's most recent novel, *Another World* (Viking Penguin, 1998), the character Nick waits by the bedside of his sick grandfather: "Nick watches him chew, thinking that any nourishment now can only prolong the agony and that perhaps he ought to be encouraging him not to eat. He thinks of Paul Morel diluting his mother's milk so that it won't nourish her. Finally, poisoning her, partly in compassion, partly in unconscious revenge because her milk had poisoned him" (51).

10. The best account of the war years can be found in Mark Kinkead-Weekes, *D. H. Lawrence: Triumph to Exile, 1912–1922* (Cambridge: Cambridge University Press, 1996). Paul Delany's *D. H. Lawrence's Nightmare: The Writer and His Circle in the Years of the Great War* (Hassocks, Sussex: Harvester, 1979) remains a useful special study.

11. Frieda's speculations refer to the possibility that Lawrence entertained sexual feelings for Hocking and may even have had an affair with him. See Kinkead-Weekes, *Triumph to Exile*, 376–81 for a balanced account of the episode.

12. See Dennis Jackson, "Literary Allusion in *Lady Chatterley's Lover*" in *D. H. Lawrence's "Lady": A New Look at "Lady Chatterley's Lover,"* ed. Michael Squires and Dennis Jackson (Athens: University of Georgia Press, 1985) 170–96.

## WORKS CITED

Adelman, Gary. "The Man Who Rode Away: What D. H. Lawrence Means to Today's Readers." *TriQuarterly* 107–8 (Winter, Spring/Summer 2000): 508–36.

Asquith, Lady Cynthia. *Diaries 1915–18*. 1968. Reprint, London: Century, 1987.

Barker, Pat. *Regeneration*. 1991. Reprint, Harmondsworth: Penguin, 1992.

Bellow, Saul. *Ravelstein*. New York: Viking, 2000.

Byatt, A. S. *Babel Tower*. London: Chatto & Windus, 1996.

———. *The Shadow of the Sun*. 1964 (as *Shadow of a Sun*) Reprint, New York: Vintage, 1991.

———. *Still Life*. London: Chatto & Windus, 1985.

———. *The Virgin in the Garden*. 1978. Reprint, Harmondsworth: Penguin, 1981.

Dunmore, Helen. *Zennor in Darkness*. 1993. Reprint, Harmondsworth: Penguin, 1994.

Lanchester, John. *The Debt to Pleasure*. London: Picador, 1996.

Larkin, Philip. *High Windows*. London: Faber & Faber, 1974.

Ondaatje, Michael. *Anil's Ghost*. London: Bloomsbury, 2000.

Ross, Michael. "Acts of Re-vision: Lawrence as Intertext in the Novels of Pat Barker." *DHLR* 26 (1995–96): 51–63.

Siegel, Carol. *Lawrence Among the Women: Wavering Boundaries in Women's Literary Fiction*. Charlottesville: University Press of Virginia, 1991.

## D. H. Lawrence in British Fiction, 1958–2001

This list contains seventy-five British works of fiction. The list would be much longer if poems, plays, feature films, television dramas, and non-fiction works (especially autobiographies or memoirs) were also included. Works first published outside Britain do not appear in the list. References to Lawrence range from a single allusion or quotation to substantial passages of discussion.

| 1958 | Kingsley Amis | *I Like It Here* |
| 1958 | Lawrence Durrell | *Balthazar* |
| 1958 | Lawrence Durrell | *Mountolive* |
| 1959 | Malcolm Bradbury | *Eating People Is Wrong* |
| 1959 | Michael Innes [J. I. M. Stewart] | *Hare Sitting Up* |
| 1959 | Keith Waterhouse | *Billy Liar* |
| 1960 | Lawrence Durrell | *Clea* |
| 1960 | Kingsley Amis | *Take a Girl Like You* |
| 1960 | Clancy Sigal | *Weekend in Dinlock* |
| 1961 | Iris Murdoch | *A Severed Head* |
| 1962 | Doris Lessing | *The Golden Notebook* |
| 1964 | A. S. Byatt | *Shadow of a Sun* (reissued as *The Shadow of the Sun*, 1991) |
| 1965 | Malcolm Bradbury | *Stepping Westward* |
| 1965 | David Lodge | *The British Museum Is Falling Down* |
| 1965 | Alan Sillitoe | *The Death of William Posters* |
| 1966 | Melvyn Bragg | *The Second Inheritance* |
| 1966 | John Fowles | *The Magus* (revised 1977) |
| 1967 | A. S. Byatt | *The Game* |
| 1967 | Angela Carter | *Shadow Dance* |
| 1967 | Angela Carter | *The Magic Toyshop* |
| 1967 | Alan Sillitoe | *A Tree on Fire* |
| 1970 | Melvyn Bragg | *A Place in England* |
| 1973 | Martin Amis | *The Rachel Papers* |
| 1973 | Angus Wilson | *As If by Magic* |
| 1974 | Melvyn Bragg | *The Silken Net* |
| 1974 | J. I. M. Stewart | *Young Patullo* |

1976 Malcolm Bradbury   "Tough at the Top" and "Room at the Bottom" in *Who Do You Think You Are? Stories and Parodies*
1977 Penelope Lively   *The Road to Lichfield*
1978 A. S. Byatt   *The Virgin in the Garden*
1979 Alan Sillitoe   *The Storyteller*
1980 Melvyn Bragg   *Kingdom Come*
1981 Keith Waterhouse   *Maggie Muggins, or Spring in Earl's Court*
1982 William Boyd   *A Good Man in Africa*
1982 Alan Sillitoe   *Her Victory*
1982 John Wain   *Young Shoulders*
1984 Penelope Lively   *According to Mark*
1985 A. S. Byatt   *Still Life*
1985 Julian Barnes   *Flaubert's Parrot*
1986 Nicholas Freeling   *Cold Iron*
1988 Mavis Cheek   *Pause Between Acts*
1988 David Lodge   *Nice Work*
1988 Peter Rubinson   *A Dedicated Man*
1989 Martin Amis   *London Fields*
1989 Carol Clewlow   *A Woman's Guide to Adultery*
1989 Penelope Lively   "The Five Thousand and One Nights" in *Beyond the Blue Mountains*
1989 Alan Sillitoe   *The Open Door*
1991 Pat Barker   *Regeneration*
1993 Pat Barker   *The Eye in the Door*
1993 Helen Dunmore   *Zennor in Darkness*
1993 Jeanette Winterson   *Written on the Body*
1994 Spike Milligan   *Lady Chatterley's Lover According to Spike Milligan* (humor)
1995 Elaine Feinstein   *Lady Chatterley's Confession*
1995 Spike Milligan   *John Thomas and Lady Jane According to Spike Milligan* (humor)
1995 Jeanette Winterson   *Art and Lies*
1996 A. S. Byatt   *Babel Tower*
1996 Philippa Gregory   *Perfectly Correct*
1996 Helen Fielding   *Bridget Jones's Diary*
1996 John Lanchester   *The Debt to Pleasure*
1997 Sean French   *The Dreamer of Dreams*
1998 Martin Amis   "Let Me Count the Times" and "Straight Fiction" in *Heavy Water And Other Stories*
1998 Pat Barker   *Another World*
1998 Alan Sillitoe   *The Broken Chariot*
1998 David Storey   *A Serious Man*

| 1999 | J. M. Coetzee | *The Lives of Animals* |
| 1999 | Nicci French | *Killing Me Softly* |
| 2000 | Margaret Drabble | *The Peppered Moth* |
| 2000 | Michael Ondaatje | *Anil's Ghost* |
| 2000 | Zadie Smith | *White Teeth* |
| 2000 | Lyn Wood | *Intense Blue* |
| 2000 | Malcolm Bradbury | *To the Hermitage* |
| 2001 | Ian McEwan | *Atonement* |
| 2001 | Iain Sinclair | *Landor's Tower* |
| 2001 | Alan Sillitoe | *Birthday* |
| 2001 | David Lodge | *Thinks—: A Novel* |
| 2001 | Sebastian Faulks | *On Green Dolphin Street* |
| 2001 | Melvyn Bragg | *A Son of War* |

# An "Englishman at Heart"?: Lawrence and the National Identity Debates

### Judith Ruderman

In an interview in the *Jewish Chronicle* in 1926, the British Home Secretary, William Joynson-Hicks—who would a few years later instigate the seizure of D. H. Lawrence's *Pansies*—explained that his chief test for granting nationalization papers to an "alien" was whether the immigrant had become "an Englishman at heart." By this standard, Joynson-Hicks had in mind assimilation into the dominant culture through adoption of its language and customs, and on the basis of this standard he deported hundreds of Jewish immigrants after World War I (Cesarini 152). Had Lawrence, Joynson-Hicks's nemesis, been put to the same test, it is problematic whether he himself would have passed, even though in many ways, including holding negative attitudes toward Jews, Lawrence was the arch Englishman. Lawrence presents an interesting case of a person who was both inside and outside of Englishness, and whose struggles at self-definition mirror those of the marginalized groups that he frequently denounced.

Lawrence lived during a period of debate about what it meant to be English, a discourse framed and animated, as it so often is, by opposition to minorities. Not surprisingly, Lawrence's writings suggest that his efforts at defining himself were integrally bound up with his characterization of the Jew, among other marginalized groups. But because he was not firmly moored in his class, nation, or gender, Lawrence was actually a man without a country, who challenged as well as transmitted central aspects of his identity as an Englishman. My essay will examine Lawrence's relationship to some cultural markers of "Englishness" in his time and pose a relationship between definitions of Englishness and Jewishness.

Critics have recently focused increasingly on the role that the Jew has played in the construction of various national identities throughout history.[1] Through the ages, majority cultures have defined themselves by reference to minorities, knowing self through opposition to other (other as defined by self); as Philip Dodd puts it, "Englishness is not so much a category as a relationship" (Dodd 12). The Jew, in whatever country, has functioned as "the quintessential minority against whom the status of minority rights was usually defined" (Biale et al. 17). James Shapiro points out in his study of Shakespeare and the Jews that England's empire-building and the Protestant Reformation destabilized the national sense of self. In such a period of transition, the Jew provided a handy way for the English to define who they were partly on the basis of who they decidedly were not. That there was no organized Jewish community in England between 1290 and 1656 may have diluted the force of day-to-day anti-Semitism (Endelman 237), but if anything, the relative absence of actual Jews must have magnified their mythic proportions during this time.

Eventually the European Enlightenment accorded human rights to groups long deprived of them, but at the same time it gave rise to the idea of "the nation, a new construct that mobilized historical traditions in the service of a new, homogeneous community, frequently hostile to recently emancipated groups like the Jews" (Biale et al. 2). Jews constituted a "question," a "problem," for the majority culture. They might live *in* the nation, but they weren't *of* it. Indeed they were often seen as antithetical to the culture's best self. A case in point is Richard Lovat Somers's rumination on the demise of England, in Lawrence's novel *Kangaroo*. Thinking of Lloyd George, Somers dismisses him handily: "A little Welsh lawyer, not an Englishman at all.... Somers gradually came to believe that all Jews, and all Celts, even whilst they espoused the cause of England, subtly lived to bring about the last humiliation of the great old England" (*K* 226). How quickly the Celt put Lawrence in mind of the Jew, that "quintessential minority."

Lawrence often expressed admiration for the Celt, unlike the Jew, as evidenced, for example, in his letters about the Cornish farmer William Henry Hocking. But he did so in a manner that suggested the Celt as a holdover from the past, thereby diminishing him in a subtle and very English way. Lawrence wrote, "There is something manly and independent about [Hocking] – and something truly *Celtic* and unknown – something non-christian, non-European . . ." (*L* ii. 664). Cornwall, he said, "isn't England. It isn't really England. . . . It has another quality: of King Arthur's days, that flicker of Celtic consciousness before it was swamped under Norman and Teutonic waves" (*L* ii. 505).

Lawrence's view of Cornwall was essentially the same as that expressed by Matthew Arnold in his lectures on Celtic literature at Oxford, which were published at the same time as that critic's ruminations on Englishness entitled *Culture and Anarchy* (1869). Arnold confined the contributions of the Celt to the past and recommended that, thus fixed in time and typed, they become something for study. A chair of Celtic languages at Oxford was the result. Meanwhile, artistic colonies established in Cornwall in the late nineteenth century further stabilized the identity of the Cornish as an ancient people, primitive and simple. The Newlyn School of painters remained firmly affiliated with such national and cosmopolitan centers as the Royal Academy, and thus it was from the standards of the core that influential commentators on the Celts, in pictures as well as words, determined the place of Celtic culture in Englishness (Dodd 12–15). D. H. Lawrence's flip remark about the Welshman Lloyd George in *Kangaroo* reflects the attitude of the dominant culture of the period, which excluded the Scots, Irish, and Welsh, not to mention the Jews.

A recent sourcebook called *Writing Englishness, 1900–1950* makes note of the marginalized cultures of Scotland, Ireland, and Wales (Giles and Middleton 3) but fails to mention the Jews. Yet immigration from Eastern Europe was one of the primary factors influencing the articulation of the politics of national identity in the early decades of this century. The English were very concerned about the mass influx that concentrated Jews in port cities and especially in London's East End. No doubt these urban immigrants helped to bolster the opposing image of unsullied ruralism as a component of true Englishness. What was perceived as an urban crisis in employment, housing, and crime led to a nostalgia for the past and the production in art and letters, music and architecture, of "a ruralist version of a specifically English culture" associated with England's south (Hawkins 63). Tellingly, the *Annals of Eugenics* for 1925–26 marshaled images of the countryside to explain the threat posed to the country's well-being by recent immigrants to England: "No breeder of cattle . . . would purchase an entire herd because he anticipated finding one or two fine specimens included in it: still less would he do it if his byres and pastures were already full" (quoted in Holmes 217). A romanticized ruralist vision helped simultaneously to neutralize the growing heterogeneity in English life by emphasizing a stable, village-based English society and to salve the wounds from the loss of imperialistic power and the horrific deaths on World War I battlefields (Rich 37–38).

D. H. Lawrence's fiction from first to last expresses a rather wistful ruralist vision, with countryside or forest embodying the natural and the good. In this way he was very "English." His mythologized versions of the rural Midlands in Nethermere and the woods surrounding Wragby Hall are meant to recapture an old England; they are specifically contrasted to urbanization and to the Jews. In *The White Peacock*, Cyril's visit to London exposes him to the frightening view that "the world was all East-end" now, with a teeming profusion of "black-mudded objects" (*WP* 281–82). Indeed Jack the Ripper's serial murders of prostitutes had all taken place in the East End late in the previous century, and most of the suspects were Jews (Gilman *Jew's Body* 112). Writers other than Lawrence would engage in extensive explorations of "darkest London," and the many examples of literature of "the double" in this period may reflect an unease with the proximity of the dangerous other and a resulting "fear of reversion to some lower point on the psychic or social or evolutionary scale" (Brookes and Widdowson 141–50). In the thirty years before the First World War, children's magazines and other popular media disseminated a propagandistic message extolling "the 'muscular Christianity' formerly reserved for the public schools, as this would be a route to combating 'degeneracy' and the 'savage' instincts of the urban poor"; the post-war legacy of a concentration on empire was the association of racial superiority with national identity (Castle 179–81).

In Lawrence's case, except for *The White Peacock*'s encoded reference to the East End Jewish poor, the writings tend to pinpoint the Jewish *rich* as the nemesis of rural England. Like poor Jews, in fact, rich Jews in early twentieth-century England were implicitly linked to prostitution. In this view, the reproduction of money through the charging of interest sexualized money and stigmatized bankers as degenerate and diseased prostitutes (Gilman *Jew's Body* 124). The entire ruralist movement in England contained an anti-Semitic element in the blaming of Jewish bankers for the untoward growth of commerce and industry (Hawkins

70), an element clearly visible in *Lady Chatterley's Lover* in the comparison of the devil to a Jewish banker (*LCL* 261). Elsewhere in Lawrence, Richard Lovat Somers complains of "the industrialism and commercialism of England, with which patriotism and democracy became identified" and pinpoints Jewish financiers as the perpetrators of this denigration of old English values (*K* 213–14).[2]

Lawrence's most extensive portrayal of the rural tradition and community appears in *The Rainbow*, in which Lydia Lensky, a Polish exile in England, is reawakened to her true self when she moves from London into the country. (Here too one finds a castigation of the Jewish financiers, to whom Lydia's father would have lost his land in Poland had he not married a German with money.) In her first months of immigration, in the city, Lydia maintains a Polish core, hiding herself in her Polish identity; but she eventually embraces Tom Brangwen and his rootedness in the English soil. She becomes "really English, really Mrs. Brangwen" (78). Yet the novel is no unalloyed paean to Englishness or to ruralism. Lydia maintains the distance of a foreigner, and her granddaughter Ursula scoffs at Skrebensky's defense of race and nation (288–89, 304–5). Lawrence was unlike Kipling and Henty, whose fictional adventure stories and history textbooks, with their images of the inferior alien, were of a piece in promoting imperialist ideas (Castle 6). Ursula seeks to "burst the narrow boundary of Cossethay"(246) in order to find her wings, not to be Anton Skrebensky's wife in India.

Indeed in his recognition of the female striving for liberation (problematized as that is in Lawrence's works), his frail health, his childhood companionship with the girls and avoidance of the boys' rough-and-tumble play, his love and practice of the domestic arts, his ambiguous sexual identity, even his literary style, Lawrence fails to evidence—although he yearns for it at times—another important cultural marker of English identity: manliness. Ralph Waldo Emerson, characterizing England in his essay on "race" in the collection *English Traits*, had noted the country's love of physical, often brutal strength as manifested in fighting, flogging, and fagging. Emerson marveled at the "great vigor of body and endurance," gushing that "other countrymen look slight and undersized beside them, and invalids. . . . [The English] have more constitutional energy than any other people do. . . . They box, run, shoot, ride, row, and sail from pole to pole"

(Emerson 34–35, 38). Needless to say, Emerson's description of these "typical" English activities does not match the experience of most English Jews of Lawrence's time, nor the popular conceptions about Jews, which attributed to this group of people such inherent bodily characteristics as flat feet (Gilman, *Jew's Body* 38–44). Although said to be exacerbated by such environmental conditions as pounding the city pavement and standing behind the merchant's counter, these flat feet ultimately revealed an ineluctably degenerate weakness that in effect disqualified the Jew from being English.

Physical characteristics were thus allied with participation in culturally sanctioned activities. In addition to sports, service in World War I was a major activity that had the benefit for cultural identity formation of manifesting not only manliness but also patriotism. Jews were suspect on the second count as well as the first, a not surprising connection. In Europe in the mid-nineteenth century, for example, the Jewish body was seen by anti-Semites as "inherently unfit for military service" (Gilman, *Jew's Body* 42), a critique that heightened in intensity as barriers to military service lessened. During World War I, the English Jew could not "win" in the popular imagination. Russia was an ally of Britain, yet the recent immigrants had fled its pogroms; Germany was an enemy, yet many of the wealthier Jews were of German origin. Much ill will was directed at Jews at this time, especially since the Russian Jews in England were not conscripted until late in the war (Lipman 139–43).

Lawrence was also suspect on both counts: a lack of manliness and a lack of patriotism. His own physical condition rendered him unfit for military service, and his national allegiance was questioned because he had a German wife. Partly out of conviction, partly in retaliation for objectionable personal treatment at the hands of military authorities, Lawrence lashed out against the war and society. He likened the soldiers he saw at Worthing in 1915 to "lice or bugs," and complained to Ottoline Morrell that "hell is slow and creeping and viscous and insect teeming: as is this Europe now – this England" (*L* ii. 331). A few months later, the literary critic of the *Star*, reviewing *The Rainbow*, used the same terms to vilify the novel and to exalt the military: "The life they lay down [for liberty] is a lofty thing. It is not the thing that creeps and crawls in this novel" (Draper 95). What Lawrence called the "soldier-spirit" he thought to be antithetical to life: in

1916 he told Cynthia Asquith that "the whole crux of life now lies in the relation between man and woman. . . . In this relation we live or die. – The soldier-spirit is fatal. . . . A man who has a living connection with a woman is, ipso facto, not a soldier, not an essential destroyer, but an essential creator" (*L* iii. 27). Several of his male protagonists of the 1920s have performed military service in World War I and suffer physical and emotional damage because of it: the gypsy in *The Virgin and the Gipsy*, Phoenix in *St. Mawr*, Mellors in *Lady Chatterley's Lover*. Though soldiers, they are "manly" in Lawrence's terms and hence for idiosyncratic reasons: they do not have the "soldier-spirit" of an Anton Skrebensky, but, instead, lead independent, sometimes nomadic lives, outsiders all. And they are enormously attractive to their female counterparts.

With manliness as an essential component of Englishness, women were marginalized. At the time of Lawrence's birth, women had no nationality of their own, but rather assumed the nationality of their husband. Lawrence's depiction of Ursula's striving for independence in the world of work and the city, repudiating her mother's fecundity, went against the grain of English norms: men and women had their separate and discrete spheres in which to work hard at stemming the tide. From earliest childhood, men and women were socialized differently, the former to protect the nation and its institutions, the latter to produce children and imbue them with the proper English values. The popular children's magazines *Boy's Own Paper* and *Girl's Own Paper* stressed, respectively, sports and war for boys, child-rearing and cooking for girls (Mackay and Thane 193–96). At least 150 youth magazines appeared between 1880 and 1918, intended to reinforce in leisure reading across classes the notions of gender, race, and nationalism that children encountered in their schoolbooks (Castle 5–8). *Women in Love* suggests the popularity of this literature when Ursula Brangwen, at her sister Rosalind's request, brings home a copy of *Girl's Own Paper* from the lending library (259).

Ursula in this same chapter of *Women in Love* repudiates the convention dictating that Birkin ask her father for her hand in marriage; in fact, Lawrence himself sought lifelong the company of independent, headstrong women like his Ursula. Yet he could not help but be influenced by the indoctrination of the popular children's literature. Indeed, he promulgated very similar ideas about the proper education of boys and girls in both "Education of the People" and *Fantasia of the Unconscious*. Like the children's magazines, Lawrence's treatises on education and on psychology set males firmly on one side of a breach and females on the other, with men responsible for "scouting, fighting, gathering provision" and women for "the immediate personal life" of raising children and keeping the hearth (*RDP* 165–66, *FU* 123). Thus did the weak-chested D. H. Lawrence—who in his salad days was an inveterate hiker—link the Emersonian "English trait" of physical prowess with manliness. His ideas about government, expressed in several letters in 1915, also dictate separate spheres for men and women: women should vote for, and govern, "the feeding and housing of the race" (*L* ii. 368).

It is not surprising that such culture-bound notions of masculinity in Lawrence's time were used to further marginalize the Jew and other minorities who posed a threat to England's sense of self. From the Middle Ages until recent times male Jews have actually been deemed "feminine," and thus doubly marginalized. A thirteenth-century scientist said that male Jews menstruated and hence were as corrupted as all females; this belief, which can be found in print into the seventeenth century, reinforced the notion that Jews, like women, were cursed by God for their sin of rejecting Jesus. It also linked the blood of menstruation with that of Christian children whom Jews were said to murder (Gilman, *Jewish Self-Hatred* 74–75); perhaps it also relates to the blood shed in the Jewish rite of male circumcision. Through the decades of the late nineteenth and early twentieth centuries, the ritual cutting of the genitalia in circumcision was associated with castration in both the popular and psychoanalytic literature, and medical science posited that male Jews, again like all females, were prone to hysteria. The influential study called *Sex and Character* (1903) by Otto Weininger (a Jewish convert to Christianity), linked Judaism with the feminine and categorized both as negative states. Such a feminized male Jew appears in Lawrence's *Women in Love* in the character of the bisexual Loerke, and also perhaps in the unnamed Jewish friend of Halliday (said to be modeled on the man Lady Ottoline referred to as "a fat dark-blooded tight-skinned Armenian Jew," Dikran Kouyoumdjian, later "Michael Arlen"), whom Pussum sneers at as a coward (*WL* 71 n. 538)—although the real-life inspirations, Gertler and Arlen, were both heterosexual.[3]

If the Jewish man has been considered feminine, hence weak, historically the Jewish woman in the modern period in Europe has often been the object of ambivalent sexual desires, exoticized in paint by Ingres and Sargent, for example, and in words by writers like D. H. Lawrence. Representative of sensuality and warmth, contrasted to the chaste, modest Christian woman, the Jewish female is both "dangerous and desirable" to the Christian male (Garb 27). Such ambivalence helps to explain Lawrence's portrayal of Mrs. Eastwood in *The Virgin and the Gipsy*, a woman whose positive flouting of conventional morality is countervened by her cosmopolitanism and materialism—qualities typically associated with the male Jew and deemed antithetical to true Englishness. On the one hand, the arrival of the Eastwoods at the campfire interrupts and postpones the acquiescence of Yvette to the gypsy's power. On the other, the Eastwoods' relationship puts Yvette in mind of the gypsy and stimulates a discussion with her sister on sex, love, and marriage. On the one hand, the denigration by "the little Jewess" of Yvette's attraction to the gypsy indicates her own ironical alliance with society's prejudiced notions of race and class. On the other, she is blasted by the rector for being Jewish, for living in an unmarried state with a younger man, and for having left her children—characteristics, except for the ethnicity, that she shares with both She-Who-Was-Cynthia and Frieda.

Mrs. Eastwood is a particularly unstable figure in Lawrence's novella. Although liberated sexually, economically, and socially, she is implicitly faulted for her mobility—for buying the Major, for moving out of her Jewish world, for taking control and exercising power. In contrast, gypsies, traditionally considered dirty outcasts and petty thieves, are wiped clean of all such charges in *The Virgin and the Gipsy*, where they are portrayed as protectors of the environment and saviors of virginal lost girls. The conflation of gypsies, blackness, femaleness, and Jewishness into a quadruply powerful signification of otherness was already to be found in Prosper Merimée's 1845 novella *Carmen* (Gilman, *Jewish Self-Hatred* 6), with which Lawrence may have been familiar (Paul Morel reads Merimée's *Colomba* in the original French [*SL* 174]). Carmen is thought to reside in all four categories.[4] In Lawrence's novella, his sympathies toward the Jew as outcast are decidedly more mixed than are those toward the gypsy. To the degree that Mrs. Eastwood is a sexually alluring and dangerous other, she is identified with the gypsy state of "blackness" and liberation. On the other hand, to the degree that she fits into the category of rich Jewess, she cannot serve as a positive role model; on the contrary, she is racially degenerate.

In the medieval and early modern period, Jews could be redeemed in Christian eyes by conversion. Indeed, conversion of the Jews was part and parcel of the English identity debates of the eighteenth century, when, reflecting the English struggle with French armies and ideas, Evangelical discourse combined religious fervor and ardent patriotism in the attempts to win the Jews to Protestantism.[5] By the beginning of the nineteenth century, Jewishness came to be seen not as a creed but as "a racial identity, one which could be observed, measured, understood and pathologized. The construction of the Jew move[d], with modernization, from the language of religion to the pseudoscientific mobilization of the category of race in the new nineteenth century disciplines of anthropology, ethnology, and biology" (Garb 22). A turn-of-the-twentieth-century German proverb encapsulated the common belief: *"Was der Jude glaubt ist einerlei / in der Rasse liegt der Schweinerei!"* ("The Jew's belief is nothing / it's race that makes him swinish!" [quoted in Gilman, *Jew's Body* 202][6]). Hierarchy based on race superseded that of class or birthright, situating the "Negro" at the bottom and the Jew somewhere between whiteness and blackness, essentially and hence indelibly other (Garb 22). The late nineteenth century has been called "the age of physiognomy"—a time when Mme. Tussaud had in mind for her wax museum the name Chamber of Physiognomy (Lee 124)—and Jews, like other marginalized people in England, were portrayed in visual and written form in certain stereotypical, unflattering ways. The dark complexion, large nose, and thick lips of the Jews constituted faces that were decidedly non-English and non-white. In the words of one early twentieth-century observer of the immigrant scene, these were "faces that were not with us at Agincourt" (quoted in Lee 124).

Lawrence manifested this aspect of the English identity debates of his time, a concentration on physical features as a window to the race. References to Jewish physical traits in Lawrence's writings usually center on the height (diminutive), the nose (prominent), and the complexion (swarthy). The first description of Mrs. Eastwood, for example, is "a very small woman, with a rather large nose"; thus she is "probably a Jewess" (*VG*

86). I address this subject in my assessment of Lawrence's attitudes toward the Jews in "D. H. Lawrence and the 'Jewish Problem': Reflections on a Self-Confessed 'Hebrophobe.' " As noted in
that essay, Lawrence, like many English, often used the word
"little" to describe Jews, as if to "belittle" them. We find him
applying this adjective especially to his publishers, booksellers,
and printers, but also to other acquaintances and friends. Some
of these people were truly diminutive in stature, but the context
and frequency of "little" make it obvious that a moral or psychological trait, not a physical one, is not the real issue. To Lawrence,
Thomas Seltzer was "a tiny Jew, but trustworthy" (*L* iv. 366).

As for the nose, it is a giveaway to the Jewishness of two characters in *Aaron's Rod*, one a landlady and the other a member of
a writer's circle in Florence. The latter character, Walter Rosen—
based on Gertrude Stein's brother Leo (Lawrence referred to Leo
as "a shitten Jew," a "nasty, nosy, corrupt Jew" [*L* iv.182])—has
a nose so prominent on his face and so central to his being that it
is said to smile (*AR* 217). In one example of the nineteenth-century pseudo-scientific literature, the Jewish nose was called the
"hawknose" and was said to indicate "considerable Shrewdness
in worldly matters; a deep insight into character, and facility of
turning that insight to profitable account." This nose was more
than an outward sign of the Jew's way with money. It was also
thought to be responsible for the inability of immigrant Jews to
speak the majority tongue without a Yiddish accent; thus, the
nose branded the Jew as an outsider not only because of its shape
but also because of its speech function (Gilman, *Jew's Body* 179–
80). Such a fixation on, and stereotyping of, Jewish physical characteristics help to explain Lawrence's own references to the
Jewish nose, an organ that he usually linked to an ineluctable
failing of the Jew. The misshapen nose resulted in a misshapen
attitude toward life. Reading the Revelations of St. John a few
months before he died, Lawrence remarked that the "Jews were
particularly pernicious, for their regeneration . . . was always
moral and through the nose" (*L* vii. 545). The so-called Jewish
nose must be the source of what Lawrence castigated as the
"Jewish nasal sort of style," the "Jewish nasal ethics," with its
emphasis on the morally righteous (*L* vii. 519, 508).

But if Lawrence thought he could spot a Jew because of that
person's appearance, he wasn't always sure whether Jewishness
signified race, religion, or nation—a common occurrence in the

early 1900s, when the terms "race" and "nation" were used loosely, interchangeably, and variously (Mackay and Thane 209). In his high school European history textbook, in the chapter on Christianity, Lawrence states that the Romans finally allowed the Nazarenes to return to Jerusalem because they had abandoned their old religion: that is, "it was recognised that a Jew was not a Jew because of his nation, but because of his religion. Nationality or citizenship or race made a Greek or a Roman or a Gaul. But religion made a Jew" (*MEH* 29–30). Yet only a few pages later, Lawrence remarks that "the Jews, the Chosen People, really did hate or despise all who were not of their own race" (*MEH* 34). The well-known letter to Mark Gertler about Gertler's painting "Merry-Go-Round" explains that only a Jew could depict the modern world's disintegration into mechanism and militarism because of his "national history" and "older race" (*L* ii. 660). In *Women in Love*, Birkin agrees with Gerald that, at least in Europe, "race is the essential element in nationality" (28). It is probably because Loerke, inspired by Gertler, is a Jew that he has no national identity, but rather is "detached from everything" and "admit[s] no allegiance" (452). Anne Fernihough argues, in her book on Lawrence's aesthetics and ideology, that Lawrence is led in part by a *völkisch* stress on the concept of organicism and "the natural" into racialized thinking that in turn leads to the portrayal of this Jewish artist, Loerke, as epitomizing the modern detachment from real life (28).

In his biography *D. H. Lawrence: The Early Years*, John Worthen notes that in Lawrence's first novel, *The White Peacock*, we find evidence of the ascendancy of the modern, framed as a problem for society and deriving no doubt from the author's personal angst. Leslie and George, says Worthen, "offer parallel but opposed kinds of twentieth-century experience: . . . the modern and permanently rootless confronting the old and gradually uprooted" (Worthen 226). Discussing a very different novel of the same period, Abraham Cahan's *The Rise of David Levinsky*, David Engel characterizes this story of Jewish immigrant life as "absorbed with the issue of what it means to be modern" (70). At issue is the admixture of a heady sense of freedom and a distressing feeling of exile. Since the modern condition is marked by discontinuity and characterized by marginalization, the Jews are the quintessential modern people, Engel asserts. Carl Jung put a negative cast on this discontinuity, complaining in 1918 that the

Jew is "badly at a loss for that quality in man which roots him to
the earth and draws new strength from below" (quoted in Gilman, *Jew's Body* 197). Lawrence would have agreed with Jung,
judging by such characters as the rat-like Loerke. Another com-
mentator on "the marginal character of the Jews," however, has
defined the marginal man more objectively, less judgmentally, as
"the individual who lives in, or has ties of kinship with, two or
more interacting societies between which there exists sufficient
incompatibility to render his own adjustment to them difficult or
impossible. He does not quite 'belong' or feel at home in either
group" (Everett Stonequist, 1942, quoted in Dench 171). This description fits the rootless and restless D. H. Lawrence. Lawrence
represented his own marginality in such characters as Phoenix,
the gypsy, Oliver Mellors, and Rupert Birkin—all of whom dance
through life with what could be called "deracinatin' rhythm," to
steal J. Hoberman's pun about the contemporaneous Jewish figure of the jazz singer, who is caught between worlds and not fully
at home in any of them (Hoberman 1).

In 1915 Lawrence confessed to Lady Ottoline, "I shall be restless all my life. If I had a house and home, I should become
wicked. . . . And wherever I am, after a while I begin to ail me to
go away" (*L* ii. 318). But unlike Joyce and Pound, Lawrence did
not celebrate exile as a state of liberation and freedom; he did not
wholly reject his own nation or nationalism in general. That he
felt a kinship with that paradigmatic modern, the wandering
Jew, is revealed in several letters (iii. 435; iv. 238, 255). That he
also wished to stop his wandering is clear from his wistful
searches for what he called Rananim, his perfect place.

Amazingly, given his attitudes toward Jews, for a short time he
even conceived of that place as Palestine. Although his letters
make no mention of the Balfour Declaration that recommended
the establishment of a Jewish homeland, his letters of the period
immediately before and for some years after that Declaration of
November 1917 show his increasing preoccupation with the idea
of Palestine. To a Jewish novelist, Louis Golding, he opined that
"a Jewish book should be written in terms of *difference* from the
Gentile consciousness. . . . Yet even in Zionists I can't really get
at any gulf between me and them. They seem like one of us English just doing a Zion stunt" (*L* iii. 690). His thought of joining
his friend David Eder in Palestine, to "Zionise it into a Rananim"
(*L* iii. 214), suggests a yearning for a homeland, even one "with

noses" (L iii. 353), and a willingness to perform his own Zion stunt of sorts.[7] Of course, Lawrence was not interested in Palestine as a Jewish homeland, merely in Palestine as an uncharted territory (somewhere like Canada or Australia) in which he could form his ideal society. His letters indicate clearly that in his imagination he had already appropriated the Jews' territory, stripped it of its Jewish associations, and made it Lawrence country. Moreover, he implied to Eder that without the "spark of magic" that D. H. Lawrence could instill in Palestine, it would be a "dead failure" (L iii. 353): "I don't believe you'll pull it off, as a vital reality, without me," he stated audaciously to his friend (L iii. 354). If anything, Lawrence's willingness to march on Zion, an idea probably scotched by Eder (L iii. 687), shows his desperation to flee England.[8]

Where Englishness—like so much else—was concerned, Lawrence was a study in contradiction. On the one hand, he could assert that he would never go "back on my whiteness and Englishness and myself. English in the teeth of all the world, even in the teeth of England" (L iv. 234). Indeed, when Frieda wrote to Mabel Dodge Luhan in 1926 about the possibility that the Lawrences might have to sell the ranch in New Mexico, she remarked that "it grieves me too much to think the ranch might go, but then we have so little money and Lawrence is so English" (L v. 598). He was not like David Eder, who advocated that Jews who settled in Palestine "must give up our pretensions to being Europeans" (Hobman 166). On the other hand, Lawrence was regularly capable of excoriating England and the English from a variety of platforms.

We live today in a contradictory, destabilized world—often called "postmodern"—in which increasing diversity and easier contact among nations and peoples are matched by a corresponding rise in nationalism and closing ranks. Ethnicity, along with race and sex, is more and more regarded as a construct rather than a given, because "identity itself is not a fixed and autonomous essence but rather an aspect of culture and therefore similarly malleable" (Biale et al. 9, 25); at the same time, "ethnic cleansing" of many kinds threatens the lives of innumerable Others. In the 1990s, the term "postethnic" appeared as a theoretical lens through which to view and deal with the insufficiency of today's identity politics. David Biale, for one, would have us go beyond the concept of the melting pot in recognizing that now as

never before, identities are being chosen and categories trans-
versed. Jews have historically had much experience with the multiplicity of identities underlying "postethnicity," and today they
exist in more of a state of indeterminacy than ever (Biale et al.
29–32).

It might well be said that the fluidity of identity that marks the
modern Jewish condition marked D. H. Lawrence's life as well.
His personal history is akin to, and illuminated by, the history of
the Jewish people, a history of *relationship* to various worlds and
an often uneasy maneuvering between them. In failing the test of
being "an Englishman at heart," Lawrence challenged the very
notions of "majority" and "minority" and pointed to the brave
(and frightening) new world in which identities of all sorts are
more liberating, but also more complicated, than ever.

## NOTES

1. Examples include Linda Nochlin and Tamar Garb's collection of essays on
the image of the Jew in nineteenth- and twentieth-century literature and art in
the United States, France, and England; James Shapiro's study of Shakespeare
and the Jews; and Bryan Cheyette's analysis of "the Jew" in modern English
literature and society.

2. Gratuitous references to Jews and money appear throughout Lawrence,
often more subtly linked to the degeneration of England. In "Education of the
People," for example, in the middle of a discussion of productive activity, Lawrence characterizes the modern bourgeois as one who engages in "the mean,
Jewish competition in productivity, in money-making" (*RDP* 157). As I note in
my article on "D. H. Lawrence and the 'Jewish Problem': Confessions of a Self-
Confessed 'Hebrophobe,'" in *Kangaroo* only the rich *Jews* are identified by
their religion, as in "Marquis Tribes von Israel" and "Mr. Hebrew Rothschild"
(*K* 310); the Christian Mr. Carnegie is labeled with his area of industry rather
than with his religion (Ruderman 102).

3. The feminized male Jew also appears in works by Lawrence's contemporaries Ernest Hemingway—as the antithesis of the rugged American hero and
as the repudiated other self of the "macho" creator—and George Orwell. See
Loewenstein for the connection between the British inculcation of the ideal of
masculinity and the shadow Jewish selves created by writers like Wyndham
Lewis, William Gerhardi, and Orwell.

4. By the mid-nineteenth century, scientists like Robert Knox (*The Races of
Men,* 1850) stated uncategorically that, based on the color of the skin and the
features of the face, Jews *were* black; and being Jewish, black, diseased, and
"ugly" were all interrelated (Gilman, *Jew's Body* 173; *Jewish Self-Hatred* 6–7).

5. Michael Ragussis demonstrates in his book subtitled *"The Jewish Question" and English National Identity* how "under the influence of England's religious revival the rhetoric of conversion became so widely disseminated that it
was used in a host of cultural projects, like [Edmund] Burke's *Reflections on the*

*Revolution in France*, which worked to define English national identity in rela-tion to both other European national identities and to Jewish identity" (8).

6. Lawrence had his own offensive German proverb about the Jews. To Max Mohr, an author who was having trouble getting his novel published, Lawrence wrote, "Ist man arm, isst man Judendreck; ist man reich, lässt man Judenweg" [If one is poor, one eats Jew-shit; if one is rich, one ignores Jews] (*L* vii. 304). This proverb refers to the prevalence of Jewish publishers at the time.

7. See Earl Ingersoll, "Lawrence's Friendship with David Eder," *Etudes law-renciennes* 11 (1995), 71–84, for an account of Eder's significance in Lawrence's life.

8. Interestingly, Lawrence's American publisher, Thomas Seltzer, had his own connection to Zionism, since his sister-in-law Henrietta Szold founded Ha-dassah, the Zionist woman's organization. If the Seltzers ever discussed either Zionism or the family's experiences in Palestine with Lawrence, they left no re-cord of the conversations. However, the "laws" that Lawrence envisioned en-acting in Palestine, embodying the notions of freedom and individuality (*L* iii. 353), he would envision again for different lands: the "aboriginal" America of the classic literature and the Australian outback of *The Boy in the Bush*.

## WORKS CITED

Biale, David, Michael Galchinsky, and Susannah Heschel, eds. *Insider/Outsider: American Jews and Multiculturalism*. Berkeley: University of California Press, 1998.

Brookes, Peter and Peter Widdowson. "A Literature for England." In *English-ness: Politics and Culture 1880–1920*, edited by Robert Colls and Philip Dodd. London: Croom Helm, 1986.

Castle, Kathryn. *Britannia's Children: Reading Colonialism Through Chil-dren's Books and Magazines*. Manchester: Manchester University Press, 1996.

Cesarini, David. "Joynson-Hicks and the Radical Right in England After the First World War." In *Traditions of Intolerance: Historical Perspectives on Fascism and Race Discourse in British Society*, edited by Tony Kushner and Kenneth Lunn. Manchester: Manchester University Press, 1989.

Cheyette, Bryan. *Constructions of "the Jew" in English Literature and Society: Racial Representations, 1875–1945*. Cambridge: Cambridge University Press, 1993.

———. "Neither Black Nor White: The Figure of 'the Jew' in Imperial British Literature." In *The Jew in the Text: Modernity and the Construction of Iden-tity*, edited by Linda Nochlin and Tamar Garb. London: Thames and Hudson, 1996.

Dench, Geoff. *Minorities in the Open Society: Prisoners of Ambivalence*. London: Routledge, 1986.

Dodd, Philip. "Englishness and the National Culture." In *Englishness: Politics and Culture 1880–1920*, edited by Robert Colls and Philip Dodd. London: Croom Helm, 1986.

Draper, R. P., ed. *D. H. Lawrence: The Critical Heritage*. London: Routledge, 1970.

Emerson, Ralph Waldo. *English Traits*. In *The Collected Works of Ralph Waldo Emerson*. Vol. 5. Edited by Douglas Emory Wilson. Cambridge: Harvard University Press, 1994.

Endelman, Todd M. "The Englishness of Jewish Modernity in England." In *Toward Modernity: The European Jewish Model*, edited by Jacob Katz. New Brunswick, N.J.: Transaction Books, 1987.

Engel, David. "The Discrepancies of the Modern: Reevaluating Abraham Cahan's *The Rise of David Levinsky*." *Studies in American Jewish Literature* 5 (Winter 1979): 68–91.

Fernihough, Anne. *D. H. Lawrence, Aesthetics and Ideology*. Oxford: Oxford University Press, 1993.

Garb, Tamar. "Modernity, Identity, Textuality." Introduction to *The Jew in the Text: Modernity and the Construction of Identity*, edited by Linda Nochlin and Tamar Garb. London: Thames and Hudson, 1996.

Giles, Judy and Tim Middleton, eds. *Writing Englishness 1900–1950*. London: Routledge, 1995.

Gilman, Sander L. *The Jew's Body*. New York: Routledge, 1991.

———. *Jewish Self-Hatred: Anti-Semitism and the Hidden Language of the Jews*. Baltimore: Johns Hopkins University Press, 1986.

Hawkins, Alvin. "The Discovery of Rural England." In *Englishness: Politics and Culture, 1880–1929*, edited by Robert Colls and Philip Dodd. London: Croom Helm, 1986.

Hoberman, J. "Deracinatin' Rhythm: Is 'The Jazz Singer' Good for the Jews?" *Village Voice* 26 (7–13 January 1981): 1, 31–33.

Hobman, J. B., ed. *David Eder: Memoirs of a Modern Pioneer*. London: Victor Gollancz, 1945.

Holmes, Colin. *Anti-Semitism in British Society 1876–1939*. New York: Holmes & Meier, 1979.

Lee, Alan. "Aspects of the Working-Class Response to the Jews in Britain, 1880–1914." In *Hosts, Immigrants and Minorities: Historical Responses to Newcomers in British Society 1870–1914*, edited by Kenneth Lunn. New York: St. Martin's, 1980.

Lipman, V. D. *A History of the Jews in Britain since 1858*. London: Leicester University Press, 1990.

Loewenstein, Andrea Freud. *Loathsome Jews and Engulfing Women: Metaphors of Projection in the Works of Wyndham Lewis, Charles Williams, and Graham Greene*. New York: New York University Press, 1993.

———. "The Protection of Masculinity: Jews as Projective Pawns in the Texts of William Gerhardi and George Orwell." In *Between "Race" and Culture: Representations of "the Jew" in English and American Literature*, edited by Bryan Cheyette. Stanford: Stanford University Press, 1996.

Mackay, Jane and Pat Thane. "The Englishwoman." In *Englishness: Politics and Culture, 1880–1929*, edited by Robert Colls and Philip Dodd. London: Croom Helm, 1986.

Metzger, Mary Jane. "'Now by My Hood, a Gentle and No Jew': Jessica, *The Merchant of Venice*, and the Discourse of Early Modern English Identity." *PMLA* 113 (January 1998): 52–63.

Ragussis, Michael. *Figures of Conversion: "The Jewish Question" & English National Identity*. Durham: Duke University Press, 1995.

Rich, Paul. "Imperial Decline and the Resurgence of English National Identity, 1918–1979." In *Traditions of Intolerance*, edited by Tony Kushner and Kenneth Lunn. Manchester: Manchester University Press, 1989.

Ruderman, Judith. "D. H. Lawrence and the 'Jewish Question': Reflections on a Self-Confessed 'Hebrophobe.'" *DHLR* 23 (1991): 99–109.

Shapiro, James. *Shakespeare and the Jews*. New York: Columbia University Press, 1996.

Worthen, John. *D. H. Lawrence, The Early Years 1885–1912*. Cambridge: Cambridge University Press, 1991.

# Lawrence and Knud Merrild:
# New Materials, New Perspectives
### Keith Cushman

In the world of Lawrence studies, Knud Merrild will always be remembered as one of the Danish painters who became friends with the Lawrences in Taos in the winter of 1922–23. In the larger world of twentieth-century art, Merrild is not so well-known, but his work is represented in such collections as the Museum of Modern Art, the Philadelphia Museum of Art, the Los Angeles County Museum, and the Art Institute of Chicago. In 1990 Merrild was one of twenty artists surveyed in an exhibit at the Santa Barbara Museum of Art titled "Turning the Tide: Early Los Angeles Modernists 1920–1956." As recently as the spring of 1998, the prestigious Hirschl & Adler Galleries in midtown Manhattan included Merrild in a four-person show of modern artists titled "Eccentric Orbits." I believe that fifty years after his death, Knud Merrild is poised to develop a more substantial reputation as a modern American abstractionist.

In the first section of this essay I will briefly tell the story of Merrild's personal and artistic interaction with Lawrence. In the Lawrence world Merrild the artist is best remembered for his portrait of Lawrence that is part of the Arensberg Collection of the Philadelphia Museum of Art, but Merrild's artistic connection to Lawrence is far more extensive than that. Merrild designed the dust-jacket of *The Captain's Doll*, and he also completed several other trial dust-jackets and sketches toward dust-jackets.

Furthermore, he is undoubtedly the most prolific of Lawrence portraitists. Most of these images have never been seen; most are unknown even to Lawrence scholars. The second section will be devoted to a consideration of two of the dust-jacket designs and a number of the portraits. Then I will provide a brief glimpse of the artist Merrild became in the years after his encounter with the

Lawrences, especially in the 1930s and 1940s. I will also discuss the enduring impact of Lawrence on Merrild the artist and man.

## I. "HE HAS A GREAT SENSE OF BEAUTY, AND IS MODERN"

In Taos, Knud Merrild and Kai Götzsche were known simply and universally as "the Danes." Merrild had arrived in New York in August 1921; he met Götzsche there through his work designing movie posters. The Danes traveled from New York City to Taos in their ramshackle model-T Ford, curious about the artists' colonies there and in Santa Fe (Dailey 7). They reached Taos in mid-1922. When Mabel decided not to allow Lawrence and Frieda to live in a cabin she owned, Lawrence rented a log cabin seventeen miles above Taos, and he invited the Danes to live in a nearby cabin. Lawrence, Frieda, Merrild, and Götzsche had hit it off, and the Danes were pleased to accept the invitation.

That winter above Taos is well-documented in Lawrence's letters and survives even more extensively in Merrild's memoir of Lawrence, *A Poet and Two Painters*, published in 1938. Merrild's practice of quoting long passages from Lawrence's writings—sometimes much *later* writings—to represent Lawrence's conversation seriously damages the book. But *A Poet and Two Painters* is nevertheless one of the most likable of the 1930s memoirs, notable for its clear-eyed, richly detailed, somewhat wry account of life with the Lawrences.

In his Preface to *A Poet and Two Painters*, Aldous Huxley describes the book's portrait of Lawrence as "perhaps the most vivid, the most objective and . . . the most disinterested yet produced" (Merrild xvii). Merrild recognized that he and Götzsche "did not possess the brilliance of [Lawrence's] mind nor the abundance of his knowledge; we had only horse sense, and knew people and the world by experience. . . . We did not play up to him, and were not afraid of voicing our opinions . . ." (Merrild 92). The "unity of manly togetherness, understanding, fidelity" (Merrild 85) that the Danes felt with Lawrence shines through Merrild's memoir.

The Danes were essentially Lawrence's contemporaries (Götzsche was born in 1886, Merrild in 1894), but in *A Poet and Two Painters* they seem rather like the teen-aged sons (almost always well-behaved) of Lawrence and Frieda. Lawrence and the Danes

enjoyed riding and working around the ranch together. Lawrence
relished the manly, physical activities they shared. As he wrote
Catherine Carswell on 17 December 1922, "We've got two Danish
artists in a tiny log cabin – they came along with us – and we all
chop down trees for our burning, and go off riding together. Altogether it is ideal. . . (L iv. 362).

The Danes loved the rough winter they spent with this "man
of strong personality and character, almost overpowering and ab-
solutely fearless" (Merrild 85), and they appreciated Frieda's
mothering. They also witnessed a few of Lawrence's rages, including "a hysterical outbreak on Lawrence's part" over Frieda's
"very nonchalant way with her cigarette" (Merrild 136–37) and,
most notoriously, his shockingly brutal treatment of the dog Bib-
bles. Frieda later told Merrild that the Danes "knew them more
intimately than any human beings before us or any after us"
(Merrild 136).

Merrild had been a champion swimmer back in Scandinavia,
and he was also a crack outdoorsman. The fact that Merrild was
both an artist and a man of easy physical prowess appealed to
Lawrence. In the year before coming to Taos, Merrild had "taken
some odd jobs as labourer, steeplejack, helping in building smoke-
stacks and in building steel and concrete construction works." He
"had been riding and handling heavy steel beams, had mixed ce-
ment and gravel by hand and hauled it in wheelbarrows on scaf-
folding, etc.—not to speak of the pushing of our automobile we
both had to do on all the steep hills across the entire country"
(Merrild 77).

This muscular Dane was also an intensely modern painter.
From 1909 to 1912 Merrild had studied at the Art and Technical
School in a small town near Copenhagen. While studying in Copenhagen at the Arts and Crafts School in 1913, he saw an exhibi-
tion of cubist painting that made him decide to become a modern
artist. The Arts and Crafts School threw him out in 1916 for vigorously advocating modern art. Subsequently he lasted only
about a year in the confining conservative atmosphere of the
Royal Academy of Fine Arts (Dailey 6–7, Meyers 421).

Lawrence's idea of having Merrild design dust-jackets for his
Seltzer first editions emerged from a "tea-party" the Danes had
for the Lawrences at their "primitive atelier" in Taos not long
after their first meeting. Lawrence wasn't at all interested in the
Danes' paintings: " 'It bores me to look at paintings,' he said.

'Why do you have to paint? There are enough paintings in the world, the art of painting is dead.'" But Lawrence was impressed with some posters Merrild and Götzsche had done for a New York film company, and Merrild also brought out some of his "own designs for ceramics, vignettes and book-plates." By the time the Lawrences had left, Lawrence "had asked me if I would care to make some designs for his books and also to illustrate his 'Birds, Beasts and Flowers'" (Merrild 16–18).

On 28 November 1922 Lawrence still thought that Merrild's surname was "Merrull," but he knew that the Danes had "no money, hardly," and he was certain that he wanted "Seltzer to let Merrull do my book-jacket designs – he is a very clever decorator – and some designs for *Birds Beasts*" (*L* iv. 344). As it turned out, Seltzer used the dust-wrapper design for *The Captain's Doll* but turned down Merrild's designs for *Kangaroo* and *Birds, Beasts and Flowers*. Subsequently, Seltzer also rejected a Merrild design for the jacket of *Studies in Classic American Literature*.

The idea of having Merrild do "some designs for *Birds Beasts*"—that is, illustrations for the individual sections of the book—never panned out. The Humanities Research Center at the University of Texas owns four brush drawings by Merrild that were intended as interior decorations for *Birds, Beasts and Flowers*. These drawings are reproduced on pages 58 and 59 of Gerald Lacy's edition of *D. H. Lawrence: Letters to Thomas and Adele Seltzer* (1976), where they are erroneously attributed to Lawrence. Seltzer did use Kai Götzsche's design for the dust-jacket of *Mastro-don Gesualdo*. (*The Captain's Doll, Kangaroo, Birds, Beasts and Flowers*, and *Mastro-don Gesualdo* were all published by Seltzer in 1923.)

From the beginning Lawrence was mindful of the Danes' poverty: they "have no money, hardly" (*L* iv. 344). On 10 February 1923, Lawrence wrote Seltzer that "when you get used to it you'll like Merrilds *Kangaroo* jacket. I didn't like it at first: now think perhaps it's the best. I do want them to have a few dollars to be able to go on their way with. Otherwise I must give them, and it's so much better for their pride if they can earn them" (*L* iv. 383). Lawrence's tone seems like that of a concerned parent. His characteristic tact and generosity are unmistakable: he would give the Danes the money they needed, but it was better if they could earn it.

Lawrence was sensitive to the Danes' penury, but that was no reason to try to convince Seltzer that Merrild should design some of his dust-jackets. Lawrence saw the Merrild of 1922 as a "clever decorator"—and as the sort of artist who was right for Lawrence's American dust-jackets. In England Martin Secker had become Lawrence's main publisher, packaging Lawrence's books in staid, uniform, cream-colored dust-jackets without any sort of visual art, clearly in an attempt to neutralize Lawrence and convert him into a safe "standard author." But by 1922 Lawrence had set his main hopes on the American market, which he perceived as younger, more adventurous, and readier for Lawrence's boldness. He believed that Merrild's designs would help sell books to this audience. Lawrence wrote his publisher that Merrild "has a great sense of beauty, and is modern" (*L* iv. 345)—high praise indeed. In any event Seltzer paid Merrild $120 for his designs for *The Captain's Doll*, *Studies in Classic American Literature*, and *Kangaroo*, though he used only the *Captain's Doll* jacket (*Letters to Thomas and Adele Seltzer* 259).

## II. Book-Jacket Designer and Portraitist

I'll begin with an account of Merrild's dust-jacket designs for Lawrence. The two I'll be discussing date from the winter of 1922–23 in Taos. Lawrence began by giving Merrild "particulars about the contents of the books and the motifs he would like me to use"; the creation of the jacket designs became a shared activity. Lawrence liked Merrild's *Captain's Doll* jacket "quite well right away," but not his *Kangaroo*."To make clear what he wanted," Lawrence "made a drawing of a kangaroo himself," and subsequently he also "made the first design" for *Studies in Classic American Literature*. Drawing together was a kind of game for the two men: "and did we have fun! Lawrence just loved to draw, he was like a child about it" (Merrild 96–97). Although Lawrence played such an active role in the design of the jackets, Merrild always stood his ground.

Merrild's colorful, witty design for the Seltzer *Captain's Doll* (Figure 1) is one of the most splendid of the Lawrence dust-jackets. Seltzer published his edition of *The Captain's Doll: Three Novelettes* in 1923. The other two "novelettes" are of course *The Fox* and *The Ladybird*. A color photograph of Merrild's jacket can be found on the front cover of the *D. H. Lawrence Review* (28:1–

Figure 1. Dust-jacket for *The Captain's Doll*

2). I discuss the jacket in my essay, "Lawrence's Dust-Jackets: A Selection with Commentary," on pages 31–33 in that number of the *DHLR*.

Merrild's bold deco-ish design is in bright colors: deep red, deep blue, light green. The captain's doll dominates the design, while the icons for the fox and Count Psanek of *The Ladybird* are much smaller. Merrild cleverly transforms the fox and Count Psanek into toys to fit in with the captain's doll, another toy. The vertical of the doll's black shirt plays against the broad horizontal black bar behind the doll to strengthen and stabilize the design. Merrild's name with "1923" below it also figures as a design element.

The jacket playfully calls attention to Lawrence's reputation for pushing the literary boundaries of sexuality. The doll's sexuality is strongly ambiguous. The doll itself is weak and passive, just the way Hannele would like Captain Hepburn to be. The doll's arms and legs are akimbo and easily manipulable, the gap between the crossed legs archetypally female. The right hand and arm dangling limply between the doll's legs are overtly but impotently male. The doll's cheek is rouged and its lips red—but at the same time the head is foursquare and manly. Furthermore, the stiff, erect head with its checkered cap is aggressively penile. Nor can the fox's erect tail and the two blue balls that represent wheels be accidental. The image of Count Psanek is less phallic, and yet the Count's head is similar to that of the captain's doll. Merrild's design seems to be telling the reader to be open to the sexuality of Lawrence's fiction while remaining alert to its complexity. The visual cleverness also suggests that the reader needn't take the sexuality too solemnly. Lawrence was pleased with the design, calling it "very gay and lively" (*L* iv. 453).

Secker published his English edition of the three novellas as *The Ladybird: The Fox: The Captain's Doll* in March 1923. Just one month later Seltzer published *The Captain's Doll: Three Novelettes* in New York City with the order of the three novellas reversed. I believe that Seltzer chose this title and this order to accommodate Merrild's jacket design. It's also noticeable that *Captains* has no apostrophe—either in Merrild's jacket design or on the spine (which features the same lettering). The apostrophe is present everywhere else in the book. Why the missing apostrophe? Because Danish, like the other Scandinavian languages as well as German, lacks the apostrophe, and no one caught the omission. (The Danish translation of *Aaron's Rod* is *Aarons Stav.*)

Figure 2 is the most advanced version of one of the rejected designs for *Kangaroo*. (Three preliminary sketches, owned by the Harry Ransom Humanities Research Center at the University of Texas, are reproduced on page 49 of *D. H. Lawrence: Letters to Thomas and Adele Seltzer*. All three are attributed to Merrild, though the one in the upper-right hand corner is clearly by Lawrence.) The Figure 2 design has a pop-cubist quality. Although *Kangaroo* is of course set in Australia, Merrild's design is strongly Southwest American, which may be a reason that Seltzer rejected the jacket. The colors—brown, green, orange—are Southwestern, the pattern at the top calls the Taos Pueblo to mind—and the kangaroo looks back at a cactus! The central image's blend of the geometric and the rounded also evokes Southwestern Native American design. The brown-and-white curvilinear kangaroo and the green-and-white curvilinear cactus seem almost like mirror images of one another (and kangaroo and cactus flower seem to be looking at one another). Could this be a witty visual depiction of Lawrence's vision of the essential oneness of the natural world?

This must be the design that Merrild "perhaps . . . liked the best." Lawrence complained, "I don't like the repetition of lines around the design. I really don't like repetitions!"—to which Merrild responded, "A repetition of lines in design, and in words and sentences in poetry, gives rhythm, a factor an artist is working with" (Merrild 122). Undoubtedly this is the *Kangaroo* jacket that Merrild submitted to Seltzer, for in a letter to his American publisher of 4 January 1923, Lawrence wrote, "Looking at Merrild's book-jacket designs again, I think that one for *Kangaroo* with the small figure in the middle is rather weak and abstract-looking: might lead one to expect something theoretic" (*L* iv. 367).

Knud Merrild did over twenty portraits of Lawrence, most of them small portrait sketches, including six that are owned by the Humanities Research Center at the University of Texas. This is an astonishing number of original images of Lawrence. Fourteen of them, passed down to Knud and Else Merrild's heirs in Denmark, have only recently come to light. With the exception of the india ink sketch used on the front and back covers of *DHLR* 27:2–3 they remain totally unknown to the public. Five of the

Figure 2.  Dust-jacket design for *Kangaroo*

HRC portraits—quite various images—are reproduced on page 50 of the Seltzer letters.

Three other Merrild portraits of Lawrence can be found in the dust-jackets of Lawrence memoirs (although few scholars have seen these very rare jackets). The best-known portrait, which probably dates from 1923, is in the collection of the Philadelphia Museum of Art. This picture belonged to Walter and Louise Arensberg—along with works by Klee, Kandinsky, Duchamp, Tanguy, Ernst, Brancusi, and Arp. Ultimately it was used in the jacket design of the American first edition of Witter Bynner's *Journey with Genius* (1951). Frieda used a pen-and-ink portrait sketch of Lawrence by Merrild on the jacket of her memoir, *"Not I, But The Wind . . ."* (1934). Finally Merrild created a wonderful 1933 sketch with watercolor of Lawrence in Taos for the dust-jacket of his own memoir, *A Poet and Two Painters* (1938). Interestingly each of these dust-jacket portraits is based on or at least related to one of the sketches at the HRC that is reproduced on page 50 of the Seltzer letters.

Add the fourteen sketches of Lawrence from the Merrild family, six portrait sketches at the HRC, the portrait at the Philadelphia Museum of Art plus the dust-jacket images of *A Poet and Two Painters* and *"Not I, But the Wind . . ."* and you have a total of twenty-three portraits. Most are pen and ink; some are in pencil and some add watercolor. No reference seems to have survived to any of Merrild's many portraits of Lawrence. None appears in *A Poet and Two Painters*, which is illustrated with photographs.

With the exceptions of the portrait in the Arensberg Collection of the Philadelphia Museum of Art and the dust-jacket picture for *A Poet and Two Painters*, Merrild's Lawrence portraits are informal—sketches rather than finished works. Most are unsigned. Although Merrild may have exhibited some of these sketches in the 1930s, he seems to have drawn them for his own amusement. Perhaps Merrild executed some of the sketches as he and Götzsche chatted with Lawrence during the long winter above Taos in 1922–23. But it must also be pointed out that Merrild drew two of the sketches on the reverse of a telephone journal dated 17 February 1928—and most of the portraits are impossible to date. The very small (5½ x 4¼″) india ink portrait, reproduced on the front and back covers of the *DHLR* (28:1–2), is found on the reverse of an 8½ x 11″ sheet on which Merrild has listed the twenty-three letters he had received from Lawrence prior to 24 January

1924. Does this date the portrait in early 1924? Or did he sketch it sometime in the mid-1930s when he was working on his memoir and wanted a census of his letters from Lawrence on hand?

Why this abundance of portraits of Lawrence? Many reasons come to mind. After all, Merrild's relationship with Lawrence left an enduring impact on the Danish painter's life and art. It was flattering to be befriended by an internationally renowned writer—a 1920s literary celebrity. Beyond that, Lawrence was a complicated, intriguing, controversial, larger-than-life figure. There were depths to be plummeted in this enigmatic man just as there were in his writings.

Lawrence provided Merrild with a powerful model of the artist's life, true to his artistic mission no matter what. He also embodied what it meant to be an authentic individual—in the terms of the period, a real man. As Merrild comments, "A man doesn't want to be weak, he wants to be strong and to be brave, even if it is a bit foolish sometimes. And [Lawrence] was a man, a real man in every respect" (Merrild 103).

So it's no wonder that Lawrence became an obsessive artistic subject to Merrild in the 1920s and 1930s. Lawrence posed a compelling artistic challenge. The only Götzsche portrait of Lawrence that seems to have survived is the picture of Lawrence in "leather shirt and blue overalls" and with "such a funny face" (*L* iv. 370, 373) completed in January 1923 and fully documented in Lawrence's letters and *A Poet and Two Painters*. (A photograph of this portrait, which now belongs to the Humanities Research Center, can be found following page 260 of *Letters* iv). It's as if this one image sufficed for Götzsche (even though after Taos, Götzsche spent much more time with Lawrence than Merrild ever did). But Merrild returned to the subject of Lawrence again and again. One picture could not capture Lawrence. Neither could ten.

Space prohibits my considering all of Merrild's portraits of Lawrence that survive. I will first discuss the Arensberg portrait in the Philadelphia Museum of Art and the portraits found on the dust-jackets of Merrild's own *A Poet and Two Painters* and Frieda's *"Not I, But the Wind . . ."*. Then I will discuss a few of the portrait sketches that remained in the Merrild family.

Walter and Louise Arensberg were major American collectors of twentieth-century art. Of the great collections of modern art assembled in the first half of the twentieth century, the Arensberg collection "is the most consistently expressive of the collector's . . . own personality—his fastidious taste, his intellectuality, and his love of the esoteric" (Brown 97–98). Between 1915 and 1920 the Arensbergs' New York City apartment had been a center for the European avant garde. Especially close to Marcel Duchamp, they assembled the greatest Duchamp collection (and at one point owned both full-scale versions of *Nude Descending a Staircase*) (Naumann 6–19, 28). Merrild was part of their artistic circle after they moved to Los Angeles in 1921. The Arensbergs purchased several of Merrild's pictures—and Merrild also painted the Arensbergs' house (Karlstrom 138).

The portrait of Lawrence in the Arensberg Collection of the Philadelphia Museum of Art (Figure 3) probably dates from 1923. It measures $10\frac{1}{2}$ x $8\frac{1}{2}''$. The portrait reverses and expands on the image in a pen-and-ink drawing at the HRC, signed and dated 1923 (Figure 4), which seems to be a sketch toward the more finished portrait. (The 1933–34 date in Arensberg's hand on the back of the Philadelphia portrait must be the date he bought it from Merrild.)

Merrild strikingly captioned the HRC sketch: "D. H. L./ dark mysterious villain himself" (*Letters to Thomas & Adele Seltzer* 50). The caption cannot mean that Merrild regarded Lawrence as a villain: *A Poet and Two Painters* easily refutes such a notion. The caption may be affectionately ironic, or Merrild may possibly have made the sketch after witnessing some "villainous" behavior by Lawrence. But more to the point, Merrild saw Lawrence as such a marvelous subject precisely because of his multi-faceted, chameleon-like personality. "Dark mysterious villain" was just one of many Lawrences—and one of many artistic possibilities.

The medium of the Arensberg portrait is unusual: Merrild applied gesso to cardboard, drew and painted the image using black chalk and watercolor on the textured surface, and then coated the picture with wax. Gesso is ordinarily used to prime canvas or wood rather than paper. The colors are rich: Lawrence's beard is rusty red, his checked jacket is in shades of light and dark gray, the chair is bright yellow. As Victoria Dailey observes, applying gesso to paper creates "an ivory-like tactile surface which Merrild manipulated to achieve the desired texture" and "a luminous quality" (Dailey 10).

Merrild's portraits always involve a reduction of three-dimensional reality to simpler forms and patterns. As in almost all his portraits of Lawrence, Merrild focuses overwhelmingly on Law-

**Figure 3. Portrait of Lawrence in the Arensberg Collection**

rence's head and face. In near-profile, the head seems almost to float free, a thing unto itself not quite connected to the triangle of Lawrence's upper body. Lawrence's hair has become a fanciful, curvilinear Arp-like shape. The dark mass of Lawrence's hair and spade-like beard contrasts with the checkered jacket (not a piece of clothing that Lawrence actually owned) and the simplified chair back. Is Lawrence sitting sideways on the chair or is the picture a modernist exercise in multiple perspective?

**Figure 4.  Sketch related to the portrait of Lawrence
in the Arensberg Collection**

Although Lawrence's face is difficult to read, the mirror-image
pen-and-ink sketch at the HRC must suggest that at least to Merrild this is the picture of a "dark mysterious villain." The stylization of hair and beard, the exaggeration of potato nose, and the
minuscule eye and sharply jutting brow all move this image in the
direction of caricature. It is also safe to venture that this is intended as a portrait of Lawrence as artist. He stares intently, but
his vision seems to be inward. The expression is ambiguous, but
Lawrence seems to be internally absorbed and brooding.

Arguably the most telling detail in the Arensberg portrait is
that tiny eye. Is this an image of the artist staring inwardly, in
contact with his vision? At the same time the image seems to suggest that the artist's necessary inward vision involves loss of contact with the world around him. A special sort of sight is paid for
with a particular sort of blindness. It is suggestive that Witter Bynner chose the Arensberg portrait for the jacket of *Journey with
Genius*, his notoriously unflattering depiction of Lawrence in
which the writer appears as angry, self-absorbed, and out of
touch with reality.

Many of the Merrild portraits of Lawrence seem to explore this
same issue of artistic vision. They also play variations on the
theme of Lawrence's ultimate unreadability. This is the context
for Merrild's dust-jacket for his own memoir, *A Poet and Two
Painters* (Figure 5).

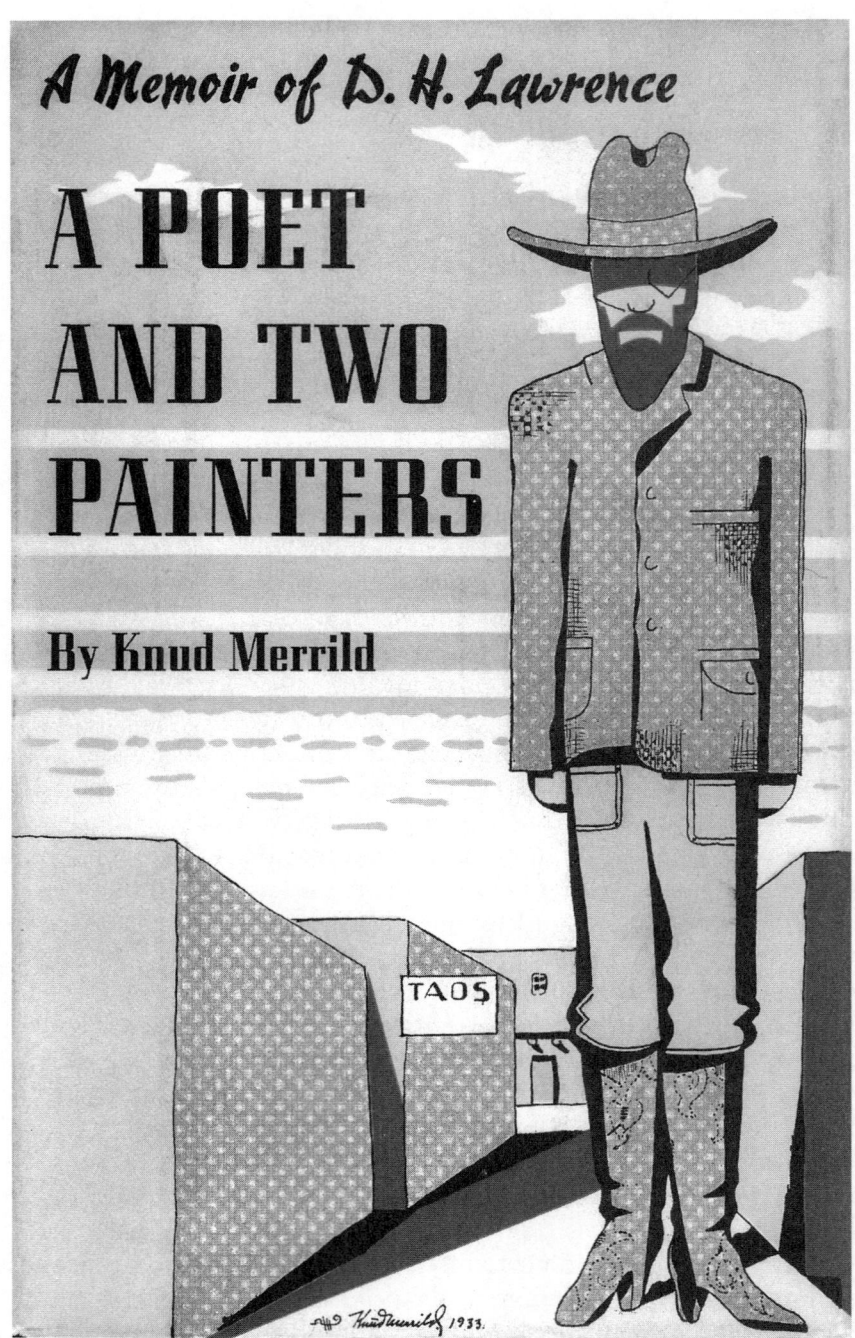

A Memoir of D. H. Lawrence

# A POET AND TWO PAINTERS

By Knud Merrild

TAOS

**Figure 5. Dust-jacket for *A Poet and Two Painters***

Our lack of knowledge concerning the history of Merrild's composition of his book renders one detail of the jacket design rather puzzling. Unlike the portraits of Lawrence found on the jackets of *Journey with Genius* and *"Not I, But The Wind . . ."* the *Poet and Two Painters* design seems to have been created specifically as a dust-jacket. It makes perfect use of the available space, leaving the upper-left-hand quadrant blank for title, subtitle, and author's name. It also directly illustrates the subject matter of the memoir. The oddity is that although *A Poet and Two Painters* was published in 1938, the jacket is signed and dated 1933.

Merrild executed this witty jacket in pen-and-ink and watercolor. A stiff, awkward, visually simplified, disproportionately elongated Lawrence in Western outfit (stylish cowboy boots, dungarees, 10-gallon-hat—though his rather ill-fitting jacket is European) dwarfs a vista of adobe buildings in Taos. Lawrence's pants, hat, and hatband, the sky, and the door to the building in the rear are all in shades of light blue. The adobe buildings on the left are pink in the sunlight, gray in shadow. Lawrence's boots and jacket are also gray. The long triangular shadow on the ground and the shadow on the building to the right are dark brown.

The design emphasizes the incongruity of the Lawrence figure, thus seemingly commenting on the incongruity of Lawrence in Taos. Some of the black outline of the lower half of the figure is so thick that it makes Lawrence into a sort of paper doll. Lawrence here is playing the gunslinger or at least the cowboy, but he's not doing so convincingly. The title, *A Poet and Two Painters*, is at Lawrence's left, but this seems to be a picture of neither poet nor painter. Three of the four adobe buildings are reduced to blank cubes, scaled down out of all proportion to Lawrence. The shadowed vista has a de Chirico feel. Is Merrild whimsically suggesting that this great man was too big for the small town of Taos?

And then there is the enigmatic mask-like face. One would say that Lawrence stares blankly ahead—except that this Lawrence *has no eyes*. Does the absence of eyes underscore the incongruity of this make-believe cowboy? Once again Lawrence's sightlessness brings to mind the issue of artistic vision. Still, the image, although satirical, seems friendly and probably affectionate, clever rather than critical. Lawrence had died eight years before the publication of *A Poet and Two Painters*; it seems likely that he would have seen the humor in the portrait. The incongruity of this dust-jacket portrait definitely conveys a point of view about Lorenzo in Taos.

The minimalist portrait sketch, executed in pencil, that Frieda used for the jacket of *"Not I, But The Wind . . ."* (Figure 6) is close to identical to another pencil sketch owned by the HRC (and reproduced on page 50 of the Seltzer letters). As with the other Merrild portraits of Lawrence I have been discussing, some will consider this sketch a caricature. Frieda barely mentions the Danes in her memoir, nor does she mention Merrild by name, although she remained friendly with him and his wife Else for the rest of their lives. Merrild is given no credit for the portrait of Lawrence on the jacket, but his signature and cypher are both clear.

The sketch's lack of aptness suggests that Frieda was using a portrait she already had in hand rather than asking Merrild to do a sketch for the jacket. This Lawrence looks vulpine and even predatory. The clump of facial hair to the right of his mouth looks like a fang, or perhaps Lawrence seems to be licking his chops. This sketch once again demonstrates Merrild's fascination with Lawrence as both icon and enigmatic psychological subject. Artistically speaking, Lawrence's head is severely reduced to a series of curves and straight lines. The forehead and brow become two straight lines at a right angle, and the brow "rhymes" with the straight line of the mouth. Lawrence's left eye is at best barely discernible, and his expression is ultimately unreadable. The sketch communicates Merrild's sense of Lawrence's mysteriousness and perhaps his sometime nastiness. Frieda apparently didn't mind putting this image on the dust-jacket of her loving memoir.

Space doesn't allow me to comment on all the Merrild portraits that were passed on to the family in Denmark after the death of Merrild and his wife. I have chosen six of the portrait sketches with the aim of illustrating some of the many different ways that Merrild perceived and portrayed Lawrence. Merrild sketched Lawrence again and again, seemingly intent both on trying out different artistic strategies and on capturing the multi-faceted personality of his subject.

Figures 7, 8, and 9 form a neat trio of images. Figure 8 was executed in Los Angeles in 1923, that is, after Merrild had left Taos—but there is no way of knowing the sequence of the three portraits. Perhaps sequence isn't really important: it is sufficient

"*Not I, But The Wind . . .*"

oᴄΘo   *By*   oᴄΘo

FRIEDA LAWRENCE
*geb. Freiin von Richthofen*

D.H.L. —

*Unpublished Letters and Material
by
D. H. Lawrence
and Memoirs by his Wife*

**Figure 6.  Dust-jacket for** *"Not I, But the Wind . . ."*

**Figures 7-8-9. Three portrait sketches**

and certainly accurate to view the three portrait sketches as variations on an iconic theme.

Figure 7—definitely a caricature—is in red pencil and watercolor; the other two are in pen-and-ink. All three images present Lawrence in the same three-quarters profile, as if he is looking over his left shoulder at the viewer. Figures 7 and 8 depict Lawrence's free-floating head, while the more realistic Figure 9 offers a suggestion of neck and shoulder below. The main differences between 7 and 8 are the eyes and the left ear. In Figure 7 the eyes are barely discernible through the thick line that represents the brow. The brow is still heavy in Figure 8, but the eyes show through. These two sketches offer variations on Merrild's by now familiar exploration of artistic sight, insight, and blindness. Lawrence has a large left ear in 7, but in 8 the ear is totally covered by hair. Indeed the main characteristic of both 7 and 8 is the aggressively filled-in hair that threatens to overwhelm the rest of Lawrence's face. The expression in 8 seems to be a scowl.

In Figure 9 Merrild's entirely different technique creates an entirely different Lawrence. Hair, beard, and moustache are represented by vigorous, visible pen strokes; Merrild has left lots of white space in Lawrence's hair. The thick, bar-like brow has been eliminated, and the eyes are almost expressive. The portrait, much softer and gentler, seems to emphasize Lawrence's humanity. This is a rather kind, debonair Lawrence. It contrasts sharply with the almost eyeless, angry-looking Figure 7 and the scowling, challenging Figure 8.

Figures 10, 11, and 12 can be seen to form another trio of images. All three are miniatures: 10 (a pencil sketch) measures $3^3/_4 \times 3^1/_8''$; 11 (a pencil sketch) measures $5^3/_8 \times 3^7/_8''$; 12 (in india ink) measures $5^1/_2 \times 4^1/_4''$. Although Merrild has minimally included Lawrence's shoulders in Figure 9 and his upper torso in Figure 10, essentially these are three images of Lawrence's head. And what different images they are.

The thumbnail Figure 10, obviously a caricature, is unusual in being full-face. The image is reminiscent of one of the pencil portraits owned by the HRC (reproduced on page 50 of the Seltzer letters and also on page 90 of *D. H. Lawrence and His World*, Harry T. Moore and Warren Roberts's pictorial biography [1966]). The style of the Figure 10 portrait is extremely reductive, moving toward abstract form. Lawrence's face, jacket, and lapel have become an exercise in straight lines and curves. His eyes are hardly more than dots attached to the long line of his brow. His nose is an incomplete circle, his moustache a series of scallops. Although Lawrence's expression is unreadable, he doesn't look cheery.

In contrast Figure 11 is a sort of portrait bust with a fully sketched realistic head in three-quarters profile atop a barely sketched torso. For once and for whatever reason, Merrild has

**Figures 10-11-12. Three portrait sketches**

created a head without notable stylization. In the midst of all his formal experiments in representing Lawrence he produces one traditional, non-modernist portrait. The image seems even a little sentimental. As usual, Lawrence's expression is difficult to read, but he does seem wary and suspicious.

Notice the similarity of the presentation of Lawrence in Figures 11 and 12. The two heads are at the same angle, and they are roughly the same (small) size. But all the fine, traditional detail of 11 gives way in 12 to radical simplification. In Figure 12 Lawrence's disembodied face dangles in space, an expressionless update of Lawrence as Cheshire cat. To change the analogy, Lawrence has been reduced to a sort of Rorschach inkblot: the viewer may make of him what he or she will. Pictorially Lawrence is now a black-and-white pattern of curves. To Merrild, Lawrence was a formal and psychological challenge to be essayed time and time again. Merrild's many portraits of Lawrence are all the more fascinating for being a series of explorations without resolution.

## III. AFTERWARDS

What of Merrild's subsequent life and career as an artist? He settled in Los Angeles in May 1923 and made that city his home for almost thirty years. He and his wife Else stayed in touch with Frieda and her new husband Angelo Ravagli, who saw the Merrilds whenever they came to Los Angeles. Michael Squires has documented the role Merrild played in helping Frieda and the dealer Jake Zeitlin sell Lawrence's manuscripts. In gratitude she gave Merrild the two manuscript versions of *Apocalypse* (which ultimately were to wind up at the Humanities Research Center) (Squires 19–20, 219–33). After Merrild suffered a heart attack in 1952, he and Else returned to Denmark, where health care was far more affordable.

In early November 1923 Lawrence wished Merrild success in his artistic career: "I hope your next shot at Fame and Fortune will bring down both birds" (*L* iv. 525). But as it turned out, Merrild could never make a living exclusively as an artist, earning most of his living as a contract decorator and a house painter. Nevertheless, he worked on. Over the years he exhibited his paintings primarily in Los Angeles, but he was also included in two shows at the Museum of Modern Art (1936, 1942) and one at the Brooklyn Museum (1936). The Los Angeles County Museum mounted a major Merrild retrospective in 1965. Unswervingly devoted to the pursuit of his artistic vision, he created a significant body of work.

Merrild was unusual among California artists of the 1920s, 1930s, and 1940s in his devotion to abstraction. He believed that abstract art was "the foundation of all art and also its essence." He was committed to "an art chiefly concerned about art, stripped of all non-essentials. Abstract art!" Needless to say, this belief led to many arguments, high above Taos, with Lawrence, who "never gave in, or even admitted the justification of abstract art" (Merrild 219, 224).

"During his years in Los Angeles, Merrild earned a solid reputation" (Karlstrom 141). At the same time, as serious as he was about his art, there was always something of the decorator about him. As an abstractionist, he is accessible and eye-pleasing. Merrild's unmistakable gifts and his accessibility, along with his connection to important historical movements, make me believe that he is ready to be rediscovered. Merrild was featured in May 1935 in a show in Hollywood called "Post-Surrealists and Other Moderns." In this show he was keeping company with Picasso, Derain, Dali, Léger, Gris, and Arp.

Victoria Dailey has "loosely categorized" Merrild's artistic phases: "decorative and Cubist-derived work of the 1920s; surrealist paintings, drawings, collages and constructions of the 1930s; and flux paintings of the 1940s" (Dailey 8). In the 1930s he was associated with the Post-Surrealists (Karlstrom 139). As Jules Langsner has commented, "Merrild's career as an artist was continuously in step with his times" (Langsner 5).

Merrild often worked in more than one style at the same time, but the mixed media piece "Primaries" (1938) (Figure 13) is a good example of his 1930s abstractions. This is a painted wood construction with corrugated cardboard, silver foil, and painted, unpainted, and flecked paper. It measures $16^{1}/_{4} \times 13^{1}/_{4}''$. With its obvious echoes of both cubism and constructivism (as well as its Miro-esque look), the work's subject would seem to be the formal arrangement of planes, colors, and textures; that is, it is "about" making art. The piece is also a study of triangles, circles, and rectangles. Merrild plays with the conventions of pictorial space, perforating the canvas (the cut-out rectangle behind the guitar, one of the two circles on the right) and thus extending the cubist vocabulary into three dimensions. The two yellow bars that seem to be frets are slatted into the guitar—another experiment in pictorial space.

The viewer must also come to terms with the piece's title. The Arp-like shape behind the guitar looks like an artist's palette—surely one of the "primaries" of the title. The colors are another. The guitar out of cubist iconography is yet another primary, but the guitar, looked at in another way, becomes a fish-like creature with staring eye and voraciously open mouth. This creature suggests one more primary: our creaturely nature. Although the piece is admittedly somewhat second-hand, its coolness and intellectual playfulness are utterly characteristic of Merrild's art.

Figure 13. *Primaries*

Merrild's most original works are his so-called flux paintings of the 1940s. The method of these paintings brings to mind Jackson Pollock's "drip paintings" in the way they introduce chance into the creative process. It should also be observed that Merrild's flux paintings, cool and detached, have little or nothing to do with the psychological deep sea diving and emotional turbulence of Pollock's masterpieces. Still, although the flux paintings are little-known—partly because Merrild was working in Los Angeles rather than New York—they play a part in the early history of abstract expressionism.

As Victoria Dailey explains, to create his flux paintings, Merrild poured

> paint onto a moistened canvas while manipulating the motion of the canvas to create different shapes until a satisfactory result was achieved. In this bold gesture, Merrild had fused the elemental forces of gravity and movement in order to create an image, and had effectively eliminated the intermediate hand of the artist. Images became pure reflections of basic natural forces. . . . (Dailey 11)

This method of painting eliminates palette-knives and brushes. Indebted to the "automatism" of surrealists like Max Ernst, Merrild called this process "painting by remote control" (Langsner 11).

The flux paintings also reveal Merrild's art at its most Lawrentian. In a pamphlet Henry Miller published on Merrild in 1945, Miller quotes Merrild on flux: "To place onself in the realm of Flux affords joy and liberation. Somewhere between life and knowledge or as D. H. Lawrence says, '—in the tension of opposites all things have their being.' In the abstract we are of all things—the Oceanic Universe that is Laotse and Heraclitus and also Dada and Surrealism" (Miller 1). Lawrence expresses a similar idea in similar language in "Indians and Entertainment": "Creation is a great flood, forever flowing, in lovely and terrible waves. In everything, the shimmer of creation, and never the finality of the created" (*Mornings* 116). As Merrild put it elsewhere, in the flux paintings he had "abandoned certitude for potentiality"(Langsner 8).

My favorite among the flux paintings is the beautiful "Littoral Flux" (Figure 14) of 1946 (that is, flux by the seashore). Victoria Dailey correctly observes that the picture evokes "the motion of sea and waves" (Dailey 12), but it should be added that this ocean is boldly depicted in red, yellow, and black against a white background. "Littoral Flux" reveals Merrild's ongoing engagement with the Oceanic Universe and his fascination with Laotse, Her-

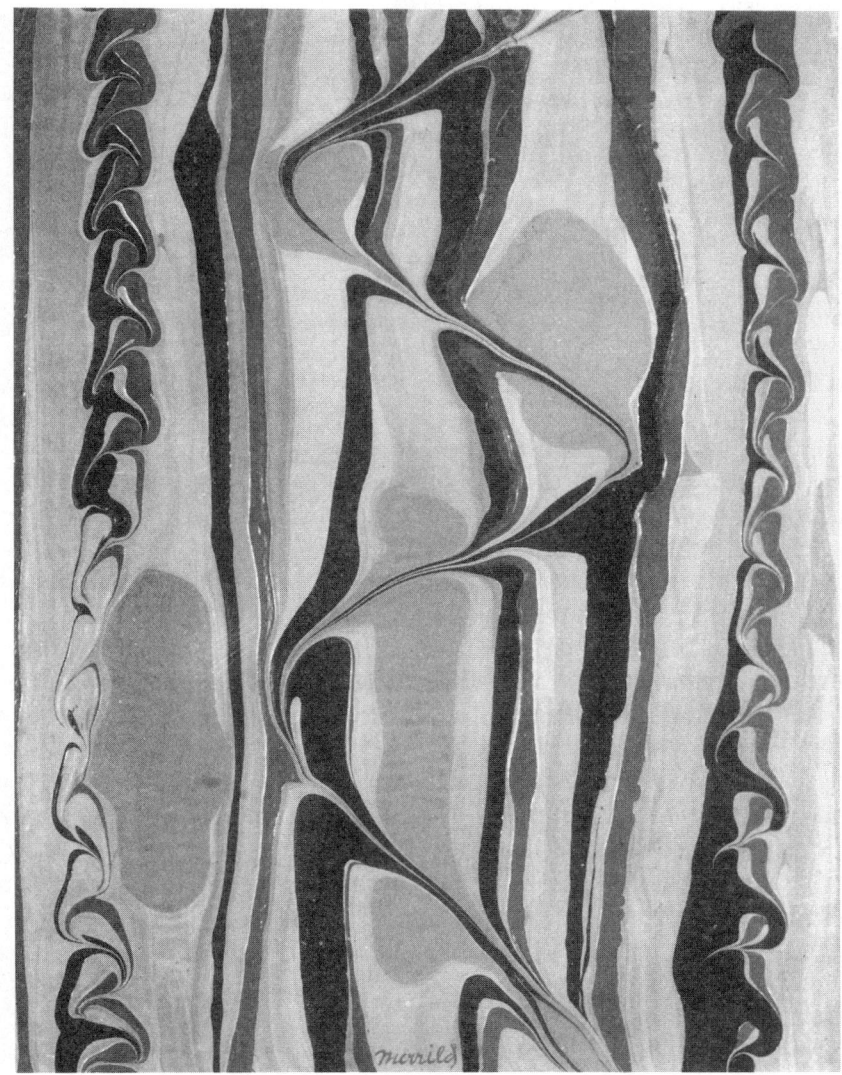

**Figure 14.** *Littoral Flux*

aclitus, and D. H. Lawrence. At the same time in purely pictorial terms it is difficult not to notice that Morris Louis is just round the corner from this elegant painting.

When Merrild looked back on the Danes' friendship with Lawrence, he remembered that they "had many things in common":

We had served apprenticeships as workers and lived among the work-
ing-classes. We had had academic training, and then as artists had
had access to the highest classes of society. (Merrild 94)

Like Lawrence, the Danes were also restless, adventurous spirits
who "had travelled far and wide" (Merrild 94). As the flux paintings demonstrate, Lawrence and Merrild shared the same dynamic, Heraclitean vision of the universe. They both also believed
that art must have serious philosophical underpinnings. Merrild
also perceived that he and Lawrence were temperamentally "at
opposite poles, he hot and I cool." "Lawrence relied considerably
on his emotions, whereas I relied on my mind" (Merrild 349).

Although Merrild had seen Lawrence's flaws and foibles up-
close, all his life he remained steadfast in his admiration for Lawrence the man and artist. Lawrence had been scorned and perse-
cuted for his writings. One of his greatest novels had been
declared legally obscene, and the unsold copies had been destroyed. But through it all Lawrence never wavered from his commitment to his art, nor did he ever compromise his artistic vision.
Even when Merrild was earning much of his living as a house
painter (ultimately he had his own company), he was never de-
flected from his true identity as a serious modern artist.

Lawrence was in Los Angeles from late August through most
of September 1923. Frieda left for England in August, and he
spent a good deal of time with Merrild and Götzsche. The three
of them fantasized about a trip to the South Seas, but finally Lawrence settled on a return to Mexico. He tried to convince both
Danes to accompany him, but only Götzsche would agree to do so.
Merrild's decision to stay in Los Angeles—indeed to stay in Los
Angeles painting houses—holds a significant lesson in Lawrence's impact on him.

Merrild was tempted to go to Mexico with Lawrence and Götzsche, "even if compelled to see and experience it through him,
and to settle and live *his* new life." But Merrild heard voices that
said to him, "You are talking Lawrence, thinking Lawrence, living and acting Lawrence, your life, your being is through Lawrence, you are saturated with Lawrence. Shed the burden of
Lawrence, his dominating, overpowering influence, and live your
own life, get out from under his shadow and grow into your own
being. . ." (Merrild 322). Merrild could best honor and learn from
Lawrence by refusing to accompany him. It was time to sail his

"own little ship," to "have the courage of my own convictions and make my own adventures in the world" (Merrild 323).

Lawrence left Los Angeles with Götzsche on 25 September 1923. He and Merrild never met again. But the artist Knud Merrild remained faithful to D. H. Lawrence for the rest of his life.

Thanks to Nancy Doll, Director of the Weatherspoon Art Gallery, the University of North Carolina at Greensboro, and Doug Dreishpoon, Curator at the Albright-Knox Art Gallery.

## WORKS CITED

Brown, Milton W. *American Painting from the Armory Show to the Depression.* Princeton: Princeton University Press, 1955.

Bynner, Witter. *Journey with Genius: Recollections and Reflections Concerning D. H. Lawrence.* New York: John Day, 1951.

Cushman, Keith. "Lawrence's Dust-Jackets: A Selection with Commentary." *DHLR* 18, no. 1–2 (1999): 29–52. Merrild dust-jacket of *The Captain's Doll,* produced on front cover.

Dailey, Victoria. "Knud Merrild: Change and Chance." In *Knud Merrild: Works from the 1930's and 1940's.* Los Angeles: Steve Turner Gallery, 1991.

Karlstrom, Paul J. and Susan Ehrlich. *Turning the Tide: Early Los Angeles Modernists 1920–1956.* Santa Barbara: Santa Barbara Museum of Art, 1990.

*Knud Merrild: Works from the 1930's and 1940's.* With an essay by Victoria Dailey. Los Angeles: Steve Turner Gallery, 1991.

Langsner, Jules. Introduction to *Knud Merrild 1894–1954: Paintings, Constructions, Collages, Watercolors, and Drawings.* Los Angeles: Los Angeles County Museum of Art, 1965.

Lawrence, D. H. *Letters to Thomas and Adele Seltzer.* Edited by Gerald M. Lacy. Santa Barbara: Black Sparrow, 1976.

Lawrence, Frieda. *"Not I, But the Wind . . ."* Santa Fe: Rydal Press, 1934.

Merrild, Knud. *A Poet and Two Painters: A Memoir of D. H. Lawrence.* New York: Viking, 1938.

Meyers, Jeffrey. *D. H. Lawrence: A Biography.* New York: Knopf, 1990.

Miller, Henry. "A Holiday in Paint." Philadelphia: Walton Press, 1945.

Moore, Harry T. and Warren Roberts. *D. H. Lawrence and His World.* New York: Viking, 1966.

Naumann, Francis. "Walter Conrad Arensberg: Poet, Patron, and Participant in the New York Avant-Garde, 1915–20." *Bulletin (Philadelphia Museum of Art)* 76, no. 328 (spring 1980): 2–32.

Squires, Michael, ed. *D. H. Lawrence Manuscripts: The Correspondence of Frieda Lawrence, Jake Zeitlin and Others.* New York: St. Martin's, 1991.

# Lawrence and the Calculus of Change

## Michael Squires

My THESIS IS THAT ACROSS LAWRENCE'S CAREER A SEQUENCE OF AD-
aptations in his prose yields a kind of simple calculus. Oppositions of character gradually turn into oppositions of culture, and
then oppositions of voice and style. In early stories like "Odour
of Chrysanthemums" and "Daughters of the Vicar," oppositions
usually develop between stark alternatives: for instance, the be-
sotted Walter Bates is also beloved; Edward Massey poses ane-
mically against Alfred Durant; and in "The Prussian Officer" the
Captain's suppressed emotion collides with the Orderly's easy
openness. But in Lawrence's mid-career these oppositions are developed or complicated (for instance, Egbert must choose between family and war, March between Banford and Henry), while
the narrator is increasingly critical of his protagonists and locates
their failures in their culture.

In Lawrence's late career the oppositions, though never aban-
doning those of earlier phases, are relocated at the level of rhetoric and style—as antinomies, or suspended oppositions—and they
yield a fusion of dissonant voices. This fusion forms a grid best
described in one of Lawrence's unique phrases—"a new motion"
that he calls "the upright through the horizontal" (*LCL* 419, 173
n. 35),[1] which means that verbal registers, moving in different directions, counter each other. Lawrence embeds opposition and
contradiction more deeply than before—into the narrator's every
strategy of presentation, from characterization to cultural critique to verbal phrase.

This reformulation offers a fresh way to interpret Lawrence's
fiction. It invites readers not to place his work in simple categories of callow and accomplished, minor and major, but rather, to
envision his work on an axis of disequilibrium and equilibrium,
of imbalance and balance, the one leading into the other. In this
reformulation Lawrence's early work provides the terms of un-

derstanding his growth as a writer. The early oppositions of character finally turn into complements which are the basis of a narrative poise that, when fully developed, preserves both rhetorical and biographical tension within Lawrence's style. The oft-cited critical paradigm of early work, masterpieces, and declining later work can be replaced—indeed ought to be replaced—by a paradigm that rejects these outdated approaches and freshly identifies, across Lawrence's career, points on an artistic axis which gradually reveals the fullest sense of his literary achievement.

This proposed paradigm of Lawrence's development can also be expressed as a sequence of three visual shapes, each evolving into the next: parallel lines (‖) that represent simple oppositions; a "T" that represents oppositions turning into frictional juxtapositions of character and culture; and finally a dagger (†) that represents the fusion of strongly dissonant voices in Lawrence's work. His own phrase "the upright through the horizontal" is his final equilibrium, where his life *and* his work achieve optimal balance. These shapes conveniently mark the evolution of a style that develops radically across his quarter-century career as a writer.

# I

For all of the surface vagaries of Lawrence's short life—world travel, a difficult marriage, assorted temptations, intense friendships that failed—his art shows a surprisingly coherent development. It is inaccurate to say that he rises grandly, then slips sadly away from those heights.[2] His art is always developing. To support my claim I look briefly at the major phases of Lawrence's creative life, but consider especially those works for which draft material exists. Why? Because Lawrence's drafts reveal those moments when conceptual change is most recognizable; they show him reassessing his characters' choices and redirecting his thought in ways that help readers calculate his stylistic evolution. When Lawrence rewrote a work, he almost always reimagined it, using altered assumptions about the nature of experience. As he reshaped his characters, he usually defined their personalities with more precision and surrounded them with a more pointed assessment of their values. Draft material helps to measure the *expanding narrative space* between a character and the narrator who describes him. Gradually, Lawrence learned to counter a character's sense of himself with the narrator's larger, ironic judgment.

In his early stories Lawrence leads his characters to make stark human choices that typically acknowledge forms of life and death: Archie the vicar's son ("The Shadow in the Rose Garden") is dead *in* life as he sits vacantly in his enclosed garden; Walter Bates ("Odour of Chrysanthemums"), routinely drunk, is dead *to* his married life with Elizabeth; and Hauptmann the repressed officer ("The Prussian Officer") and beautiful Mary Lindley ("Daughters of the Vicar") have denied the sensual life of their bodies. But when Lawrence reworked "Odour of Chrysanthemums," he transferred the simple opposition between husband and wife into the more subtle opposition between Walter's wife and Walter's mother—both women feeling jealous, both appropriating his dead body, both allied in mild class antagonism. Lawrence also transformed their sentimental hovering over the man's dead body to a more considered—even calculated—understanding of marriage, its failure, and the consolation that Elizabeth Bates (cold realist that she is) can wrest from her now-more-controlled grief: "she knew she had never seen him, he had never seen her, they had met in the dark and had fought in the dark, not knowing [each other]" (*PO* 198). Death—opposed to the life stirring in her womb—yields Elizabeth a secret consolation. Lawrence transforms a simple emotion into a mature recognition.

As he contemplates these early characters, he often makes *risk* the template of revision, because risk leads them most readily to stark moral choices. When he rewrote "Two Marriages" into "Daughters of the Vicar," he allowed Louisa Lindley to articulate her pure, regenerative feeling more assertively. When she washes Alfred's back in the draft version, Lawrence stresses not their attraction but their embarrassment. In his revision she pulls down their barriers to find a vital center of connection: "Her feeling of separateness passed away. . . . There was this living centre. Her heart ran hot. She had reached some goal in this beautiful, clear, male body" (73). Her earlier hesitancy turns firm with resolve. Across class, across culture—and against her family's strong opposition—she reaches her "goal" but at the cost of having to go to Canada with a man in many ways foreign to her. It is entirely possible that Alfred will offer her only physical appeal: for in the draft version Lawrence openly cites Alfred's lack of depth—"he's not introspective" (233)—but in revision suppresses it. Indeed, Louisa envisions their marriage as "a fabric made out of [Alfred's] energy of tenderness" (246). The opposition between them softens into a more subtle complementarity. Cultural differences, now muted, frame the story without shaping its style.

Similarly, as Lawrence refines *Sons and Lovers,* the opposition between Paul Morel and Miriam Leivers gains surprising complexity. In a scene from chapter 7, where the two characters stand flooded with light from a huge orange moon whose potency sets Paul's blood aflame, Lawrence needed to account for Miriam's inadequacy as Paul's sexual feeling mounts. Initially, Lawrence saw the two characters as simple opposites, Miriam transfigured in her spiritual purity, Paul transfixed by the agony of his desire: "She stood beside him, forever like his attendant angel. Her face, slightly golden with moonlight, was lifted towards him: the same stillness, the same humility about the closed mouth, the same pure confidence. . . . He wanted to smack her face, to beat away its holiness" (*SL* fac. 254). Against her angelic holiness, his resistance comes strong and surging, ready even to smash her spiritual perfection. Holiness must be humiliated.

But in revision Lawrence complicates Miriam's emotional stance. Now he makes her "half aware" of Paul's sexual passion, so that she can gaze at him in wonder even as she uses her sanctity as a shield to protect herself from such knowledge: "But somehow she denied him. She was expecting some religious state in him. He wanted the answer of her blood to his. But it never came. Still mystical and yearning, she was half aware of his passion, and gazed at him, wondering" (*SL* fac. 254). She loses her purity of motive even as she transcends the flesh. Lawrence widens the space between Miriam's spiritual virginity and the narrator's sympathy for her.

The final printed version treats Miriam with mounting disdain. The narrator can no longer acknowledge the value of her purity. Her face, no longer "slightly golden with moonlight," is now "covered with the darkness of her hat"—shadowed and suspect; and her "pure look of faith and yearning" becomes a more self-conscious "she was brooding" (*SL* 215). Lawrence mutes her religious ecstasy, turning her radiance from impersonal exaltation to covert manipulation. Gradually she comes to resemble a human

Gothic arch, weighted with layers of brooding, personal concern. She links Louisa Lindley and Gudrun Brangwen.

## II

If Miriam is gradually distanced from both Paul and the reader, Lawrence's portrait of Gudrun Brangwen and Gerald Crich shows him also refining his artistic stance—increasing the complexity of their response while he more painfully separates them from their vital connection to the Midlands town of Beldover. As he casts *The First Women in Love* (1916) into *Women in Love* (1920), his revisions illustrate the change that initiates his middle phase, when he prefers not oppositions but juxtapositions, and when he moves away from binaries toward ambivalences. Gudrun's increasing power over others is balanced by Gerald's declining power; her subtle confidence is measured by his creeping lassitude. Her vitality, however diabolical it becomes, gains strength because of the upper-class hollowness that afflicts Gerald; for he, like Edward Massey before him, more and more symbolizes a class in crisis whose values leech the vital forces of life. For Gerald the outward and the inner struggle become one. His emptiness and doom are his culture's.

Early in the novel, when Gudrun rows Gerald across the lake, his injured hand having curtailed his ability to maneuver, she seems distant from him in the boat—he cannot, as he wishes, hold her. Unable to shift, she tells him she cannot easily move "unless you want to tip us both into the water" (*FWL* 163). But in revision Lawrence added a sentence that confirms her growing control: "She caressed him subtly and strangely, having him completely at her mercy" (*WL* 177). Later, when her fingers wander over the features of his handsome face, Lawrence wrote emphatically, "How perfect and *other* he was—but how perfect!" (*FWL* 305), which he subsequently changed to "How perfect and foreign he was—ah how dangerous!" (*WL* 331), to signify the kind of knowledge Gudrun will need to discover his complex essence. Lawrence now juxtaposes Gerald's *perfection* with his *danger*.

During Winifred Crich's drawing lesson, Lawrence complicates Gerald as an icon, reversing Gudrun's earlier admiration for him when, awed by his thrusting vigor as he swims, she cries, "God, what it is to be a man!" (*WL* 47). Having observed that Gerald's black clothes "sat well on his well-nourished body" (*FWL* 218), Lawrence then cut the following sentence from *Women in Love*: "he was keen and bright and full of energy" (*FWL* 218). In Lawrence's revision Gerald perceives himself differently. He acquires a measure of pathos. His bondage to fate, which cripples his power, manifests itself more fully in *Women in Love*, where he becomes less efficient and more vulnerable.

Gradually, when the exterior attraction of Gerald and Gudrun can no longer hide the interior rupture that has exposed "the obscene beyond" inside them (*WL* 242), their friction encompasses a new sense of loathing. In the rabbit scene, when Gerald and Gudrun look at each other with diabolical recognition, Lawrence adds a pregnant sentence to *Women in Love*: "He was unconfident, he had qualms of fear" (242). Gerald's superficial control of the kicking rabbit only hides the interior disintegration that had begun even before his father's death. After Gudrun kisses him, she realizes that the precious sensory knowledge of him would certainly fill her. Nonetheless, what Lawrence added to *Women in Love* clarifies her gain: "For he was so unsure, so risky in the common world of day" (*WL* 332). The template of risk defines her search too. Like Louisa Lindley, she rejects the opportunity for social advancement with a well-positioned husband. She risks the possibility of marriage, then concludes that Shortlands would offer her the kind of inner death that Mary Lindley discovers with Edward Massey in "Daughters of the Vicar." Gudrun's demand to *know* brings her to the abyss of Gerald's interior life, where his "fatal halfness" seems (even to Birkin) to appear a "wholeness" in a man with such limited self-knowledge (*WL* 207). She can excoriate his inadequacy in an idiom still located mostly within her own mind, not within the narrator's. The conflict Lawrence discovers is personal and cultural but not yet rhetorical. His fiction has reached the "T" of frictional juxtapositions.

In a later scene in which Gerald goes to Gudrun for release, anguished at having lost first his father and then his inner connection to the mines, Lawrence's addition (in my italics) clarifies the direction of the man's evolving characterization: "Now [while Gerald slept beside Gudrun in Beldover] she was driven up against his perfect sleeping motion like a knife white-hot on a grindstone. *There was something monstrous about him, about his juxtaposition against her*" (*FWL* 320, *WL* 346). His "perfect" motion grates against his "monstrous" identity. The word *juxtaposi-*

*tion* aptly defines the growing sense of alienation that separates characters from their culture. Tortured by his isolation from work, family, and self, Gerald goes to Gudrun to be healed; but after she has satisfied his desire, even she, lying in an anguish of heightened consciousness, senses the "awful, inhuman distance which would always be interposed between her and the other being!"(*WL* 346). Their connection to the community of Beldover shorn, their alienation intensified, the novel cuts them from their roots.

In sum: alive to a new vocabulary of strife, Lawrence captures a new complexity in his characters. With increasing clarity, his revisions capture the personal—and cultural—downfall of a man like Gerald, whose opening stance as a proud industrial magnate yields to his equally complex search for death. The pathology of his emotional and spiritual illness, unfolding with extraordinary precision, compels the reader's sympathy. In mid-career, as Lawrence came to prefer juxtapositions, a character's risk becomes more extreme: death is now a more definitive result of character flaws.

Once Lawrence had come to know well such people as John Middleton Murry, Katherine Mansfield, Philip Heseltine, E. M. Forster, Ottoline Morrell, and Bertrand Russell, he recognized that their superficial appeal hid deplorable contradictions: Ottoline Morrell vilified Frieda while decrying the Easter 1916 uprising in Dublin; the homosexual Forster composed novels about heterosexual love; the handsome Murry was enervated by his own aimless welter of emotions; and Philip Heseltine said he despised the woman he married. Thereafter, protagonists with inner defects fascinated Lawrence. His personal experience had enlarged the range of his fiction by showing him that, under an attractive surface like Gerald's, a person's integrity may be a sham.

In the mid-career short story "England, My England," which evolved across several years, Lawrence voices oppositions to show the narrator's sympathy turning against both a character and his culture, while the style turns ironic. The narrator shifts, for instance, from a neutral sentence in 1915—"Gradually [Winifred] began to get dissatisfied with her husband" (*EmyE* 221)—to a far more pedestrian sentence in 1922—"Poor Winifred was like a fish out of water" (17)—the cliché part of the distance he was interposing between reader and character. Or in 1922 he adds the sardonic exclamation, "There you are. There it was: always the same" (18). Folded within the narrator's tone lies a potent irritation. Lawrence gradually discovers a colloquial, democratic voice which he ratchets up into mockery, its annoyance twisted and compressed like a spring. This voice, at odds with the sympathetic creation of character, emerges soon after *Women in Love* was revised.

In the 1915 version of "England, My England," Evelyn Daughtry's death-wish arises from his personal inertia; Winifred, his wife, stronger than he, tries redirecting his energy but only sets them—says the narrator—"in opposition," "as if fated . . . to destroy each other" (220). Their daughter's wound, accidental and awful, slowly turns into Evelyn's own psychological wound, as a "horrible paralysis" comes over him (222). Unable to fix the condition he helped to create, he slowly becomes "nullified in the midst of life," his "corrosive" smile expressing his inner emptiness (223). This emptiness is neither inert nor, as one would expect, susceptible to his wife's manipulation. Instead, vibrating to the ideal of soldierly service to his country, his emptiness fills itself with thoughts of war; he is thrilled to become "an agent of destruction," to "kill or be killed" (225–26). His death collapses but does not resolve the opposition between domesticity and militarism; as in *Women in Love*, the conflicts are juxtaposed.

In 1922 Lawrence shortened the story's ending, the man's death coming more quickly to throw the emphasis on the protagonist's family life, which cannot sustain him. The couple's opposition has been muted, made suggestive rather than strict. Having renamed his protagonist, Lawrence now explores Egbert's psyche for emotional insight, and finds not what he had found in 1915, a simple split between sensation and consciousness (227), but a suspended opposition: "He heard [the German bullet] in his ears, but he heard it also in his soul, in tension" (32). This early example of antinomy provides one piece of the calculus of change. In his excellent *D. H. Lawrence: Life Into Art*, Keith Sagar says that at the story's close Lawrence's irony yields to identification (155). Although at first I agreed, a closer look persuades me otherwise. To put the matter in a paradox: the distance between protagonist and reader increases *even as* the portrait of Egbert is more intimately realized, and—here is the crux—the expansion of Egbert's family context is countered by the narrator's pointed irony, even at the end. The narrator's interrogation of the dying Egbert's mind, with its sequence of seventeen questions, too closely sustains the narrator's early, flippant use of questions—for instance, "But Egbert! What are you to do with a man like Egbert?" (13)—to allow the irony to be forgotten. It permeates the whole story. This antinomy expresses the "tension" between two competing valuations of a character in crisis: the public and the personal, the one sharply at odds with the other.

In the first version of *The Fox* (1918), Banford resembles the 1915 Evelyn Daughtry. Both cling to a stronger woman; both are centrifugal characters pushed away from their familial center into death; both are powerless against their antagonists. But rewriting *The Fox* in 1921 gave Lawrence another chance to test Banford's character. He allows her to carry her selfish inner nature to its conclusion: she subconsciously seeks the felled pine tree just as Evelyn had sought death in the war, or Gerald in the snow. Given the chance to stretch themselves into destiny, these characters stretch in the same way. To the 1921 Banford, Lawrence adds a matrix of mother and father, but he also adds her jeering manner ("Who me, mind myself?" she cries mockingly [*Fox* 65]); for Egbert, Lawrence expands the power of Winifred's father, thereby enhancing *that* family matrix too. In revision Lawrence takes an inner defect—as he had with Gerald Crich and the pair of men in "The Prussian Officer"—and works that defect to a conclusion: death. Why death? Because death is connected (if only superficially) to the war; but, deeper than that, it is connected to Lawrence's phobia (at this time) of same-sex coupling, which also generated a terrifying uncertainty, as his portrait of Bertie Reid in "The Blind Man" (1919) testifies. In the barn Maurice Pervin's groping exploration of Bertie's face is like a rape that leaves him "haggard, with sunken eyes," unable to "bear" this sudden access of sensual knowledge (*EmyE* 63). In mid-career the panic that drives Lawrence toward sexual certainty brings death into the plot, but it brings irony into the style.

## III

Later in Lawrence's career, characters take shape from rather different assumptions. No longer is Lawrence centrally interested in looking below a character's attractive surface—like Egbert's or Gerald's or even Bertie's—and discovering an emptiness. Now

Lawrence stands farther away, energized by fresh hostility, judging characters whose culture and values he has sharply scrutinized. That culture can be hard with resistance—Mexico, New Mexico, the Midlands, Australia—or equally alive with potent stimulation. But it affects a character more painfully, and in a style more complicated with energy. In Lawrence's third stage— the vertical through the horizontal, imaged as a dagger (†)— anger and hostility stand in brutal opposition to modes of patient landscape creation; sympathy harbors disgust.

The multiple versions of Lawrence's last two novels allow the fullest calculation of his new stance. In *Quetzalcoatl* (1923) Lawrence positions Kate's immersion in exotic Mexico against her distaste. The opposition, for her, is taut not with risk (as in Lawrence's early stories) but with anxious uncertainty. Swaying dangerously between the poles of her nature—her need to embrace, her need to recoil—she is emotionally vulnerable. Fascinated by the rituals of a bold new Quetzalcoatl religion, she finds her spirit drawn to Mexico and her sexual self awakened by both Ramón and Cipriano. Yet she realizes at last that she cannot be part of Mexico, old or new. Whereas Louisa Lindley is finally untouched by her antagonists, Mary and Edward Massey, Kate is made ill by the forces she resists. Uprooted from Europe, her family now little more than a memory, she has lost the emotional strength to seize upon what is healthy in a foreign environment. She must be reimagined.

Lawrence's 1925 rewriting of the novel as *The Plumed Serpent* allowed him to alter Kate's role in the transformed Mexico that Ramón and Cipriano envision but also to suppress the "vertical" counterforce of his style. One expects Kate to drop her cloak of ambivalence, to immerse herself in the bold plan to resuscitate Mexico from its spiritual malaise—which she almost does, gathering her fine courage into a firm resolve. But given all of Lawrence's personal emotional upheavals in 1924, including Frieda's more robust animosity toward Brett, he disbelieved now in giving women any power that was not anchored in male enterprise. Hence Kate takes a different kind of risk in *The Plumed Serpent*: she yields her female integrity in order to honor men—not men who are her equals, but men who pass "beyond what she knew, beyond her depth" (*PS* 67). Kate's charm now derives not (as one might expect) from her vitality or her intellectual acuity, but from another source: "Her great charm," says the narrator, "was her soft repose" (81). She could be Connie Chatterley, sitting quietly at Wragby, sewing, attentive to the intellectuals around her. Gradually Kate loses her courage. She cannot shape her environment to contain her destiny.

In *The Plumed Serpent* Kate has tired of oppositional friction. Spiritually sick, she craves salvation. She feels dizzy, dazzled by Ramón's white trousers and jacket, touched to the quick by his remote godliness and sensual body. In her weakened state, she responds most fully now to those who are strong—Cipriano and his "magnetic power" (82), the boatman flush with "great strength and energy" (89), Ramón exhibiting his "powerful will" (167). They enact her waning resolve. She yearns passively for someone—even unknown gods—"to put the magic back into her life" (103). The "vertical" hostility typical of Lawrence's later work expresses itself in denying Kate the power to act.

By 1925 the structural oppositions of early stories like "Daughters of the Vicar" have become a collapsing set of antinomies. *The Plumed Serpent*'s closing chapters show Kate, bound now to Cipriano, acting out a role of "supreme passivity" (311) and becoming Malintzi, the Quetzalcoatl deity. Kate is the Woman Who Rode Away—but rescued now rather than sacrificed to the Indian gods. When, for instance, Kate sits alone on the beach of Lake Sayula, repelled by all she sees, her response is muted into passivity as Lawrence turns *Quetzalcoatl* into *The Plumed Serpent*. Here is *Quetzalcoatl*:

> "I've had enough of this," she said rising. "I'm going back to Europe."
>
> She looked westward at the receding lake, the lousy shore, the lumps of women at the water's edge: the dilapidated-looking villas and the mockery of a white church with its two fingers to heaven: the scarlet flame-tree, the dark mangoes. And she smelt the smell of Mexico, excrement, human and animal, dried in the sun on a dry, dry earth: and mango leaves: and clean air with refuse and a little woodsmoke in it. And she said again:
>
> "I loathe Mexico. I loathe it. I'm going back to England." (*Q* 144)

Kate, her senses in simple revolt, sounds more like Louisa Lindley than Egbert. The smell of Mexico is excremental, the white church a mockery, the whole country loathsome.

But in *The Plumed Serpent*, Kate's stance goes slack when Lawrence alters the dialogue. Here is the key sentence: " 'But the day will come when I shall go away,' she said to herself"—quietly "rocking once more on her verandah" (218). She pauses. Now she is old, tired, glad for the haven she has found. Artistically it is a low point, the revised novel bereft of the vertical narrator "positioning" the horizontal plane of Kate's life. The novel is a relapse.

In Oaxaca, Mexico, the water and the food presented constant dangers; gradually Lawrence's resistance failed. His prolonged illness as he rewrote this novel therefore complicates what one says about either his style or his revision process. In *The Plumed Serpent* Kate yields her sexual self—and lets her soul succumb too. Mexico mesmerizes her. She is March married to Henry. In anguish, both March and Kate brood over the inadequacy of their marriages. But the narrator's understanding of the two women has changed. On the high cliffs of Cornwall, March, at the close of *The Fox*, believes she "*would* be an independent woman to the last.—But she was so tired, so tired of everything" (*Fox* 70). When Henry extends his hands to March shortly after Banford's death, she bestows upon him a look "of helplessness and submission" (*Fox* 66). Her resistance falters; she will yield. At the end of *The Plumed Serpent*, Kate is dwarfed by the narrator: "As an isolated individual, she had little or no significance. As a woman on her own, she was repulsive, and even evil, to [Cipriano]. She was not real till she was reciprocal. To a great extent this was true, and she knew it" (*PS* 388). In those last four words, "and she knew it," Kate simply confirms the narrator's judgment. Her voice is squashed into submission, just as at the novel's close she comes to her Mexican saviors not for love but "to make a sort of submission" (443), and to beg them to keep her. The vertical counterforce briefly disappears. It is the victim of illness.

It is no surprise that Connie Chatterley extends Kate's characterization. Connie has the same fear of the future, the same moderate income, the same refined personality, a similar experience of men and marriage, and a powerful desire to locate a lover outside her expected social range. But the most interesting question is this: Does Kate's characterization provide the template for a novel with a different subject matter?

From the first version of *Lady Chatterley* (1926) to the last (1928), Lawrence also sends Connie to a place that is foreign to her (the strange traps in the gamekeeper's hut resemble the *ollitas* and *rebozos* in Mexico), and increasingly motivates her to submit to her destiny with an unlikely man. Like Kate, Connie has understood her destiny ineptly from the false clues her culture has supplied. She *thinks* she wants cerebral stimulation—conversation, leisure, privacy. Nevertheless, because her courage is indominable, Lawrence protects her (as he does not protect Kate) from becoming effaced by male dominance. Motivated by deep inner needs, and inspired by the natural beauty around her, Connie more forcefully sets up acts of discovery. In each version, for instance, Lawrence further enhances her appreciation of the male body. He lets her view it from more and better angles, and finally, not from her superbly articulated consciousness at all but in a camera shot—"the erect phallos rising darkish and hot-looking from the little cloud of vivid gold-red hair" (*LCL* 209). The phallos is, Connie knows, a clear revelation of godliness: "Like another being!" (*LCL* 210). The three versions of the novel become like a miniature case study of Lawrence's writing career: the first version full of activity and yearning, the second version more complex and anguished, the final version alone transcending what Lawrence had earlier written. As he revises his characters in the three-version *Lady Chatterley*, he gives them a strength that characters like Egbert and Kate could not command. Connie's and Mellors's newfound inner strength arises from their *unconscious* identification with the cosmic forces of the universe.[3] Their rootedness, because it is deeply spiritual, gives them an unshakable identity. Their courage lies in profound repudiation of their culture.

At the level of rhetoric and style, the motive of repudiation is also very much at work, defining Lawrence's last phase. In each version he actively seeks antinomies as a mode of expression. He urges Connie toward more intense sexual feeling but entraps her more deeply in the social class to which she feels bound. Sexual liberation and social constraints pass through each other like opposed angles—the vertical through the horizontal—and create a unique texture. In the final version Lawrence can push his characters to extreme forms of behavior (for instance, Connie acquiescing to anal intercourse, Mrs. Bolton allowing Clifford to fondle her breasts, the narrator fully venting his hostility toward modern society): while at the same time Lawrence can reposition his characters' explosions of feeling into the stylistic texture of the novel. The explosion of intense feeling is now concentrated in the novel's central technique of dismantled contradictions.

In chapter 13, for instance, Connie imagines an emotionally

neutral zone where her "fugitive dreams of a friendship between these two men [could blossom]: one her husband, the other the father of her child. Now she saw the screaming absurdity of her dreams. The two males were as hostile as fire and water. They mutually exterminated one another" (*LCL* 192). This is Connie's view. But, one must ask, does an attentive reader find the two males, under the surface, to be hostile? In truth, Clifford and Mellors are clear complements. An attentive reader must read beneath the narrative surface and in opposition to the characters' feelings about each other, as these brief examples illustrate:

- Both men acknowledge physical limitations: Clifford is paralyzed; Mellors is frail and troubled by a cough.
- Both at first recoil from others—Clifford from anyone but "personal servants" (15), Mellors from "any further close human contact" (89).
- The war deeply affected both men—Clifford loses his legs and sexual potency, Mellors the devotion of his beloved Colonel.
- Both link the core of themselves to the earth: Clifford finds solace in the mines, Mellors in the pheasants and cows.
- Both men are married to women who commit adultery.
- In the wood both men lecture Connie about the power of the ruling classes.
- Both men are highly articulate—Clifford in his speeches to his wife, Mellors in his final letter to Connie.
- Clifford is arrogant with his servants, Mellors with Hilda and Duncan Forbes.
- Clifford demands subservience from Mrs. Bolton; Mellors from Connie when he requires her "to be a passive, consenting thing, like a slave" (247).

Take away their class conditioning, and hence their values, and these men are very similar. Both are forceful advocates of a tenable philosophy of life. Both are admirable in identifying personal goals and then achieving them, right down to the peace that both find in a woman's body. The point is that the novel's energy is now directed sometimes with, sometimes against, the novel's surface grain.

Lawrence's late prose captures the central contradictions of his own experience. A ferocious energy, compounded of the disappointment and betrayal in his personal life, now pulls plot and characterization in opposed directions. In the novel's action Lawrence captures a displaced version of the freshly balanced voices he has learned to control. The vertical counterforce in the style is positioned to incorporate a heavier weighting of biographical pressures than ever before. When, for instance, Connie leaves England and goes abroad, Lawrence includes in the novel's second version a drumroll of annoyance which builds to the narrator's chagrin:

> She came to hate . . . those bright holiday faces round the board, the genial sense of plenty of money, the flippant assertion of care-free-ness, the hard, insentient chatter of people enjoying themselves by will to do it, and the exasperating but never-ending attempts to be funny, to be witty, to be humorous! Oh humour! Oh that deadly cog-wheel sense of humour which starts so many automatic little souls spinning with a sort of self-satisfaction! (*FSLC* 488)

Following a list of targets within Connie's point of view, the last sentence tears open the envelope of her consciousness. The dismissive "automatic" and the condescending "little souls" position a second voice *through* Connie's, so that Lawrence's narrative of her awakening is fused with recoil.

Lawrence's revision in version 3 confirms the new direction in his style, the exclamatory lament about smug people turning into acid loathing:

> But in her inner consciousness she was keeping touch with the other man. She mustn't let her connection with him go: oh, she mustn't let it go, or she was lost, lost utterly in this world of riff-raffy expensive people and joy-hogs. Oh, the joy-hogs! Oh "enjoying one-self"! Another modern form of sickness. (*LCL* 256)

Connie's urgent appeal for connection is like a cross-grain to the narrator's hard contempt. The revision—more compressed and contemptuous—adds the slang phrase "riff-raffy" to augur the new level of disrespect that punctures Connie's "connection" to Mellors. The voices collide. In this more complex mode, Lawrence fuses her secret warmth for Mellors with a social norm ("enjoying oneself") which he can mock, down to the final flippant fragment. His linguistic "register" sustains one kind of irony while it masks another. Indeed, the narrator, though he impugns the excesses of his culture, protects Connie by placing her emotional freedom in complex opposition to the way her inherited money permits her, at the novel's close, to consider purchasing a farm for Mellors. She rejects her culture, but not its privileges. Lawrence's final version of the novel hides her naked admission in the first version: "If she had to belong to a class, let it be to the ruling class" (*FSLC* 117).

Near the end of his life, Lawrence tried to position all the pressures of his life outside the circle of conventional expectation, and to keep them suspended there. The suspension is the key. Years earlier, in *The Rainbow*, Ursula had imagined beasts' eyes lurking outside the lighted circle of knowledge (405); now Lawrence's narrator has moved outside the circle, trying to hold in suspension not just conscious and unconscious forces but all the external and internal forces that had buffeted him. He aimed to squeeze them into a single capacious voice, as in "My soul softly flaps in the little pentecostal flame with you, like the peace of fucking. We fucked a flame into being. Even the flowers are fucked into being, between sun and earth. But it's a delicate thing, and takes patience and the long pause" (*LCL* 301). This voice, where Lawrence and Mellors are closely identified, is the voice of an *outsider*. The words he chooses marginalize him. Lawrence's revision pushes him into an extreme position. Just as Mellors is evicted from Wragby, sent away from his mother and wife and child, so the language he chooses places his letter outside the boundary of narrative convention. Indeed, Lawrence himself moved increasingly away from convention—living in a foreign country (Italy), publishing his work privately (in Florence), often refusing medical treatment (for his tuberculosis), and acquiescing to Frieda's infidelity (with Angelo Ravagli). Now, in Lawrence's writing, the vertical counterforce is stronger, heavier, weighted with estrangement. There is no voice like it in English fiction. It belongs only to the late Lawrence.

It would be wrong to conclude that Lawrence's revisions always move in a single direction, or that Lawrence rigidly develops his art from structural to stylistic to rhetorical oppositions: all three are intertwined, always. But what the calculus of change finally means is that the contradictions that so many critics have found in Lawrence's work yield to forms of accommodation, in which eventually the pressures of Lawrence's life and art command equal voice. And here lies the importance of viewing the career as a whole. At the end—when Lawrence had reached a kind of spiritual equipoise—he could bind together character and voice in extraordinary balance, rarely with strain or compromise. The simple oppositions at the outset of his work are gradually transformed into a grid of cultural oppositions, which in the late career can be dismantled into a grid of voices whose horizontal and vertical forces are at last balanced into "a new motion."

## NOTES

1. The full passage reads: "She [Connie Chatterley] felt him coming, the far-off thrill of dawn, thrilling up out of the sensual depths. It came with a new motion, the upright through the horizontal, and with it a wild new trilling of dawn" (TSR reading).

2. See, for example, F. R. Leavis, *D. H. Lawrence: Novelist* (Chicago: University of Chicago Press, 1956), 69, 74; Harry T. Moore, *The Priest of Love: A Life of D. H. Lawrence* (New York: Farrar, 1974), 425; and Keith Sagar, *D. H. Lawrence: Life Into Art* (Athens: University of Georgia Press, 1985), x.

3. This link is not fully articulated until "A Propos of *Lady Chatterley's Lover*" in 1929.

# The Life of the Son/Sun and the Death of the Mother in *Sons and Lovers*

## Gavriel Reisner

SOPHOCLES'S *OEDIPUS REX* CONTAINS NUMEROUS REFERENCES TO "the place where three roads meet," the location where Oedipus "cuts down" Laius (412–13). Invocations of the "triple crossroads" haunt the thought and language of the play's characters. Repeated questions about tragic events at a fated spot dismantle the illusions of Oedipus and Jocasta. Thus, the number *three* looms over the text, or the performance, as a numerical signifier more important than any of its thematic or technical significations. Similarly, the audience is left with a sense of the ternary, the threefold idea or form, as a disrupting power that will explode the play.

The deconstructiveness of the threefold concept echoes in the reading of Lawrence. In essays like *Study of Thomas Hardy* and *The Crown*, Lawrence writes about a duality of experience, expressed by the conflict between a Male "movement toward discovery" and a Female "movement toward the origin." Yet a mysterious "third thing," a "Holy Ghost" emerges from the Lawrentian clash of oppositions to reconfigure the dualistic structure.[1] In later novels the "third thing" refers to an emotional or psychic state of being between (and within) Male and Female partners. In the autobiographical *Sons and Lovers*, the third thing refers to a force of experience not comprehensible in terms the novel associates with either the Mother or the Father.

Turning to a reading of some central scenes in *Sons and Lovers*, episodes rich in psychoanalytic suggestion, we confront a difficult-to-conceptualize "third thing" in relation to three writers: Lawrence, Freud, and Lacan. All three writers create dualistic systems that generate a deconstructive third term. Freud in *Beyond the Pleasure Principle* is concerned with the conflict between Life and Death, taking these concepts as both literal and figurative. Lacan divides our human modes of perception and expression into what he calls the Imaginary (visual) and Symbolic (verbal) orders of experience. Freud's Death and Life and Lacan's Imaginary and Symbolic have a parallel dynamism, for each concerns a clash between a moving forward, a progression, and a moving backward, a regression.

The movements toward Life and Death in *Beyond the Pleasure Principle* culminate in the mysterious Beyond, a state of being or experience irreducible to either category. Similarly, the third Lacanian mode, the Real, is defined as the unrepresentable, precisely that in human perception and expression that eludes both the Imaginary (visual) and Symbolic (verbal) orders. Hence, we have three writers who work with a dualistic system exceeded by a third force which the dualism itself generates.

My reading of *Sons and Lovers* follows the paradigm of a dualistic view that moves beyond itself. It begins with some early scenes between Paul, Gertrude, and Walter; the scenes concern Paul's struggle away from deathly and Imaginary patterns toward vitality and the Symbolic. The argument continues in a series of encounters between Paul and Miriam, where we trace Paul's achievement of the Symbolic, although he approaches it by an Imaginary path. The last section is about a return to the Oedipal triangle in a climactic scene of death and fire, as intense as a blinding by the Real. My reading will connect the Freudian Beyond and the Lacanian Real through the trope of fire.

Lawrence, like Freud and Lacan, struggles with the problem of love, an emotion found in the imperiled area beyond need. Eros is felt in the vital encounter with a separate reality, an Other to whom we turn for something that is neither survival nor reproduction. (In biological terms, *love is excess*.) Yet the going forward finds its complement in a going backward, a repeating. All three writers find *repetition* at the heart of love and work with the paradigm of *transference-love*. Transference occurs in a doubling between the inner world and the outer, a condensing of an object from the psychic reality of the past with an object in the social reality of the present.[2]

The going forward in love is a positive quest, the drive beyond necessity Lacan calls *desire*.[3] The going backward is a negative quest, the turning away from energy which Freud finds in the death-drive, and which resembles desire as an anti-desire, a desire not to desire. Both forms of desire narrate themselves in the repetitions of fiction, in dreams, fantasies, and literature; each describes a tendency in a literary-psychoanalytical romance. The duality of a transference leading backward to archaic objects, to what Daniel Weiss calls "the mother in the mind" (39), or forward to contemporary objects, what we can call "the partner in the world," is elaborated in Lacan's Imaginary and Symbolic orders.[4]

Repetition of experience suggests the regression to visual psychic images, that is, objects of fantasy merged with the subject and apprehended in the Imaginary mode. But, repetition can move forward toward primarily Symbolic encounters, relationship based on the more objectified interchanges of speech. The Symbolic is characterized by the perception of others as subjects rather than objects, for speech is the medium of the subject, the one recognized as an *agent* of desire. Lacan identifies the Imaginary with a fixedness of images and the Symbolic with the flexibility of words: the dynamism of language fragments (in a positive shattering) the stasis of visuality. The Imaginary is about repetition in locked position, the repetition-compulsion, while the Symbolic describes an open position, the struggle of perception to emerge from repetition in the play of language.

In *Sons and Lovers*, repetition is felt most poignantly in relation to the loss of love and loved objects. The disappearance and death of beloved figures in the novel derives from a continuous substitution-play. Characters constantly replace one another as objects of desire: this leads to a male series of objects, Walter, William, Paul, Baxter, and a female series of objects, Gertrude, Miriam, Clara.[5] The idea of the transference helps explain not only *actions* but *affects* in the novel. The pained emotional states, the helplessness and rage which dominate *Sons and Lovers*, develop from conflicting drives toward the contemporary objects and the original source of desire. In the passions of Paul Morel a primary internal image operates like a "stereotype plate" to connect the women chosen in the external world in a "psychical 'series'" ("Dynamics" 100).

Thus, in the moonlit garden scene, the bonding between Gertrude and Paul describes a genetic merger, mother and son united not only in body but in soul (psyche *is* soul in the original Greek). Gertrude experiences mystical self-loss under the white moon, but the "shiny, pale air" (34) which surrounds her also pervades her body, and a metaphorical field unifies mother and unborn child. Recalling that the Lacanian Imaginary erases boundaries between self and other,[6] the encounter introduces *the genesis of the Imaginary*, the beginning of an unbordered, energetic field, an unspoken oneness of feeling and existence which inscribes the tendency to return to perceptual oneness in subsequent encounters.

Such merger occurs during Paul's later life-endangering illness. His sickness, following the mother's self-absenting despair at the death of his older brother William, appears as a ghostly disintegration of personality: "One night he tossed into consciousness, in the ghastly, sickly feeling of dissolution, when all the cells in the body seem in intense irritability to be breaking down, and consciousness makes a last flare of struggle, like madness" (171). He is saved by turning to her "breast," yet rises "white and fragile" from his sickbed, as if maternal rebinding were the only protection against total self-dissolution. The quality of the description, with its presentation of borders more energetic than physical, indicates the Imaginary, the state of being where emotional and visual recognition by the Other, the Imaginary Other inseparable from the self determines the continued existence of the self.[7]

In the classic psychoanalytic pattern (and Lacan's work does, however obscurely, "return to Freud") the father provides a counter-strength, a vital intensity countering the mother's deathly intensity. After the illness, Walter presents Paul with a paternal gift, "a pot of scarlet and gold tulips. They used to flame in the window, in the March sunshine, as [Paul] sat on the sofa chattering to his mother" (171). The father's outburst of color and life suggests a dialectic between *dissolution* and *resolution* within Paul.

Yet the father's role significantly alters Lacan's manner of linking sexual gender and experiential order. Lacan identifies, though not in a one-dimensional fashion, the Imaginary with the maternal and the feminine, and the Symbolic with the paternal and the masculine.[8] The Symbolic begins with the Name-of-the-Father, the demanding negative of the *Non/Nom-du-Père*. The father's *No!* expresses the incest prohibition against the son's Imaginary fusion with the mother. Accepting the *No!* of the father, the child receives the name of the father; he or she, enlisted into linguistic codes, speaks to separate from visual merger and enter into human culture.

Yet in Lawrence the empowering *Non/Nom-du-Père* cannot be

inscribed in language *per se*. The father in *Sons and Lovers* is excluded from innovative language by both his own sensuous nature, which finds modes of expression other than the verbal, and the mother's effective denial of his authority-in-language.[9] The atmosphere in the Morel home denies the force of the father's words, yet tacitly affirms the force of his performance *at work*. Thus in Lawrence male authority is achieved by a kind of subterfuge against the civilizing force of language. Walter's practical skills, his manual abilities that can rise to a creative artisanry, achieve the Lacanian "play of signifiers," *but without words*. The "play of signifiers" refers to representational fertility and contains, therefore, concurrent suggestions of sexuality. Paul's passage toward the Symbolic order occurs, thus, in a detour around language, through another kind of language, an *Imaginary language* operating in combined Imaginary/Symbolic tropes. Paul—or Lawrence—replaces the *Name-of-the-Father* with the *Made-of-the-Father*.

Thus, Paul follows his father, as Lawrence followed his father, *using words to make things*. Paul makes paintings as Lawrence makes natural and cosmic tropes and, particularly, as he writes persuasive dramatic actions that may be analyzed in *relation to* (though not *translated into*) psychoanalytic ideas. Hence, the Lawrentian moon, which projects a white net of light around highly imagined or fantasized scenes, can be reinterpreted in a Lacanian context. Remembering that Lacan uses "stage" in the double sense of physical place, a dramatic platform, and psychic time, a developmental period (*Écrits* 5), the moon, in Lawrence, illuminates the "stage" of the Imaginary.

If Lawrence invokes the moon as the representation of early fusionary stages between mother and son, Freud and Lacan use the sun to describe the later disturbed relations between father and son. Discussing the psychotic judge Schreber, Freud sees his fantasies about the sun as externalizations of, precisely, the *uninternalized father*, with the son, therefore, rendered incomplete and damaged. Failure of internalization for Freud is reconceived as a failure of Symbolization by Lacan. The father who remains unreachably distant—*foreclosed* rather than *repressed*, that is, *expelled* rather than *buried*—is described in a memorable formulation: "It was incorrect to say that the perception which was suppressed internally was projected outward . . . [rather] what was abolished internally returns from without," in the form of the sun that Freud describes as a father-symbol (*Schreber* 71).

Lawrence, of course, like Whitman and other writers before him, took the sun as a vital source. But the sun recalls its psychoanalytic symbolism when Gertrude Morel confronts the sun/son in a manner that *reverses* her own urge-to-absorb her child:

> Mrs Morel watched the sun sink from the glistening sky, leaving a soft flower-blue overhead, while the western space went red, as if all the fire had swum down there, leaving the bell cast flawless blue. The mountain-ash berries across the field stood fierily out from the dark leaves, for a moment. . . .
>
> She thrust the infant forward to the crimson, throbbing sun, almost with relief. . . . Then she put him to her bosom again, ashamed almost of her impulse to give him back again whence he came. (50, 51)

The sun is the source of creative generativity, proliferating in a strength and purity of color. As psychic parable this refers to the energy of the father, a vital phallic energy, reflecting itself in receptive space, bestowing its signifying strength to achieve a positive transfer where *the sun engenders a son*.[10] In the creative transfer from father to son there is a receiving of the *benefit* of paternal power. Hence sunlight reappears in figures like "the mountain-ash berries" etched in fiery form. The moment of landscape-painting brings to mind the transfiguring attention paid to nature in Lawrence's poetry. Suggesting the opposite of the disturbed process suffered by Schreber, it leads to a *foreopening*. In an anticlimax Gertrude returns the child to her "bosom," closing him into the smaller compass of her being. She secludes him from the "crimson, throbbing sun," an image which in its transformativeness can be connected to the Lacanian Phallus, and the Phallic metaphor bears similar intensity in Lacan and Lawrence.

With this notion of the prototypical sun—the Lawrentian-Freudian-Lacanian son/sun—we may look differently at the figurative use of fire, correlate of sun, in the food-burning scenes in *Sons and Lovers*. Asked to guard his mother's bread, Paul's task is to maintain productivity in an environment of moderate heat, the degree of its intensity controlled by the mother.[11] The bread, with its Ceres-like maternal suggestions, represents his continuing subordination to the figure of original life-sustenance. Hence,

Weiss associates the bread with Gertrude's "heart" (42). She sustains by mother-love, and the bread is the product of controlled heat, of the moderately productive environment created when a boy lives within his mother's recognition.

But its metaphorical significance alters with the progress of the scene. It contains three similar but different, metonymical[12] encounters between Paul and Miriam Leivers, his first lover. Miriam duplicates Gertrude's dominating will in her own possessive spirit. Paul, a visual artist who represents Lawrence the verbal artist, shows Miriam a rose he has prepared as a fashion prototype:

> The spread cloth with its wonderful reddish roses and dark green stems, all so simple, and somehow so wicked looking, lay at her feet. She went on her knees before it, her dark curls dropping. He saw her crouched voluptuously before his work, and his heart beat quickly. (241)

Lawrence paints with words in a merger, both Imaginary and Symbolic, of visual and verbal forms. His character Paul similarly employs chromatic forms to refer back to the father in an Imaginary/Symbolic floral rendering, his language that of color and design. The "wickedness" of Paul's pattern suggests its erotic quality, Symbolic in the Lacanian sense, a sign of free, independent, outgoing making. Interestingly, Paul's rose exemplifies *art nouveau*, the style that began modernism in architecture and the applied arts, its stylistic newness antiquating the nineteenth-century reliance on the past for aesthetic approaches and ideological convictions. *Art nouveau*, its name suggesting newness, forswears the influence of domineering priority. Paul's particular design, a classic *art nouveau* rose-pattern, intertwines male and female representations in a decorative eroticism.

Miriam responds to the design with devotion disguising sexuality, her genuflection both a tribute to Paul's spirit and a submission to his body. The atmosphere begins to suggest a mutual erotic quest. But as Miriam remains bent over the painted cloth, Paul abandons the tension between them in deference to a prior responsibility:

> 'By Jove, the bread!' he cried.
> He took the top loaves out, tapped them vigorously. They were done. (241)

Miriam remains on her knees, in sacrifice or communion, and talks about the cruelty of the rose, but Paul remains true to filial obligation. Retreating from Eros, he converses with an intimacy recalling his childhood sickbed. He begins

> to talk about the design. There was for him the most intense pleasure in talking about his work to Miriam. All his passion, all his wild blood went into this intercourse with her, when he talked and conceived his work. She brought forth to him his imaginations. (241)

Miriam repeats the dissolutional position, the original unbordered relationship with the mother, reversed in power but perpetuated in essence. Paul dominates their communication, his strength restricted to the Imaginary mode in a verbal egocentricity that banishes the relations of desire. He closes the woman into the secondariness of undesiring and perceives her as a blank vessel of reception: "She did not understand, any more than a woman understands when she conceives a child in her womb" (241). Miriam's substitutive role occurs in the regressive area where aesthetic experience retreats from the Symbolic back to the Imaginary, a withdrawal from the desire of the other.

In the denial of the desire of the other a symbolism-of-Eros is replaced by a symbolism-of-Thanatos. For Paul uses language, but the words produce an unhealthy psychic intimacy. In an earlier discussion the bright fusion between Paul and Miriam is like light pervading separate selves, a transfusion of language itself:

> She wanted to draw all of him into her. It urged him to an intensity like madness. . . .
>
> He was discussing Michael Angelo. . . . [T]here he lay in the white intensity of his search, . . . almost inhuman as if in a trance. (232)

The scenes, which fulfill an element of desire in both of them, are mentalized, abstract, and rarefied into the area of psychic sublimation. They present an enervating transference and are more devitalized, indeed, than his actual relationship with Gertrude. For the transference to Miriam essentializes the most destructive dimension of the connection to the mother, crystallizing the deathliness of the Imaginary.

As the atmosphere between Paul and Miriam becomes increasingly morbid, another young woman, Beatrice, enters the room in Symbolic provocation:

He bent forward to her to light his cigarette at hers. She was wink-
ing at him as he did so. Miriam saw his eyes trembling with mischief,
and his full, almost sensual mouth quivering. *He was not himself,* and
she could not bear it. As he was now, she had no connection with him,
she might as well not have existed. She saw the cigarette dancing on
his full red lips. She hated his thick hair for being tumbled loose on
his forehead. (244; my emphasis)

The action is presented from Miriam's point-of-view, and, despite its visuality, introduces her consciousness to a different
mode of perception. Miriam gazes at Paul and Beatrice while the
observed moment, a cinematic shot, affords insight into the one
who gazes. Miriam observes an Erotic contact distanced in the
visual field of a crossover between the Imaginary and Symbolic
modes. Indeed Miriam and Paul are now traversed—pervaded, vi-
olated—by the Symbolic. In Lawrentian language they are separate selves, no longer fused in oneness; the alienated strangeness
Miriam feels arises because separateness releases Eros. Seeing
his autonomous desire, the Imaginary Other who is not her also
represents her in a sexual encounter. (Miriam's sexuality can
only be experienced through the Other.)

Here Lacan gives the Lawrentian action added depth while
Lawrence gives the Lacanian categories added drama. The cinematic shot shows the advantages of the Lawrentian/Lacanian
juxtaposition, indeed of the alignment of literature and psycho-
analysis in critical analysis. In its visual realization of sexuality
the novelistic cinema-shot shows the Imaginary doing the work
of the Symbolic—the picture can lead to the end of picturing.

Watching the encounter between Paul and Beatrice, Miriam
*duplicates* the mother, appearing as a censuring presence placing
the Symbolic under limitation. Paul's not being "himself" indicates his separation from the Imaginary self frozen in the fantasy
world with Miriam; instead, the cigarette lights up the Symbolic
in a point of masculine fire. A play of substitution occurs when
Miriam is the essential non-participating (in that sense invisible)
third in a sexual play between Paul and Beatrice. The small
drama is predicated on the silent presence toward which it feigns
indifference, with the triangulated event conditioned upon its
witness.

In his excitement, Paul forgets prior obligation. Miriam, in her
restrictive maternal guise, reminds him of the bread, now

burned, and emitting "bluish smoke" from the oven door (244). Paradoxically, Beatrice transfers responsibility for the burnt bread to Miriam, correctly predicting that Gertrude will come to a corresponding conclusion. The complete confidence with which she shifts blame derives from *unconscious knowledge*, a certitude based on silent transmission.

As an image before Miriam's eyes, Paul and Beatrice together represent the form of that which Miriam cannot possess but infinitely desires. Paul becomes the desired Other who waits at an uncrossable distance, the beloved Other who performs a desired-prohibited action, and Beatrice is Miriam's *alienated self-other in action*. Miriam, the one who gazes, looks into experience, *an experience that in its visuality is itself like a mirror*. She finds the Other that both is and is not her, that her ego both embraces and rejects. This is that other-in-the-mirror that we first encounter in very early childhood, the *petit objet a'* that both is and is not the self.[13] Beatrice emerges as the duplicate of Miriam's desire, the object of desire that helps define the ego and, finally, *her own passionate unconscious*. Miriam now turns, explicitly, to the Phallic Paul: "Why might she not press his body with her two hands. It looked so firm and every whit living. And he would let other girls, why not her?" (246).

From there we move to the third scene on the metonymic path, Miriam's reading out loud from her "diary of her inner life, in her own French" (246). Miriam allows erotic play in the defamiliarized speech of a foreign language, a defamiliarization that can release the unconscious. Miriam's composition traces the welling-up within her of erotic feeling transformed into metaphor: sunlight replaces the drained color of morning before sunrise, its transfiguration communicated by the bedroom window going from *blême* to *jaune*, pallor to color. The whole creation affirms an erotic wish, a dreamlike wish-fulfillment. The sunrise suggests the accession of male presence reified in the sun/son. Miriam's feeling of *terreur* recalls the beautiful opening of Rilke's *First Duino Elegy*, its description which claims that "Beauty's nothing / but beginning of Terror we're still just able to bear" (21). In its Lawrentian variation, exceedingly close to Rilke, this would appear as: terror is the beginning of Eros we cannot endure but creatively-destructively embrace. In Lacanian language the passage might suggest that the acquiring of the Symbolic freeplay of erotic or intellectual pleasure (*jouissance*) entails a dreadful beginning.

But Paul is unable to respond to the erotic play element behind Miriam's verbal disguise. Miriam remains distant from Eros not because she lacks desire, but because hers is a conditional desire experienced as a tremulous and secondary passion-in-the-mirror. Her erotic feelings emerge reflectively and require affirmation from the Other. In the relationship between Paul and Miriam the unconscious speaks fearfully (their conscious speech often stammers). Paul responds to Miriam's tentative Eros with a cruel refusal. His unconscious discourse expresses itself in action, a *no* of the lover, *non de l'amant*. The *no* reveals itself in Paul's flinging down of the pencil (247), an expression of Phallic withholding (the Lacanian use of psychoanalytic terms includes and expands upon their traditional sense). The pencil is handled similarly in an earlier scene, a moment of demonic acting-out: "Once he threw the pencil in her face" (189). Later, incensed at her inability to master algebra, Paul barely controls his rekindled fury: "And still, when he saw her eager, silent, as it were blind face, he felt he wanted to throw the pencil in it" (189). He feels threatened by her *Imaginary blindness*, by her projection of the preconceptions of desire. She is unable to react to what she actually sees because she inhabits the world she self-protectively imagines. Yet, "flinging down" the pencil, Paul is himself caught in the regressive compulsion-to-repeat experienced by the one who cannot yield to the erotic. He yields, rather, to the regressive unconscious will. Saving the bread is an act translatable as the protecting of the Paul in Gertrude, the keeping of the child in the womb.

Yet Gertrude can interpret the scorched bread as a sign of filial betrayal. After his mother's return Paul encounters a doubled image, with Gertrude's domestic sexuality repeated in the matronly disapproval of his sister: "Annie, her blouse unfastened, her long ropes of hair twisted into a plait, went up to bed, bidding him a very curt goodnight" (250). Annie reinforces the mother's silent, powerful withdrawal. But soon after, Paul and his mother, beginning with a conventional good-night embrace, enter into "a long, fervent kiss." During their incestuous action Gertrude explicitly *discards* the father, "And I've never—you know, Paul—I've never had a husband—not really—" (252). Deep pauses separate her rhythmic words, her breath's verbal spaces inviting Paul to enter.

The father's arrival interrupts their forbidden contact; in a stark confrontation the characters return to a conflict before language, the rudimentary Oedipal triangle of mother-father-son:

> Morel came in, walking unevenly. His hat was over one corner of his eye. He balanced in the doorway.
> "At your mischief again?" he said, venomously. . . .
> He went into the passage, hung up his hat and coat. Then they heard him go down three steps to the pantry. He returned with a piece of pork-pie in his fist. It was what Mrs Morel had bought for her son.
> "Nor was that bought for you. . . ."
> "Wha-at—wha-at!" snarled Morel, toppling his balance. He looked at the piece of meat and crust, and suddenly, in a vicious spurt of temper, flung it into the fire.
> Paul started to his feet. . . .
> He would at that moment dearly have loved to have a smack at something. Morel was half crouching, fists up, ready to spring. . . .
> "Right!" said Paul, his eyes upon the side of his father's mouth, where in another instant his fist would have hit. He ached for that stroke. (252–53)

Walter's dignity is undermined by drunkenness and a vision-blocking hat, but he thrusts instinctively to the point with the hostile word "mis/chief." That word is curiously appropriate, almost as if he found, instinctually, its fundamental, perhaps original, meaning. The charged term suggests the violation, the *missing*, of the *chief* law of civilization, the incest-taboo, and emerges like a single primordial speech-act to assert paternal authority at the very moment of its breakdown. Subsequently, Morel forswears speech in a stuttering that still expresses outrage at faithless action and useless language.

Yet he succeeds in annihilating a central Symbol. The climactic sequence engages two signifiers, the one devouring the other. The pork-pie serves as ritualized object conferring masculine supremacy. This wife/mother's choice between father and son, the power confirmed through ritual consumption, recalls the rivalry of *Totem and Taboo*. Paul, like the sons in Freud's essay, consumes what belongs to the father, the use of food allowing an act of representative incorporation—which in Freud's essay occurs through the father himself, the sons usurping his position by cannibalizing him (*Totem* 140–46).

But in *Sons and Lovers* the father avoids being overthrown by the son. This reassertion of paternal supremacy occurs through the domestic fire, the family hearth (burning *Walter's* coal). Morel takes the symbol of masculine victory, the pork-pie which the mother had conferred on her dominant male, and sacrifices it to the fire. Fire is a version of the sun, a Symbolic alteration representing its capacity for reformation, the reallocation of sun-energy to other objects. But in a blaze of primal fire, Morel not only reasserts his own dominance, but also reminds Gertrude that only he can pass on that dominance, that the mother cannot transmit *the Non/Nom du Père*.

This primal assertion of fatherly supremacy leads to the violent rebellion of the son. The entire encounter follows the sequence in *Totem and Taboo* where the sons' destruction of the father follows his patriarchal assertion and sexual dominance. Strangely, Paul's aggression targets the erogenous (also verbal) zone of his father's mouth. In an uncanny pun the language of destructive desire, the "stroke" for which Paul "aches," conflates the blow to the father with the harm suffered by the mother. It is the mother who appears to receive a "stroke," its terrible evidence appearing mutely at her mouth. The feature Paul wished to strike in the father marks itself in blood on the mother's drained face:

> But he heard a faint moan from behind. His mother was deadly pale, and dark at the mouth. . . . She began to struggle with herself. Her open eyes watched him, although she could not move. (253)

The forbidden attack on the father is eerily mirrored in the near-death of the mother: what Paul fails to do to the one he nearly does to the other, the unsettling transformation reflecting a forgotten parental bond. Desiring to avenge himself, Paul discovers that *to injure the father is to injure the mother*. (After an extended deferral, Oedipus made the same discovery.)

Under the deep shadow of paternal resentment and reflexed through parents whose indivisibility remains inexplicable, we approach the atmospheres of the third Lacanian order, the inarticulable *Real*. Real/ity extends to two key areas. There is first the sexuality of the mouth, the father's aggression against a Phallic trope incorporated by the stronger feminine trope. Its female sexuality extends to death and something unspeakable, a blurring of life-identity by maternal blood. Then we have the unbearable *gaze from the depths of death.* The erotic gaze, we realize, is indis-severable from the sexual body, for the gaze is the body-animat-ing window and mirror of desire. The death gaze reflects the separation of the psyche from the body, propelling the reader into mysticism or terror.

Parental bonding shows a Real finality shattering the subject's narcissistic illusions. Neither the Imaginary nor the Symbolic se-miotic network can allow full unification with the mother or full replacement of the father. The fantasy of omnipotence, of pos-sessing the body of the mother by usurping the authority of the father, is destroyed by paternal *power* and maternal *mortality.* Paul has been doubly assaulted, facing the father's hostility to him, and the mother's collapse, aggressive toward both father and son. The scene, which consumes not only the Imaginary and the Symbolic representations, but also the process of representa-tion itself, leaves its characters vulnerable before the abyss of the Real. ("Everybody tried to forget the scene" [254].)

In a moving passage in the *Four Fundamental Concepts* (59), Lacan explores the disturbing reverberations of fire as the Sym-bol which removes the screen of the Symbolic. He analyzes the "dream of the burning child," a dream that plays an important role in *The Interpretation of Dreams* (5: 509). It concerns a be-reaved father who dreams his dead son comes to him to say: "Father can't you see I'm burning?" The father then awakens to find that the watchman had fallen asleep and that the boy's body had been burned by a fallen candle. Freud reads the dream as an interchange of dream and reality, with the reality of the fire dis-rupting the dream, and the dream itself the fulfillment of the father's understandable wish for his son to be alive a little longer.

Lacan takes this further. Like Freud he sees the dream as an entrance to death, but adds that the fire signals the boy's return from the Freudian Beyond, for unbearable and unformed fire sug-gests an "underlying" Real/ity.

> But the terrible vision of the dead son taking the father by the arm designates a beyond that makes itself heard in the dream. Desire manifests itself in the dream by the loss expressed in an image at the most cruel point of the object. . . .
> *Father, can't you see I'm burning*? This sentence is itself a fire-brand—of itself it brings fire where it falls—and one cannot see what is burning, for the flames blind us to the fact that the fire bears on the *Unterlegt*, on the *Untertragen*, on the real. (*Concepts* 59)

Bowie connects these passages to the traumatic dreams of *Beyond the Pleasure Principle* with their introduction of traumas-beyond-integration, to which the subject helplessly returns, and the traces of which are found in the Real that exists beyond the pleasure principle (105). His point is that the child's statement in the dream repeats the important reality preceding the dream, that the death of the child is repeated in the verbal fragment, and the unfathomable Real evokes death itself in a special sense. For it evokes unfathomable death, Coleridge's "death-in-life," a state not only beyond the power of the individual will but also beyond the power of articulable language.

The relevance of this to the food-burning scenes, which are concerned with loss and rejection, is that the mother momentarily dead in the world of life contrasts with and parallels the child (in the dream) momentarily alive in the world of death. This is an uncanny border-crossing, strengthened in the novel by the gaze of the dead mother, the stare from eyes of death that gaze from a paralyzed body. For if the boy in the dream defies death to live a moment longer with the father, the mother defies life to bind her son to her own dying body, to unify with him in the impossible Real, which can only mean, *to have him, literally or figuratively, die with her*.

Therefore, Paul remains desperately weak until he takes his mother's life to return life to himself. Similarly, after this moment of confrontation Walter is broken, for Gertrude resides elsewhere, already beyond him. The scene beginning with the father's defeat of the son, incinerating his connection to the mother in an Imaginary blaze, ends with both men helpless before the maternal invocation of the Real.

Notably, the earlier, more accessible orders begin with *the maternal image*, with the Imaginary going toward her in fusion and the Symbolic going away from her in translation. The Real emerges in a stark, originary Oedipal context, revealing itself when the original object of desire appears to *defeat her Imaginary representation*. In *Sons and Lovers*, as in such works as *Oedipus Rex* and *Hamlet*, the Real is the mother as she exists separated, vulnerable, but unsusceptible to connection. In *Oedipus Rex* and *Hamlet* the death of the mother concludes the main action, with maternal death decreeing the closure of the play at the point when the condensation of imaginative meaning, the literary, comes to the end of its play. The Real appears at the end of language, coming to its end before the mother in her dying, which is another way of saying *the unImaginable mother*. The body of the mother in its dying expresses the ultimate unreachableness of the psyche/soul of the mother. Thus, in *Sons and Lovers*, the Death-of-the-Mother erases the Name-of-the-Father.

## Notes

1. See Daleski 31. For a discussion of "the third thing" and "the Holy Ghost" see Ben-Ephraim, "Achievement" 136–37.

2. Freud describes the transference in the three early essays on "Dynamics," "Remembering," and "Transference-Love." The "Dora" case-study ends with a searching analysis of the transference (112–22), while *Beyond the Pleasure Principle* contains speculative discussions of the concept (18–23). Laplanche and Pontalis note that its orthodox reading refers to "*transference during treatment*" (455; their emphasis), but Freud expands the transferential process to include "normal" experience (*Beyond* 21).

3. Laplanche and Pontalis interpret Lacanian desire as that which exists beyond both need and demand. Need is aimed at a real object and can be satisfied, while demand is addressed to real others as a demand for love. But desire is a relation to fantasy that cannot be fulfilled (483). Lacan's cryptic statement, "man's desire is the desire of the Other" (*Écrits* 264), presents desire as an interweaving of fantasies between self and other, an unresolved continuous play of meaning and wanting. Freud's discussion of death as the cessation of energy (and therefore desire), the grateful winding-down of the organism because *the end of all life is death*, takes place in *Beyond* (36–39; Freud's emphasis).

4. For a description of the three orders see "The Split Between the Eye and the Gaze" in Lacan's *Four Concepts* (67–78). Among the useful works on Lacan—and critical introductions are nearly indispensable in reading him—are the studies by Bowie, Ragland-Sullivan, Wilden, Muller and Richardson, and Payne.

5. The term "object" is employed here, but it would also be possible to use the term "figure"—an "object" for the character involved in the transference is a "figure" for the artist who creates the fiction.

6. Bowie finds the Imaginary in "the order of mirror-images, identifications, and reciprocities. It is the dimension of experience in which the individual seeks not merely to placate the Other but to dissolve his otherness by becoming his counterpart" (92).

7. Lacan does not use the word "self," preferring the term "subject." Freud rarely uses "self," but develops the modern concept of "ego." Lawrence uses "self," "being," and "ego," alternatively, intuitively, depending on context. All three writers connect *desire* to *being*. I am looking for that combination of force and feeling when, for the sake of general communicability and comprehension, I use the common term "self."

8. The distinction between Imaginary and Symbolic comes out most clearly in Lacan's reading of the *fort/da* game in Freud's *Beyond*. The use of the syllables *fort! da!* to replace the absent mother (absent in body, voice, and gaze) is the passing to the further order, for "the moment in which desire becomes

human is also that in which the child is born into language" (*Écrits* 103). That language is the language—the law—of the father: ambivalent, transformative, prohibitive.

9. Earl Ingersoll traces the Imaginary in Walter and the Symbolic in Gertrude back to the early relationship between the parents. Gertrude is attracted to Walter's face and body, while Walter is attracted to her demeanor and language. Worthen discusses the conflicts between Lydia and Arthur Lawrence in relation to language. Lydia with her middle-class background proudly spoke the "King's English" and disdained Arthur's working-class dialect. Arthur Lawrence's imitations of standard English were greeted by the laughter of his wife Lydia and son David Herbert (Worthen 61).

10. Critics have written on the sun-sequence in terms of masculinity, reminiscent of Lacan for whom the Phallus is the signifier of desire. Thus, L. D. Clark notes that Gertrude wraps "the child in her motherhood" to prevent its belonging to "the sun or the orbit of life" (58). Jack Stewart explores the cultural ramifications of sun and fire in Lawrence, noting their identification with the cultures and peoples of the South, as water and ice reflect the cold North, and the "dialectic of North and South becomes a dialectic of life and death" (135). Wilden points out that the sun/son homophone creates an indistinguishable union in speech if not in writing: "if the schizophrenic says 'I'm the black sun,' the psychiatrist may well catch the significant ambiguity of 'sun,' but how would the literary author spell it?" (185).

11. Seeing it in positive terms, Cynthia Lewiecki-Wilson takes the mother-son relationship as a mutual "participation in the creative unconscious" (76). Wary of a certain sexist bias in earlier psychoanalytic Lawrence criticism, Lewiecki-Wilson underestimates how threatening the mother-related unconscious is for Paul.

12. The two principles of literary organization described by Roman Jakobson, the *metaphorical*, where one image *enfolds* another, and the *metonymic*, where one image *introduces* another, exist inseparably when love involves the search, the finding yet not-finding, of an original object. There is a tension between the metonymic series of lovers and the metaphorical hidden lover within the apparent lover. For a discussion of Lacan's application of Jakobson's two basic registers of language, metaphor ("the relation of similarity," related to Freudian condensation), and metonymy ("the relation of contiguity," related to Freudian displacement), see Wilden 238–49.

13. Lacan organizes being into 1) the speaking subject; 2) the *small object, a'* (*petit objet a'* for *autre*), with which it identifies, but which it cannot have; 3) the ego which models itself on the object it cannot have and is divided commensurately; and 4) the unconscious or *large other, A'*, which speaks through the subject. It is important to remember that the small object *a'* is first encountered in early childhood in the unified mirror-image as the Imaginary self-other that at once reifies and alienates the ego. (One both is and is not one's image in the mirror, so that, as Wilden puts it, "the *moi* is an Imaginary construct" [160]). Lacan's *Schéma L*, which lays out this pattern, is found in *Seminar II* (243).

## WORKS CITED

Ben-Ephraim, Gavriel. "The Achievement of Balance in *Lady Chatterley's Lover*." In *D. H. Lawrence's "Lady": A New Look at "Lady Chatterley's*

*Lover,"* edited by Michael Squires and Dennis Jackson. Athens, Ga.: University of Georgia Press, 1985.

Bowie, Malcolm. *Lacan*. London: Fontana, 1991.

Clark, L. D. *The Minoan Distance: The Symbolism of Travel in D. H. Lawrence.* Tucson: University of Arizona Press, 1980.

Daleski, H. M. *The Forked Flame: A Study of D.H. Lawrence.* Evanston, Ill.: Northwestern University Press, 1965.

Freud, Sigmund. *Beyond the Pleasure Principle.* 1920. In *The Standard Edition of the Complete Psychological Works of Sigmund Freud*, translated under the general editorship of James Strachey in collaboration with Anna Freud. Volume 18:1–63. London: Hogarth Press and the Institute of Psycho-Analysis, 1953–74.

——. *The Case of Schreber.* 1911, 1912. *SE*: 12:1–84.

——. "The Dynamics of the Transference." 1912. *SE*: 12:97–108.

——. *Fragment of an Analysis of a Case of Hysteria ("Dora").* 1905. *SE* 7:1–122.

——. *The Interpretation of Dreams. SE* 4–5.

——. "Observations on Transference-Love." 1915. *SE*: 12:157–71.

——. "Remembering, Repeating, and Working-Through." *SE*: 12:145–56.

——. *Totem and Taboo. SE*: 13:1–161.

Ingersoll, Earl G. "Gender and Language in *Sons and Lovers.*" *Midwest Quarterly* 37 (1996): 434–47.

Jakobson, Roman. "Two Types of Language and Two Types of Aphasic Disturbances." In *Fundamentals of Language.* The Hague: Mouton, 1956.

Lacan, Jacques. *Écrits: A Selection.* Translated by Alan Sheridan. New York: Norton, 1977.

——. *The Four Fundamental Concepts of Psycho-Analysis.* Edited by Jacques-Alain Miller. Translated by Alan Sheridan. New York: Norton, 1981.

——. *The Seminar of Jacques Lacan: Book II, The Ego in Freud's Theory and in the Technique of Psychoanalysis 1954–55.* Translated by Sylvana Tomaselli. New York: Norton, 1991.

Laplanche, J., and J.-B. Pontalis. *The Language of Psycho-Analysis.* Translated by Donald Nicholson-Smith. New York: Norton, 1973.

Lewiecki-Wilson, Cynthia. *Writing Against the Family: Gender in Lawrence and Joyce.* Carbondale: Southern Illinois University Press, 1994.

Mack, Maynard, et al., eds. *The Norton Anthology of World Masterpieces.* New York: Norton, 1997.

Muller, John P., and William J. Richardson. *Lacan and Language: A Reader's Guide to Écrits.* New York: International Universities, 1982.

Payne, John. *Reading Theory: An Introduction to Lacan, Derrida, and Kristeva.* Oxford: Blackwell, 1993.

Ragland-Sullivan, Ellie. *Jacques Lacan and the Philosophy of Psychoanalysis.* Urbana: University of Illinois Press, 1987.

Rilke, Rainer Maria. *Duino Elegies.* Translated by J. B. Leishman and Stephen Spender. New York: Norton, 1963.

Stewart, Jack F. "The Vital Art of Lawrence and Van Gogh." *DHLR* 19 (1987): 123–48.

Weiss, Daniel A. *Oedipus in Nottingham: D. H. Lawrence*. Seattle: University of Washington Press, 1962.

Wilden, Anthony, ed. *Speech and Language in Psychoanalysis: Jacques Lacan*. Translated and with commentary by Anthony Wilden. Baltimore: Johns Hopkins University Press, 1968.

Worthen, John. *D. H. Lawrence: The Early Years 1885–1912*. Cambridge: Cambridge University Press, 1991.

# "Records of Pain and Hope Now Spent": Elegy and Expenditure in *Amores*

## Holly Laird

> The term poetry, applied to the least degraded and least intellectualized forms of the expression of a state of loss, can be considered synonymous with expenditure; it in fact signifies, in the most precise way, creation by means of loss. Its meaning is therefore close to *sacrifice*. . . . [F]or the rare human beings who have this element at their disposal, poetic expenditure ceases to be symbolic in its consequences; thus, to a certain extent, the function of representation engages the very life of the one who assumes it. It condemns him to the most disappointing forms of activity, to misery, to despair, to the pursuit of inconsistent shadows that provide nothing but vertigo and rage. (Bataille 120)

## I

GEORGES BATAILLE'S STRIKING DESCRIPTION OF POETRY AND OF THE poet's life as forms of expenditure and loss seems especially apt when applied to the poetry and the life behind the poetry of D. H. Lawrence's book of elegies, *Amores* (1916). Of all his volumes of poems, this one alone is dedicated to the poetic "mourning" that Bataille analogizes to uneconomical and nonintellectual indulgence, for example, in luxury, in war, or in "perverse sexual activity," all of which have "no end beyond themselves" (118). As Lawrence put this in describing the autobiographical sequence of these poems, in "the sick year after" the death of his mother, "everything collapsed, save the mystery of death, and the haunting of death in life. I was twenty-five, and from the death of my mother, the world began to dissolve around me, beautiful, iridescent, but passing away substanceless. Till I almost dissolved away myself, and was very ill" (*Poems* 851). As he wrote in a characteristic elegy, "I reel with disseminated consciousness, / Like a man who has died" ("Dolor of Autumn," *Amores* 75).

What Lawrence most distinctively adds to Bataille's description of poetry as expenditure is an insistent sense of recurrent conflict. Rebecca West once said that "a writer composes a book in order to put down what the warring elements in him think on some subject which interests them all, and to arbitrate between them" (168). So too, for Lawrence, as I have argued elsewhere, conflict textures his writing in every phase of his career as a poet (*Self and Sequence*). Thus even the elegiac experience of wasting away was articulated and theorized as a process of struggle or, in Lawrence's vocabulary, of "opposition" between antagonistic people, selves, principles (*L* ii. 638). Correlatively, conflict became a vehicle for dissolution.

Bataille argues (in the sentence concluding the passage cited in my epigraph) that "the poet frequently can use words only for his own loss; he is often forced to choose between the destiny of a reprobate, who is as profoundly separated from society as dejecta are from apparent life, and a renunciation whose price is a mediocre activity, subordinated to vulgar and superficial needs." As Lawrence expressed this in "Blue" (retitled "The Shadow of Death" in *Collected Poems*),

> The clouds go down the sky with a wealthy ease
> Casting a shadow of scorn upon me for my share in death; but I
> Hold my own in the midst of them, darkling, defy
> The whole of the day to extinguish the shadow I lift on the breeze.
> (*Amores* 119)

But while the Lawrence of *Amores* would quickly have agreed he had chosen the "destiny of a reprobate" in opposition to that of the "ordinary me" (*Poems* 850, 852), the choice between them was less clear, less easily pursued than Bataille and Lawrence himself sometimes suggested. The conflicts themselves between the reprobate and ordinary man, between others' beliefs and his own, between the hope for new forms of life and the certainty of wartime death, between the "death-paean[s]" of the past and the "swoon[ing]" hope of "futurity" (*Poems* 181) wore Lawrence down, even while enabling the production of an elegiac sequence of poems.

While a number of Lawrence's most widely esteemed early

poems—including "The Wild Common," "Discord in Childhood," "Snap-Dragon," and many of the early love poems, not only the elegies to his mother—were first collected in *Amores* in 1916, today's critics rarely pay much attention to this book or its circumstances. When, in the course of his development of volume 1, "Rhyming Poems," for *Collected Poems* in 1927 to 1928, Lawrence rewrote and rearranged this verse and combined it with three other books of his poetry,[1] he inadvertently also prepared for neglect of this early book. Readers naturally perceive volume 2, titled more boldly "Unrhyming Poems," as the volume in which Lawrence's poetic "demon" has "his say" (*Poems* 28).[2] Several decades ago, Abbie Potts wrote an essay on the elegiac in Lawrence's work, and the few specialist books on the poetry touch on individual poems among the elegies, but with the exceptions of Gail Porter Mandell's *The Phoenix Paradox*, my *Self and Sequence*, and, to a lesser extent, M. J. Lockwood's *A Study of the Poems of D. H. Lawrence*, they do not grapple with the book or sequence in its entirety.[3] MLA's online bibliography includes no listings at all for *Amores*. The second volume of the Cambridge biography, which covers the years from 1912 to 1922, devotes only half a short paragraph to it (Kinkead-Weekes 301).

This last fact springs, of course, in part from the timing of *Amores*, which was produced long after the first drafts of the elegies were composed; scholars have habitually taken interest in individual poems rather than poetic sequences or verse books, and biographers focus on dating the original compositions of poems (though often by guesswork) rather than on subsequent periods of revision and publication. John Worthen and others trace the first drafts for these poems to the years before 1912 and the elegies mostly to December 1910 and the year 1911 following Mrs. Lawrence's death (*Early Years* 488–91). Thus the first volume of the biography rather than the second discusses individual poems that appeared in *Amores*. Although the second volume devotes considerable attention to the place and significance of revisions for Lawrence's novels and philosophy during these years, it makes no attempt to characterize the development of *Amores*.

Lawrence created *Amores*, however, in a pivotal juncture in his career, a moment when he was struggling, from underneath the dead hand of the war and the banning of *The Rainbow*, to relaunch his career. The elegies thus traverse two separate periods in his life in both of which he faced major struggles with death.

In 1916, these struggles included wrestling with his own illness, with personal and professional losses, and with the deepening world war, not only with the recollection of his past life with his mother and her death. Given the extensive consideration already devoted to the place of individual elegies in the years of his mother's illness and death, this essay shifts the focus, then, to the period when *Amores* was produced, to why and how *Amores* should matter to readers of Lawrence, and to the disappointments, struggles, and oppositional thought specific to this interlude and these poems—their "expenditures" of pain.

## II

In 1916, Lawrence yielded to, even while he fought, several of the faces of death in life. He revised and arranged the elegies for *Amores* during a pause in one of the most serious of his illnesses—an illness nearly equalling in severity those of 1901 and 1911. He fell ill after failing not only to reprieve *The Rainbow*, but also to live within Lady Ottoline Morrell's circle and to build Rananim with Philip Heseltine. England itself seemed to Lawrence to have died or to be on the brink of death, as the losses mounted around him; and as usual he experienced and embraced such death from within, almost ceasing to hope for the rebirth all "natural" deaths portended for him. Throughout this time, he also fought with Frieda over their friends, their marriage, his beliefs, and his past. While enacting a process of conflict, grief, and mourning for his mother in the elegies that seemed newly fresh to Lawrence during the disappointments and the illness of 1916, the elegies also became materially implicated in these later events. As Bataille suggests, "representation engage[d]" his "very life."

Thus Frieda vented some of her fiercest hostility at what became one of *Amores'* central poems—"The Virgin Mother" (originally titled "My Love, My Mother")—inscribing hatred of Lawrence and of his sentiments about his mother in the margins of the college-notebook version of this poem (Note on Poem 68, Ferrier 2:101; Worthen, *Early Years* 411–12). "I hate it" is scrawled next to three of the stanzas, and she appends a long note mocking lines in which he celebrates his freedom from "each heart's home-life" (thanks to his mother's death) and notifying him of her decision to leave him "free"—that is, alone and "lonely" "for some days." In this note, she accuses him, above all, of "Misery, a sad, old woman's misery you have chosen, you poor man, and you cling to it with all your power." "I have fought," she claims, "I have nearly killed myself in the battle to get you into connection with myself and other people, sadly I proved to my self that *I* can love, but *never* you." "I know your secret and your despair," she taunts, "I have seen you are ashamed." This passage speaks sadly indeed of Lawrence's intense misery and conflict with others, particularly with Frieda. Both Worthen and Mark Kinkead-Weekes chalk up this incident to earlier battles between Lawrence and Frieda in Germany in 1912 or 1913 (*Early Years* 412; Kinkead-Weekes 21), but whenever she first inscribed her graffiti, they confronted Lawrence as he returned to these manuscripts in January 1916 to revise and arrange his elegies. After publishing his first book of poems, *Love Poems and Others*, in 1913, Lawrence had reported, "I thought the book awfully nice – I loved it. F[rieda] refuses to have sufficient respect for it – but there, she *would*. There are in it too many heroines other than herself" (*L* i. 462). But rather than now gathering the poems he had written about Frieda, he returned to the old notebooks, full of the same "heroines," above all his mother.

The title *Amores*, of course, speaks elegantly of old "loves," functioning as both subject and object, honoring Lawrence's multiple loving and lovers, both wanted and unwanted, desired and imposed. Derived from two of Lawrence's college notebooks, the earlier one containing "Latin notes" (Ferrier i. 26), these poems brought his not so ancient past flooding back, "strange and far-off, unreal, and yet, in another mood, so near and *navrant*" (*L* iii. 61). In these poems, he futilely wrestled to transform his "dull" lovers and himself with the "Fire-threshing anguish" of sexual passion ("Last Words to Miriam," *Amores* 43), much as in the present of 1916 he had failed to transmute even the small circle of his friends and his wife with a shared passion for Rananim. In 1915 and 1916, Lawrence was especially torn between Frieda and a new heroine (though not a lover)—Ottoline Morrell. Lady Ottoline supported Lawrence during his sickness, but she did not admire Frieda and thus continually courted Frieda's resentment. Although Lawrence stuck by Frieda in these quarrels, he dedicated *Amores* to Lady Ottoline, thereby setting his resistance to Frieda in indelible print.

Situated between the failure to publish *The Rainbow* and the writing of the first *Women in Love*, *Amores* played an integral part also in Lawrence's wartime sagas. (Lawrence began to write *Women in Love* in late April 1916 when his poems were in press.) The first *Women in Love* failed to find a publisher, but as Worthen explains in his discussion of this version of the novel, this book was "poignantly addressed . . . not to a post-war world disillusioned with society, and resigned to its fate [as was the 1921 version], but one actually fighting a war" ("The First" 23). "Appropriately for a novel which has the war so much in focus," Worthen argues, the relationships of the first *Women in Love* are characterized far more than the revised 1921 version by "conflict and uncertainty" (14). "The book frightens me," Lawrence wrote, "it is so end-of-the-world" (*L* iii. 25). But *Amores* told the story of Lawrence's more personal confrontation with the "end-of-the-world" before he fictionalized it in this novel.

In addition, *Amores* became the object of a disappointing episode in London, which Lawrence subsequently transformed into the well-known Pompadour Café scene in *Women in Love* (380–86), so that *Amores* acquired a crucial fictional role within this *roman à clef*. Not coincidentally, the Pompadour Café scene occurs immediately prior to Ursula and Birkin's exodus from England and is pivotal in representing the London society that Gudrun and Birkin—and also Lawrence—disgustedly rejected. Commentators are aware of the actual incident at the Café Royal behind this scene, but they never, to my knowledge, do more than note the role of *Amores* in it. Since in the novel Lawrence replaced the book of poems with a letter by Birkin, scholars tend to see the incident as self-parody, mocking the preachiness of Lawrence's own letters.

The choice of a letter rather than a book of poems in this scene has narratological advantages, but that does not mean Lawrence found the real-life ridicule of *Amores* insignificant. This change was necessary, most obviously, because Birkin is not a writer; in addition, a letter is less open to public ridicule (ridicule of it is more offensive) since it is more private than a published book of poems. Yet his friends' mockery of this very personal book insulted Lawrence no less than if they had exposed one of his letters. He probably saw it too, as I will shortly demonstrate, as an indication of their rejection of the poems' larger aims and of the poet-Lawrence's stance as "The Prophet"—the title he chose in 1916 for one of the newly wrought poems in *Amores*:[4]

Ah, my darling, when over the purple horizon shall loom
The shrouded mother of a new idea, men hide their faces,
Cry out and fend her off, as she seeks her procreant groom,
Wounding themselves against her, denying her fecund embraces.

(41)

Some key images in Birkin's letter in fact had appeared previously in *Amores*. When Birkin writes to Halliday (the fictionalized Heseltine), pleading with him to seek "the living desire for positive creation, relationships in ultimate faith, when all this process of active corruption with all its flowers of mud, is transcended," Halliday's group laughs giddily at the possible allusion to Halliday's lover, the Pussum, as a "flower of mud" and connects this phrase also with Baudelaire's *Fleurs du Mal* (*WL* 383–84). Previously, in a poem "Lotus Hurt by the Frost" (retitled "Lotus and Frost" in *Collected Poems*), Lawrence may also have been working under the inspiration of Baudelaire's poems, though he added a direct allusion to this classic decadent text only later in the 1921 version of *Women in Love* ("We're all flowers of mud.—Fleurs—*hic*!—du mal!"[*WL* 384]). But in both versions of the novel, as in the poem, he was also seeking an opposing, unBaudelairian principle, "the living desire for positive creation" (cf. *FWL* 351–52 with *WL* 383). So in the poem "Lotus Hurt by the Cold," Lawrence wrote of his own "flowers of mud": "How many times, like lotus lilies risen / Upon the surface of a river, there / Have risen" in his blood "glimmers of my hope," in a "sensitive beautiful blossoming of passion," until "naked for her in the finest fashion / The flowers of all my mud swim into sight" (*Amores* 84). (The earliest extant version of this poem appears in a typescript sent to Amy Lowell probably in 1916, for consideration for *Some Imagist Poets*—see Ferrier i. 13, 34; Vasey MS E320.5.) The beloved of this poem denies Lawrence as thoroughly as did the London group, turning "A look of hate upon the flower," so that his "lotus buds of love sink over / To die unopened" (84–85). The anecdote of "Lotus Hurt by the Cold" catches Lawrence in the act of inditing his metaphysic within the contours of his recollected experience well before he reproduced this philosophy as a sermon for others in his novel.

While the scene in the Pompadour Café is parodic, it leaves little doubt as to whose side the novel is mostly on. When Gudrun hears the ridicule being heaped on Birkin's letter, she reacts with Lawrence's angry passion: "I could have *killed* them! . . . It's a thing that *cannot be borne*—. . . . I feel I could *never* see this *foul* town again—. I couldn't *bear* to come back to it" (385–86). So Lawrence told S. S. Koteliansky in reaction to the mockery of his poems:

> When I think of London, the Café Royal – you actually there, and Katharine [*sic*: Katherine Mansfield] – terror overcomes me, and I take to my heels, and hide myself in a bush. It is a real feeling of horror. I dare not come to London, for my life. It is like walking into some horrible gas, which tears one's lungs. Really – Delenda est Carthago. (*L* ii. 649–50)

Lawrence's association of this incident with apocalypse clearly indicates how, after having represented the process of complete dissolution in the poems of *Amores*, its subsequent fate in the hands of quondam allies became in its turn lodged in his imagination as a representation of England's self-willed demolition.

Lawrence had taken pride in the construction and publication of *Amores*, as is amply attested in volume 2 of the Cambridge *Letters*. He wrote to his agent, J. B. Pinker, on 24 January that he was "putting together a very nice book of poetry," and the next day, to Amy Lowell, that "I find I have such a lot of poems, now, and such nice ones. I can make a most beautiful book" (513). On 1 February, he announced to J. D. Beresford, "I have got ready a book of poetry here – quite ready – which I think is a great work to have done" (520). With the poems at the printer on 16 April, he wrote to Dollie Radford (herself a poet), "There is something peculiarly exciting and delightful about a book of verse, more than about prose" (596). (Ten days later he announced to Lady Cynthia Asquith that he had begun work on another novel, the first *Women in Love* [*L* ii. 601].) Lawrence cared a great deal about the arrangement he had devised as well: he did not at first want to return to Duckworth, who had published his first book of poems, in part because he "didn't like the form [Duckworth] gave it"; in a postscript to Pinker, Lawrence added, "I don't want the MS. altered at all from what it is now" (31 January; 519). On 1 February, he informed Ottoline Morrell that the poems "make a sort of inner history of my life, from 20 to 26," and so it is not surprising to see him on 2 February reiterating his request to Pinker: "I don't want it altered" (521, 522).[5]

Even while still working on the poetry, he began reflecting philosophically on it, as he typically did when finishing a book, thereby further endorsing *Amores*. In a letter of 27 January 1916 to Dollie Radford, he remarked "that there, in the poems, at last, living has come to perfection and to an unchanging absoluteness, that is completely satisfying" (516). Intriguingly, this statement anticipates Lawrence's famous description of "poetry of the past" and "of the future" which he seemingly abjured in favor of a "poetry of the present":

> The poetry of the beginning and the poetry of the end must have that exquisite finality, perfection which belongs to all that is far off. It is in the realm of all that is perfect. It is of the nature of all that is complete and consummate. This completeness, this consummateness, the finality and the perfection are conveyed in exquisite form: the perfect symmetry, the rhythm which returns upon itself like a dance where the hands link and loosen and link for the supreme moment at the end. Perfected bygone moments, perfected moments in the glimmering futurity, these are the treasured gem-like lyrics of Shelley and Keats.
>
> But there is another kind of poetry: the poetry of that which is at hand: the immediate present. (*Poems* 181–82)

There assuredly is at least one other kind of poetry in many of the poems in *Look! We Have Come Through!* and still other kinds in the poems that followed it, whereas Lawrence's description of a poetry of "futurity" and a poetry of "bygone moments" beautifully characterizes quite a few elegies in *Amores*.

In the long segment of *Amores* that focuses on the death of his mother, his lyricism rises from a Lawrentian version of the Keatsian nightingale in "The Bride" to a Shelleyan "futurity" in "The Mystic Blue." As Lawrence says in "Poetry of the Present," "when we hear a nightingale, we hear the pause and the rich, piercing rhythm of recollection, the perfected past. . . . The nightingale's triumph is a paean, but a death-paean" (181). In "The Bride," his mother "dreams her dreams / Of perfect things," and her "dead mouth sings / By its shape, like the thrushes in clear evenings" (*Amores* 62). In later poems like "Elegy," as in "Poetry of the Present," "The [Shelleyan] lark may sound sad, but with the lovely lapsing sadness that is almost a swoon of hope" (181). So Lawrence writes, "I am willing to come to you now, my dear, / As a pigeon lets itself off from a cathedral dome / . . . / To fall like a breath within the breathing wind" ("Elegy" 133; retitled "Call Into Death" in *Collected Poems*). The elegiac sequence in *Amores* thus gradually emerges from Keatsian "recollection" in an oscillating progress that climaxes in the book's last poem, "The Mystic Blue." In "Poetry of the Present," Lawrence writes of Shelley's poetry that "It seems when we hear a skylark singing as if sound were running forward into the future, running so fast and utterly without consideration, straight on into futurity" (181). So too in "The Mystic Blue":

> Out of the darkness, fretted sometimes in its sleeping,
> Jets of sparks in fountains of Blue come leaping
>
> . . . . . . . . . . . . . . . . . . . . . .
> All these pure things come foam and spray of the sea
> Of Darkness abundant, which shaken mysteriously,
> Breaks into dazzle of living, as dolphins leap from the sea
> Of midnight and shake it to fire, till the flame of the shadow we see.
>         (*Amores* 137–38; retitled "Blueness" in *Collected Poems*)

Yet with Lawrence's usual complexity—as these lines from "The Mystic Blue" further suggest—this poetry of "perfection" had some wished-for Lawrentian dynamic qualities. Both in the first passage cited above from "Poetry of the Present" and in the poetry, its "consummateness" moves—directly echoing the philosophy of the *Study of Thomas Hardy*—with the vital rhythm of "a dance where the hands link and loosen and link" (*Poems* 181; *Hardy* 61), more specifically, in *Amores*, a dance between the son and his mother and lovers. The images used in "Poetry of the Present" to evoke Lawrence's poetry of "finality" also recall Walter Pater's famously oxymoronic figure of the "gem-like flame," a figure of the instant moment lived to its fullest (Pater 189).[6] Meanwhile, the figures of the lotus and the mud show up in a later passage in "Poetry of the Present" as images for poetry "of the present": "Let me feel the mud and the heavens in my lotus. Let me feel the heavy, silting, sucking mud, the spinning of sky winds. Let me feel them both in purest contact, the nakedness of sucking weight, nakedly passing radiance" (*Poems* 182).

In 1916, Lawrence already believed that what "gave poetry

form" was not some external set of rules but, again as in his *Study of Thomas Hardy*, a vital principle of "opposition" between the living and the dead, the flame and the gem, the flower and the mud, and, of course, past and future. The opposition suggested in "Lotus Hurt by the Cold" thus undergirded not only the philosophy of Birkin's letter in *Women in Love* but also Lawrence's philosophy of poetry in 1916. As he told Catherine Carswell on 22 July,

> I think [your] poem is [. . .] good – but of death, too deathly. There is not enough of the *opposition* of life to give it form . . . – it falls before it reaches the borderline of art, because there is not quite enough *resistance* of life to bring that solid equilibrium which is the core of art, an absolute reached by the sheer tension of life stubborn against death, the two in opposition creating the third thing, the pure resultant, absolved, art. (*L* ii. 638)

So too, despite the perpetual agonies and sense of the finality of death reenacted by Lawrence's elegiac sequence, his metaphysic of "resistance . . . the sheer tension of life stubborn against death" meant that the general direction in which *Amores* moves is optimistic.

What I would emphasize, nonetheless, is precisely the "sheer tension," not only of "life stubborn against death," but reciprocally of death "stubborn" against life—the enervating conflicts surrounding and recounted in this volume—because, despite his resilience, Lawrence as a man and a writer continually found these conflicts returning, old wounds reexpressing themselves, leaving Lawrence and his poetry "spent" (Ferrier ii. 60). Indeed, when Lawrence was writing *Look! We Have Come Through!*, he thought of it too as his "last work for the old world," "a sort of final conclusion of the old life in me – 'And now farewell' is really the motto" (*L* iii. 90, 87).[7] *Look! We Have Come Through!* is not entirely a "poetry of the present" any more than *Amores* was entirely a "poetry of the past." Still more ironically, although Lawrence had insisted upon completion of *Look! We Have Come Through!* that this would be his "last book of poems . . . for years to come. I have reaped everything out of my old notebooks" (*L* iii. 86), he in fact returned twice to these notebooks, first, for his miscellaneous book misleadingly titled *New Poems* (1918) by his publisher Martin Secker and, second, for some of the verse in a small book of war poetry, *Bay* (1919). Finally, in his *Collected Poems*, Lawrence combined the elegies not with his love poems to Frieda in *Look! We Have Come Through!*, but with the poems "which belong to the war . . . written mostly in 1917 and 1918" (*Poems* 28). Gathered together in this way in the bulky volume 1 of his *Collected Poems*, these poems form a single, extended death sequence, "luxuriating" (as Bataille might have put it) once again in dissolution.

If *Amores* had enacted tensions only between life and death, between recollection and futurity, critics today might like the poems better. But, in addition, tension between the conventional and the unconventional runs through this book in both theme and form. (Such tensions persisted, I would argue, in later poems, but in more innovative and less Romantic forms, for example, in the dramatizations of this conflict in Lawrence's relationship with Frieda in *Look! We Have Come Through!* or in the deliberate play between the commonplace and the mythic in *Pansies*.) The poet of most of the elegies was a neo-*fin-de-siècle* poet. Reading Lawrence's *Collected Poems*, an early twenty-first-century sensibility enjoys and admires the harmonic breeziness of "Unrhyming Poems" more readily than the windy harmonics of "Rhyming Poems." Yet a different, more Georgian sensibility may find much to appreciate in the early poems. As Mandell points out, the initial reception of both *Love Poems and Others* and *Amores* was generally warmer than for any of his subsequent books of poems (76). When the book was out, its *TLS* reviewer showered praise on *Amores* for its "poems of passion," its Whitmanesque "robust sincerity," the "understanding and force" in this expression of "the love-fever," and "the sincere and deliberate fitness of matter to manner." This reviewer believed that readers "must be interested, sometimes charmed, sometimes repelled, but always forced to share the experience" (10 August 1916). Eunice Tietjens, the reviewer for *Poetry*, wrote that *Amores* "sets Lawrence definitely in the front ranks of English poets" (February 1917).

Lawrence himself seemed to dismiss these poems as conventional when he ensconced them in "Rhyming Poems." But as I showed in *Self and Sequence*, although he devoted far more time and energy to the rearrangement and final revision of "Rhyming Poems" than to any other part of his 1928 collection, he also kept the elegiac sequences themselves almost entirely intact (61–78; see also Mandell 10–11, 13–14). As other scholars have noted,

Lawrence's struggle with the "ordinary me" was not merely a rebellion against external rules and forms but an existential conflict among the poet's variant selves.

In "The Notion of Expenditure," Bataille sees orthodox conformity to convention or to utilitarian ends as producing a world of illusion utterly opposed to the attractions of nonproductive, anti-authoritarian self-expenditure:

> [T]o the small extent that a man is incapable of yielding to considerations that are either official or susceptible of becoming so, to the small extent that he is inclined to feel the attraction of a life devoted to the destruction of established authority, it is difficult to believe that a peaceful world, conforming to his interests could be for him anything other than a convenient illusion. (117–18)

Lawrence would probably not have approved of his French contemporary if he had learned about him; Bataille's "excremental" philosophy, as André Breton thought of it, took a more extreme, decadent form than Lawrence's (Stoekl xi). But Lawrence repeatedly asserted Bataille's fundamental opposition between, on the one hand, emotionally and economically prudent social orders and, on the other, the uneconomical excesses of vitality in art, in sex, and in mourning. Lawrence seems to have believed and in *Women in Love* fictionalized the belief that, to cite Bataille yet again, "a human society can have, just as [a man] does, an *interest* in considerable losses, in catastrophes that, *while conforming to well-defined needs*, provoke tumultuous depressions, crises of dread, and, in the final analysis, a certain orgiastic state" (117). But while such "disarmingly savage" needs (117) might be "orgiastic" and even necessary for personal and social restoration, they also took form in debilitating cycles of illness, "condemn-[ing] him to the most disappointing forms of activity, to misery, to despair" (120). As a survivor, Lawrence turned nearly as often to conventional means of support as to the unconventional defiance of his art.

Unlike Bataille's poet, "forced to choose" between a life as a retrobate and a life dictated by "vulgar" needs, Lawrence often failed to make such a choice or simply refused to choose. One might argue, in any case, with Bataille's argument in particular that excessive activities like luxury and war are uneconomical. Certainly, for Lawrence, as he frequently reminded Pinker, poetry served as an important economic resource even while serving as nonproductive self-expression or as a site for the transgression of established authority (where one could catch "a glimpse of chaos," as Lawrence later asserted; review of *Chariot of the Sun, P* 255).[8] Lawrence occupied both sides of the opposition between his "commonplace me" and the "demon" who played havoc on convention (*Poems* 852).

Thus in 1910 the poet who wrote the three famous elegies, "The End," "The Bride," and "The Virgin Mother," was both brazen and commonplace. On the one hand, this poet brought some demonically new things into literature. In "The End," he painfully acknowledged a mother's multiple selves as opposed to one reliably loving self: "Oh that you had never, never been / Some of your selves, my love, that some / Of your several faces I had never seen!—" (Ferrier i. poem 66). In the original version of "The Virgin Mother" ("My Love, My Mother"), he frankly admitted the son's impassioned betrothal to his mother: "And so, my love, Oh mother, / I shall always be true to thee" ("The Virgin Mother" Ferrier i. poem 68). The poet of *Amores* exposes a man's chaotic passions and in doing so transforms masculinity. Moreover, he did so with some crisp ironies, as when, in "The Bride," he carved the cruel face of death in life: "My love looks like a girl tonight / But she is old" ("The Bride," Ferrier i. poem 67).

But, on the other hand, this poet in the selfsame poems deployed orthodox poetic sentiments and diction, as in "The End," where he claims he no longer has "any hope / To heal the suffering, or to make requite" (*Amores* 61)—lines which suggest that the ever-dutiful son owes his mother consolation and has failed her in her need. This sentimental poet admired his chaste mother as she slept, prettily, in the ballad-like "The Bride," "like a maiden, and dreams her dream / Of charming things." In the 1910 "My Love, My Mother," Lawrence devoutly assured her that

> Twice I am born, my mother
> As Christ said it should be,
> And who can bear me a third time?
> —None love—I am true to thee.

Perhaps in response to Frieda's intense criticism of this poem, in *Amores* Lawrence eliminated the three lines in which he invokes Christ and asserts that no one "can bear" him "a third time." Instead he writes, "And this is the life hereafter / Wherein I am true," for

> Our ways are different now;
> You are a seed in the night-time,
> I am a man, to plough
> The difficult glebe of the future
> For God to endow.
>
> (*Amores* 64)

Lawrence obviously struggled with conventionalities of this sort; similar changes occur in other elegies in *Amores* (in 1916, "maiden" became "bride," and "charming things" became "perfect things" in "The Bride"). But Frieda's dismissal of "The Virgin Mother" was comprehensive enough that this kind of revision did not rescue it, and especially in the context of this long eulogistic sequence, poems like "The Virgin Mother" remained unequivocal tributes to Mrs. Lawrence. It was not possible for Lawrence entirely to divorce the demon from the faithful son. Acknowledging this himself, the third elegy ends (like many others in this volume) with the speaker "helpless":

> Spare me the strength to leave you
> Now you are dead.
> I must go, but my soul lies helpless
> Beside your bed.
>
> (*Amores* 65)

The conflict I outline here is thematized in the poem "Martyr," which Lawrence seems originally to have intended as the first poem in this book, though he subsequently rejected it for *Amores*.[9] In his Cornwall notebook, he wrote,

> let it not be said
> I quailed at my appointed function, turned poltroon.
> . . . . . . . . . . . . . . . . . . .
> Does my red heart rebel, do my still hands
> Complain of that which they have had to do?
> Never let it be said I was poltroon
> At this my task of living . . .
> . . . . . . . . .
> And if the Vast, the sleep that still grows richer

Have said that I, this mote in the body of sleep
Must in my transiency pass all through pain,
Must be a dream of grief, . . .
. . . : shall I then turn
Poltroon, and cry out to the vast, spread, silent God
To alter my one speck of doom, when round there flames
The whole great conflagration of all life

. . . . . . . . . . . . .

Shall I, less than the least red, half-dark grain
Of flesh within the body of sleep, . . .

. . . . . . . . . . .

. . . cry out to spare
The stress that crushes me to an atom of fire
                    (Vasey MS E320.2; see also Ferrier 2: poem 150)

This poem complains both about the speaker's ordinary, daily lot
and about the unusual nighttime grief he must suffer, both about
his smallness and about the vast "anguish of this life." In the
end, that vastness crushes him to a "speck of doom," and so his
anguish becomes indistinguishable from his daily lot—his ap-
pointed function. Far from rebelling against such a Catch-22, he
is reduced to questioning his own complaint.

This Lawrence was a "martyr," his conflicts so intense as to
fester, and in 1917 when he published the poem, after all, among
the opening retrospective poems of *Look! We Have Come
Through!*, he revised and retitled it "Martyr à la Mode" in a self-
parodic gesture akin to that of his transposition of *Amores* into
Birkin's letter in *Women in Love*. Many of the elegies actually
published in *Amores* show Lawrence less extinguished than this:
a martyr perhaps, but one who moves through mourning as if by
means of a moebius strip, discovering—in the oppositional, yet
also dynamically rotating and "dancing" figuration found in this
volume—flame in shadow and the shadowy core of flame: "shake
it to fire, till the flame of the shadow we see" ("The Mystic Blue,"
*Amores* 138).

Given the recurrent pattern of defeat and self-defeat in Lawrence's life and career at this time, however, it was perhaps inevitable that, despite his investment in *Amores*, he should also
register ambivalence toward it. In one of the dedications he
drafted, he told Lady Ottoline he had written the poems in order
to dispose of them: to be free to "forget" them, these "records
of pain and hope now spent" (Ferrier 2:60; Vasey MS E320.2).

Lawrence's expenditure of feeling had partly broken the bounds of convention, but investment in that expenditure left him spent and ready to dispose of his poems. The dual process of Lawrence's recollection of these elegies and love poems—both nostalgically in the backward-looking memories they exposed and more literally in his rewriting and reorganization of them into a future-looking book of poems—left him once again on the downswing, wanting only to "forget" their embarrassments of both "pain and hope." As scholars and interested readers, though, I suggest that we respectfully ignore Lawrence in that latter mood and get to work remembering *Amores*.[10] As Francis Bickley once hinted, in a 1916 review of *Amores*, these elegies are the poems where we find most vividly represented Lawrence's long "expenditure of spirit in a waste of shame" (110).

## NOTES

1. In "Rhyming Poems," Lawrence combines the verse from *Amores* (1916) with *Love Poems and Others* (1913), *New Poems* (1918), and *Bay* (1919).

2. "Unrhyming Poems" includes the volumes *Look! We Have Come Through!* (1917) and *Birds, Beasts and Flowers* (1923), and unlike the volumes collected in "Rhyming Poems," these two retain their original titles and most of their original organization in *Collected Poems*.

3. New sources of information have become available since these books appeared, including the Cambridge biographies and the "Cornwall" notebook (Vasey MS E320.2), which is now held by the University of Nottingham Library.

4. Prior to its appearance as this four-line poem in *Amores*—that is, in two earlier manuscripts and in a version published in 1909 in the *English Review*—these lines constituted the fourth stanza of a poem about Lawrence's experiences as a schoolteacher, "Discipline." "Discipline" too was revised for *Amores* and separated from "The Prophet," thus allowing "The Prophet" to be dissociated from the theme of school discipline. In *Collected Poems*, however, Lawrence revised "Discipline" yet again and placed it immediately after the slightly retitled "Prophet."

5. The sixty poems in *Amores* were arranged as follows: (1) Tease, (2) The Wild Common, (3) Study, (4) Discord in Childhood, (5) Virgin Youth, (6) Monologue of a Mother, (7) In a Boat, (8) Week-night Service, (9) Disagreeable Advice, (10) Dreams Old, (11) Dreams Nascent, (12) A Winter's Tale, (13) Epilogue, (14) A Baby Running Barefoot, (15) Discipline, (16) Scent of Irises, (17) The Prophet, (18) Last Words to Miriam, (19) Mystery, (20) Patience, (21) Ballad of Another Ophelia, (22) Restlessness, (23) A Baby Asleep After Pain, (24) Anxiety, (25) The Punisher, (26) The End, (27) The Bride, (28) The Virgin Mother, (29) At the Window, (30) Drunk, (31) Sorrow, (32) Dolor of Autumn, (33) The Inheritance, (34) Silence, (35) Listening, (36) Brooding Grief, (37) Lotus Hurt by the Cold, (38) Malade, (39) Liaison, (40) Troth With the Dead, (41) Dissolute, (42) Submergence, (43) The Enkindled Spring, (44) Reproach, (45) The Hands of the Be-

trothed, (46) Excursion, (47) Perfidy, (48) A Spiritual Woman, (49) Mating, (50) A Love Song, (51) Brother and Sister, (52) After Many Days, (53) Blue, (54) Snap-Dragon, (55) A Passing-Bell, (56) In Trouble and Shame, (57) Elegy, (58) Grey Evening, (59) Firelight and Nightfall, (60) The Mystic Blue. For a chart that tabulates the different sequencings of the verse in *Collected Poems* and *Amores*, see *Self and Sequence* 243–48.

6. It is worth noting that Lawrence admired Swinburne as well as Shelley at this time as among the greatest poets. On 11 September 1916, Lawrence wrote to Barbara Low in thanks for books she had sent him, and in it he praises both Swinburne and Shelley:

> I lie in bed and read [Swinburne], and he moves me very deeply. The pure realisation in him is something to reverence: he is [. . .] very like Shelley, full of philosophic spiritual realisation and revelation. He is a great revealer, very great. I put him with Shelley as our greatest poet. He is the last fiery spirit among us. How wicked the world has been, to jeer at his physical appearance etc. There was more powerful rushing flame of life in him than in all the heroes rolled together. (*L* ii. 653–54)

See also Murfin's discussion of Shelley's influence on the poetry and on "Poetry of the Present"; Murfin omits mention of Pater (35–37, 41–42, 63–92).

These facts complicate Kinkead-Weekes's account of one of Frieda and Lawrence's harshest moments in May 1916 when Lawrence nearly "beat her to death" (319). Drawing on one of Lawrence's uses of Shelley in the *Study of Thomas Hardy*, Kinkead-Weekes reads Frieda's taunt earlier in the day (described by Katherine Mansfield in a letter) that "Shelleys Ode to a Skylark was false" (319) as indicating Frieda's knowledge that "It represented for him . . . the extreme of mental and spiritual consciousness as opposed to the life of the body and the blood. . . . [H]is fury is a sure sign that there was something hatefully accurate in the charge" (322). The evidence suggests, however, that Lawrence admired "Ode to a Skylark" at the time of this argument and did not see it as sheerly "mental"; thus Frieda's attack would have been pitched directly at the Lawrence of *Amores* much as, earlier, she had aimed directly at the Lawrence of the manuscript version of "The Virgin Mother."

7. Frieda was predictably eager for this volume, adding in a postscript to one of Lawrence's letters to his agent J. B. Pinker (17 November 1916) that "L-has enough of very beautiful poems (different and *better* than the two first vol.) for a book" (*L* iii. 34–35). Lawrence does not seem to have begun work on this volume, however, until the last week of January 1917 (*L* iii. 84).

8. The fact that economic need continually counted among Lawrence's several motives in publishing his poems has unfortunately misled some scholars into underestimating their value and interest. For Lawrence himself, economic and noneconomic motives often could not be extricated from each other. If he had a primary motive, however, it was surely to see his writing into print, and during the war, he could not publish his novels.

9. I wish to thank the staff of the University of Nottingham Library for permission to study and transcribe the poems in this notebook; it contains a preliminary list of poems, which "Martyr" headed—but Lawrence then crossed it out.

10. The poems of *Amores* and *New Poems* have been digitalized by Steven van Leeuwen of Columbia University and may be found on the web at www.bartleby.com.

## Works Cited

Bataille, Georges. *Visions of Excess: Selected Writings, 1927–1939*. Edited by Allan Stoekl. Translated by Allan Stoekl, with Carl R. Lovitts and Donald M. Leslie, Jr. Minneapolis: University of Minnesota Press, 1985.

Bickley, Francis. "D. H. Lawrence." *Bookman* 51 (October 1916):26–27. Reprinted in *D. H. Lawrence: The Critical Heritage*. Edited by R. P. Draper. London: Routledge & Kegan Paul, 1970.

Ferrier, Carole. "The Earlier Poetry of D. H. Lawrence: A Variorum Text." Vols. 1 and 2. Ph.D. diss., University of Auckland, 1971.

Kinkead-Weekes, Mark. *D. H. Lawrence: Triumph to Exile 1912–1922*. Cambridge: Cambridge University Press, 1996.

Laird, Holly. *Self and Sequence: The Poetry of D. H. Lawrence*. Charlottesville: University Press of Virginia, 1988.

Lockwood, M. J. *A Study of the Poems of D. H. Lawrence: Thinking in Poetry*. New York: St. Martin's, 1987.

Mandell, Gail Porter. *The Phoenix Paradox: A Study of Renewal through Change in the Collected Poems and Last Poems of D. H. Lawrence*. Carbondale: Southern Illinois University Press, 1984.

Murfin, Ross C. *The Poetry of D. H. Lawrence: Texts and Contexts*. Lincoln: University of Nebraska Press, 1983.

Pater, Walter. *The Renaissance: Studies in Art and Poetry: The 1893 Text*. Edited by Donald L. Hill. Berkeley: University of California Press, 1980.

"Poems by D. H. Lawrence." Review of *Amores*. *Times Literary Supplement*, 10 August 1916, 379.

Potts, Abbie. *The Elegiac Mode: Poetic Form in Wordsworth and Other Elegists*. Ithaca: Cornell University Press, 1967.

Stoekl, Allan. Introduction to *Visions of Excess Selected Writings, 1927–1939*, by Georges Bataille. Edited by Allan Stoekl. Minneapolis: University of Minnesota Press, 1985.

Tietjens, Eunice. "A Book by Lawrence." Review of *Amores*. *Poetry* 9 (February 1917): 264–66.

Vasey, Lindeth. "A Checklist of the Manuscripts of D. H. Lawrence." In *D. H. Lawrence: A Calendar of His Works*, by Keith Sagar. Austin: University of Texas Press, 1979.

West, Rebecca. "The Art of Skepticism." *Vogue*, 1 November 1952, 114–15, 168.

Worthen, John. *D. H. Lawrence: The Early Years 1885–1912*. Cambridge: Cambridge University Press, 1991.

———. *"The First 'Women in Love.'"* *DHLR* 28 (1999): 5–27.

# Movement, Space, and Rhetoric in Lawrence's Travel Writing

## Jack Stewart

IN ATTEMPTING TO REASSESS LAWRENCE'S TRAVEL WRITING, I WILL focus primarily on his sense of movement and space and his verbal stylization, through combination and selection, of contingent experience. Lawrence responds more directly to the world in his travel writing than in any other genre, and the rhetorical structures with which he maps the terrain or depicts people substantiate or modify that response and his vision. First, I emphasize his sheer appetite for travel and experience, his intensified "acts of attention" (*P* 262) that, reaching beyond visual surfaces, express an ontology of space and motion. Next, I examine his representation of space and movement in perceptual frames that combine visual and kinetic, spatial and human dimensions, and in panoramic or close-up scenes structured by metonymy or synecdoche. Finally, I tune in to rhetorical devices and speech genres (including diatribe, self-parody, and sociolect), through which Lawrence dramatizes his own prickly persona or satirizes others (often by synecdoche). While the verve and variety of Lawrence's writing cuts across literary genres, some of his most vibrant perceptions and self-expression are found in the travel books.

Lawrence traveled in search of health and renewed being to lands "where the salt [had] not lost its savour" (*SS* 117). Conceding that illusion and disillusion are inevitable aspects of travel,[1] he affirmed "contact" as his prime motive. Differences of place, class, custom, and race made contact more stimulating. Lawrence was impelled to travel by a need for change, action, movement, and discovery. "Comes over one an absolute necessity to move," he exclaims at the beginning of *Sea and Sardinia* (7)—an inner necessity that is the outcome of pent-up creative drives. Paul Fussell observes that Lawrence "has the true traveller's high metabolic equipment to sustain his boundless curiosity and the

151

boundless energy feeding it" (147), and Lawrence himself propounds a vitalist ethic of movement in "The Crown," where "the goodness of anything depends on the direction in which it is moving" (*RDP* 285).

Lawrence's restlessness recalls R. L. Stevenson's manifesto: "For my part, I travel not to go anywhere, but to go. I travel for travel's sake. The great affair is to move. . ." (163). As a traveler, Lawrence delights in movement, change, freedom, and challenge. To his restless curiosity and desire for experience Lawrence adds a surpassing ability to record moments of being in touch with earth, sea, sky, places, and people. Anthony Burgess says that his poetic expression "is not the result of the creative process, it is the creative process itself" (110). His travels were journeys of discovery, combining outward acts of attention with a perennial quest for awareness. Of Italy he wrote: "Strange and wonderful chords awake in us. . . . Italy has given me back I know not what of myself, but a very, very great deal. She has found for me so much that was lost: like a restored Osiris" (*SS* 117). Change stimulates creativity, and the expanded consciousness of travel helps the writer reclaim hidden substrata of the self. Like Birkin in *Women in Love*, Lawrence is "a chameleon, a creature of change" (92); on his return from Sardinia, he experiences one such metamorphosis: "The human being is a most curious creature. He thinks he has got one soul, and he has got dozens. I felt my Sardinian soul melting off me, I felt myself evaporating into the real Italian uncertainty and momentaneity" (*SS* 170). He shares this fluidity of being with Laurence Sterne's sentimental traveler, who remarks: "whatever is my situation, let me feel the movements which rise out of it. . ." (*Sentimental Journey* 161).

In *Twilight in Italy* (1916), Lawrence's restless intellect finds symbolic meanings in what he sees. The connection between experience and reflection gives that first travel book its coherence— even if parts, like "The Spinner and the Monks," might be subtitled "Man Thinking in a Landscape." *Twilight* is more static and contemplative than *Sea and Sardinia* (1921), where Lawrence's perceptions are mobile and instantaneous, as well as prophetic.[2] The Sardinian diary, a continuous narrative of a ten-day journey, is more intrinsic to the genre. Burgess calls it "[his] outstanding travel book . . . and by far the best introduction to his *oeuvre*" (110), while Paul Fussell claims it "celebrate[s] sheer kinesis, and to that degree it is at the center of Lawrence's whole enterprise" (158). *Mornings in Mexico* (1927) is a spatial and cultural exploration of landscapes and people, in which Lawrence reinterprets tribal dances and the rituals of animistic religion. *Etruscan Places* (1932), while it contains some of his finest writing, is primarily a "curve of return" to a lost culture and a final testament of Lawrence's life-values. As such, it lies beyond the scope of the present study.

Inset glimpses of the writer give life to landscapes, as in "San Gaudenzio," where Lawrence describes how he

> used to sit and write in the great loft of the lemon house, high up, far, far from the ground, the open front giving across the lake and the mountain snow opposite flush with twilight. . . . [T]he old disused implements of lemon culture made shadows in the deserted place. Then there would come the call from the back, away above: "Venga, venga mangiare." (*TI* 165)

While similar scenes come to life with much immediacy in the letters, here a complex of space and sound, past and present, familiar and strange, combined with iterative tense and retrospective mood, give the recollection an emotive vibration. But *Twilight* also contains active images of movement. On the return journey from Switzerland to Italy, Lawrence writes: "It was a good thing to be out of doors, with one's pack on one's back, climbing uphill" (207). Having passed Sunday churchgoers in black suits, he shelters from rain under a bush and "was so glad to be there, homeless, without place or belonging, crouching under the leaves in the copse by the road, that I felt I had, like the meek, inherited the earth" (208). The feeling recalls Birkin, naked among pinetrees and primroses, rejecting the social world (*WL* 106–8). But Lawrence, committed to the "old effort at serious living" (*WL* 302), is more than a back-to-nature hiker or sightseer: he explores the ecological relation of people to place and work to life. Places visited exist in social and historical contexts, although Lawrence's intuitive vision preempts the kind of historical notes supplied by Baedeker or dug up by Norman Douglas in *Old Calabria* (1915). For Lawrence, "place" is a sensory/imaginative complex of surface and depth, vision and detail.

Tackling an Alpine journey, "I set off myself, up the valley between the close, snow-topped mountains, whose white gleamed above me as I crawled, small as an insect, along the dark, cold

valley below" (*TI* 212). The dual perspective on man and mountains allows the writer to rise above his toiling personal self and
regard it with wry detachment. Yet Lawrence's style conveys
more about himself than it states; at an inn near the Gothard
Pass, "I sat in the utter isolation and stillness. . . . And I listened
for any sound: only the faint noise of the stream. And I wondered,
Why am I here, on this ridge of the Alps, in the lamp-lit, wooden,
close-shut room, alone?" (217). In his lostness and loneliness, he
adds, rather bleakly: "The kingdoms of the world had no significance: what could one do but wander about?" (217). More positively, Birkin proposes to Ursula: "And we will wander about on
the face of the earth . . . and we'll look at the world beyond just
this bit" (*WL* 362).

The novelty and uniqueness of travel writing lie in the impact
of place on personal experience. Paul Theroux exclaims: *"No one
has ever described the place where I have just arrived:* this is the
emotion that makes me want to travel" (*Pillars* 363). The same
is true, in a higher degree, of Lawrence's descriptions, which retain the freshness of original perceptions thanks to an eidetic
memory[3] that allows him to highlight and recombine details in
significant patterns. This visual memory has its own principles of
emphasis or elision, as illustrated by the narrator's reconstruction of a group scene in "Italians in Exile":

> Quick, vivid, and sharp, the little Giuseppino was always central.
> But he seemed almost invisible. When I think back, I can scarcely see
> him, I can only see the others, the lamplight on their faces and on
> their full, gesticulating limbs. . . . All their faces are distinct . . . all
> their bodies are palpable and dramatic.
>
> But the face of Giuseppino is like a pale luminousness, a sort of
> gleam among all the ruddy glow, his body is evanescent, like a
> shadow. (*TI* 198)

Lawrence can't see Giuseppino clearly because the anarchist
leader is a secret sharer or alter ego. Such identification dissolves
physical outlines, as with images of Birkin, his face "in the shaft
of ruddy, copper-coloured light. . . gleaming like fire" (*WL* 35).
Giuseppino, like Birkin or the vine-grafter Il Duro,[4] is a dark mirror of the self that blurs the separate identity of the other.

As well as landscapes and "soundscapes," Lawrence composes
"smellscapes" and "bodyscapes,"[5] to which I will add ocean-

scapes or "motionscapes" that combine physical sensations with spiritual impulses. In *Sea and Sardinia*, Lawrence celebrates movement, giving full play to kinetic and visceral sensations of travel by sea or land, ship, foot, train, or bus. On the voyage out, slow wavelike rhythms and rolling repetitions embed the ship's motion in the lilting movement and liquid sounds of Lawrence's alliterative language:

> [T]here is something in the long, slow lift of the ship, and her long, slow slide forwards which makes my heart beat with joy. It is the motion of freedom. To feel her come up—then slide slowly forward, with a sound of the smashing of waters, is like the magic gallop of the sky, the magic gallop of elemental space.... One is free at last—and lilting in a slow flight of the elements, winging outwards.... I wished in my soul ... that one might float in this wavering, tremulous, yet long and surging pulsation while ever time lasted: space never exhausted, and no turning back, no looking back, even. (*SS* 30–31)

Lawrence's dream of sailing the world revives: "[L]ife itself would be in the flight, the tremble of space.... Space, and the frail vibration of space, the glad lonely wringing of the heart" (47). Here Lawrence foregrounds "elemental space" and ontologic motion.

Travel is at once escape[6] and confrontation, liberation from routine and a search for more authentic experience. In transit between fixed points, Lawrence experiences the motion of his own being, its sheer dynamism. He reinvokes his dream of finding "three masculine, world-lost souls" and "saunter[ing] on along with them, across the dithering space, as long as life lasts!" (*SS* 48). His delight in voyaging for its own sake inspires him to compose a paean to space and motion, freedom and creativity, in which he plumbs the oceanic experience of boundlessness. Space produces a dialectic of perceiver and perceived, engaging "all the mighty world / Of eye and ear,—both what they half create, / And what perceive" (Wordsworth).

In the compositional rhythm of his travel-writing, Lawrence balances acts of attention and recollection, sensation and imagination. Elements of projection and symbolism transform the image of space, as a "Minoan distance" lends enchantment to the eye:

> Magic are high lands seen from the sea, when they are far, far off, and ghostly translucent like ice-bergs. This was Sardinia, looming like

fascinating shadows in mid-sea.—And the sailing ships, as if cut out of frailest pearl translucency, were wafting away towards Naples. (*SS* 48)

Once landed, Lawrence and the queen-bee, Frieda, set off to explore the island. Fulfilling Stevenson's mandate "to come down off this feather-bed of civilisation, and find the globe granite underfoot and strewn with cutting flints" (163), Lawrence finds his "very feet in contact" with the "deep[ly] sparkl[ing]" granite of Sardinia (*SS* 81–82), discovering a sensory affinity with that harsh land. Contrast and change are stimulating, whatever the direction, and morning in Mandas meets with his desire to have "room for [his] spirit": "Wonderful the bluish, cold air, and things standing up in cold distance. After two southern winters . . . this bleakness and this touch of frost in the ringing morning goes to my soul like an intoxication" (81). He and Frieda go for a walk and "[s]he too feels *space* around her, and freedom to move the limbs: such as one does not feel in Italy and Sicily, where all is so classic and fixed" (82). Here Lawrence exults in a liberating sense of space that is harsher and more challenging than that of cultivated southern landscapes. At Nuovo, where a carnival is taking place, they bivouac at an inn and Lawrence creates an intimate moment of being that resonates to a surrounding soundscape:

> The q-b made a little tea on the spirit-lamp, and we sat in bed and sipped it. Then we covered ourselves up and lay still, to get warm. Outside the noise of the street came unabated. It grew quite dark, the lights reflected into the room. There was the sound of an accordion across the hoarseness of the many voices and movements in the street: and then a solid, strong singing of men's voices. . . . (*SS* 135)

The reader experiences this scene all the more sharply because of its dramatic viewpoint, with strongly marked accents of inside and outside, darkness and light, silence and sound.

In *Mornings in Mexico*, motion is a matter of panoramic perception rather than visceral sensation. In "Market Day," where the writing is more alert and poetic than in the first three essays, everything seems to be in circular or spiral motion—clouds, mountains, dust, hawks, palo blanco flowers, organ and candelabrum cactuses. Reflections inspired by figures in a landscape give rise to a metaphysic of space and motion:

Strange that we should think in straight lines, when there are none, and talk of straight courses, when every course, sooner or later, is seen to be making the sweep round, swooping upon the centre. When space is curved, and the cosmos is sphere within sphere, and the way from any one point to any other point is round the bend of the inevitable, that turns as the tips of the broad wings of the hawk turn upwards, leaning upon the air like the invisible half of the ellipse. If I have a way to go, it will be round the swoop of a bend impinging centripetal towards the centre. (*MM* 80–81)

When Lawrence is most alive to the "spirit of place," he sees birds, animals, people and their biorhythmic movements in a symbolic light. His vision is Heraclitean and Vorticist. The villagers who have been to market "have had their moment of contact and centripetal flow. They have been part of a great stream of men flowing to a centre, to the vortex of the market-place" (*MM* 91). The principle of motion sends them converging toward the center and draws them back to the periphery, in a curving rhythm of attraction and release that transcends individual wills. Lawrence places vital social impulses above economic motives. His vision of native life, relating to primitive religion in *The Plumed Serpent*, links spiral movement with the "spark of contact": "Every curve plunges into the vortex and is lost, re-emerges with a certain relief and takes to the open, and there is lost again. Only that which is utterly intangible, matters. The contact, the spark of exchange" (*MM* 92). From picturesque travel writing Lawrence aspires to cosmic vision, and "Market Day" shows the range and depth of his response to landscape, space, and motion.

In "Indians and Entertainment," "The Dance of the Sprouting Corn," and "The Hopi Snake Dance," Lawrence describes tribal dances as symbolic rituals. The corn-growing song inspires a dithyramb on "the throbbing, pulsing, clapping rhythm that comes from the dark, creative blood in man, to stimulate the tremulous, pulsating protoplasm in the seed-germ" (*MM* 106). The rhythmic singing and drumming establish an equilibrium between the racial blood, magnetized to the earth's center, and the "lonely circulating of the separate human existence" (107). The rhythmic Dance of the Sprouting Corn displays a progressive downward movement "towards the earth's red centre," and "as the men wheel round, their black hair gleams and shakes, and the long fox-skin sways, like a tail" (127). Lawrence is fascinated with ritual movement: the men and women are "all going subtly round in rings. Then slowly they change again, and form a star. Then again, unmingling, they come back into rows" (129). The purpose of the ritual is to accomplish "the mystery of germination, not procreation, but *putting forth*, resurrection, life springing within the seed" (132).

Lawrence's travel writing combines the paradigmatic axis of *metaphor*, on which images substitute for objects, with the syntagmatic axis of *metonymy*, on which acts of seeing are reconstructed (see Jakobson). Metonymic style places details in a varied and arresting order: it is an art that conceals art, highlighting intrinsic qualities and connections. The reader assimilates both the separate impact of objects in a series and the way they form spatial patterns. The apparent lack of structure in lists gives an unimpeded view of objects, seen in physical rather than mental proximity, although the need to connect and compare is implied. Metonymy puts the accent on contingency ("thereness") rather than causation; its tactics are selection ("thisness") and presentation ("whatness"). The reader's attention travels along a line, assembling data and impressions. Metonymy thus provides an apt medium for travel writing—as could be copiously illustrated from modern masters of the genre, such as C. M. Doughty, Robert Byron, Lawrence Durrell, and Bruce Chatwin, as well as Lawrence. Metonymic style has much in common with the "nomadic art" that Chatwin describes as "asymmetric, discordant, restless, incorporeal and intuitive . . . with a compulsive tendency towards ornamentation" and a love of "violent" color (*Anatomy* 98). ("Corporeal" should replace "incorporeal" if these attributes are to be applied to metonymy.) Coordinating items in disjunct series liberates the travel writer from byways of exposition and subordination, so that he can concentrate on physical surfaces, colors, and forms of objects.

Metonymy expresses the stimulus and momentum of a perceptual process, metaphor its imaginative associations. Metonymic representation of space and movement is evident in "Market Day," where Lawrence constructs a large-scale panorama from a series of fragments:

And away on the footslope lie the white specks of Huayapa, among its lake of trees. It is Saturday, and the white dots of men are threading down the trail over the bare humps to the plain, following the dark twinkle-movement of asses, the dark nodding of the woman's head as she rides between the baskets. . . . [T]he white specks of men, like sea-gulls on plough-land, come ebbing like sparks from the *palo blanco*, over the fawn undulating of the valley slope. (*MM* 81–82)

Visually this panoramic set-up, with the eye singling out, adding to, and comparing details, reminds one of Van Gogh's drawing of *The Crau from Montmajour* (May 1888) or of Japanese *ukiyo-e* art, but here the dots and specks are in motion. Lawrence surveys the gathering crowd from a wide-angle vantage point and a phrase like "twinkle-movement" fuses visual and kinetic in a pluri-sensory term. Movement, singly or in groups, is syntagmatically marked by staccato conjunctive or adverbial openings ("And," "Down"); present participles with chiasmic variations ("running, trotting, ebbing along" / "threading with ebbing, running, barefoot movement"); and directional signals encoded in prepositional phrases ("towards the town," "above the stagnant green of trees," "away under the opposite fawn-skin hills").[7] The visual progression from moving figures to shapes that mark their goal links spatial with human dynamics.

The pleasure of such sketches lies in the writer's technique, which, as in Zen painting, conveys a whole ethos through casual but precise touches. Siegfried Wichmann explains that "[the] driving force in the Far East is Zen painting, called *zenga*, which is directly connected to poetry" (391). He points to Japanese painters who "follow 'the line which sets everything in motion', the line which presents the traces of movement in flecks, beams, dots and strokes. . . . The swelling and decreasing motion of the brush is like a reflector of the artist's personality" (399). So Lawrence's line of sight, articulated in imagery and syntax, expresses communal movement and also the personality of the viewer. He controls the angle of vision and selects details with a single purpose—to dramatize the influx of people from margins to center. The sense of being *in* this artfully constructed scene is implied by the helpful direction, "You will know [the road] by the tall walking of the dust" (*MM* 82). The animated road is "like a pilgrimage" (*MM* 83), but, unlike Bunyan's straight and narrow way, it is a curving path on which a human flow stirs up dust in a familiar circuit.

Lawrence's metonymic style conveys movement and rhythm in

a panoramic view of ox-wagons among foot-travelers (see *MM* 83–87). Suppressing main verbs, highlighting participles ("rowing," "rolling," "swaying"), insistently echoing adverbs and prepositions ("Onwards"; "On, on"; "Past"), suspending closure by parenthesis and scanning, Lawrence's style simulates the act of looking in slow rhythms that focus attention on moving forms. The wide-ranging "metonymic 'set-up'" is followed by "synecdochic 'close-ups'"[8] of the Zapotec and Serrano people. Lawrence projects a theory of blind impulse onto these unknown "primitives," whose eyes are "black and bright and wild, in the dark faces. They have no goal, any more than the hawks in the air" (84–85). The impression of unmotivated impulse is increased by the conjunction of physical close-ups with cultural distance, which iconicizes the "other," but produces a purely specular or speculative image. Lawrence's "primitivism" shows imaginative empathy with the native people, by placing them in a wider context of vital movement, but in doing so it displaces them from human social contexts that would constitute their reality for an anthropologist. Meanwhile, the image of their unfocused gaze appropriates or subsumes their identity.

Presenting rhythm and ritual in "The Dance of the Sprouting Corn," Lawrence combines "synecdochic 'close-ups'" with metaphoric defamiliarization:

> Bit by bit you take it in. You cannot get a whole impression, save of some sort of wood tossing, a little forest of trees in motion, with gleaming black hair and gold-ruddy breasts that somehow do not destroy the illusion of forest. (*MM* 125)

The visual effect of fragmentation and oscillation, obliterating individual identity, is increased by the sequential medium of writing.

The structural "predominance of metonymy," in describing place, "predetermines the so-called 'realistic' trend" (Jakobson 92) in travel-writing, which is oriented towards random events and multiple details. The concrete conciseness of Lawrence's seeing produces synecdochic series, as when he compares hands spread out on a table in *Twilight in Italy* (174–75). The close-ups of individual hands attract attention, while their juxtaposition implies contrasting lifestyles. Metonymic movement focuses on one thing after another, bringing out differences or similarities within a common framework. One such set-up, in Sardinia, structures the act of looking and brings together a series of objects in motion (see *SS* 95). The directional signal, "Down the high-road," subtends a long sentence including six parallel uses of the neutral verb "came," inverted to throw focus forward on advancing objects of attention—"wild half-ragged men on ponies," "four wide-eyed cows," "three delicate, beautiful merino sheep," "an ancient, ancient man with a stick," "a stout-chested peasant," "a straggle of alert and triumphant goats." The syntactic and semantic series set in motion by guided looking achieves symmetrical closure when "everything came to a halt."

In some of his most hallucinatingly vivid descriptions, Lawrence sets up the scene metonymically, then expands its significance metaphorically. As he maps the environs of Orosei (*SS* 148), adverbial phrases ("Away to the right," "To the left," "upwards and inland") set up directions for looking, as in Hemingway's prose.[9] Lawrence keeps the language simple, with geographical nouns and plain visual adjectives, in order to lay the groundwork for an ecstatic, metaphoric vision of the flowering almond trees. So intense is the act of seeing that it reproduces itself metaphorically in "the hot eyes of the individual blossoms" (148).

The gusto of travel derives from the freedom of an observing self on holiday, mind relaxed and senses open, as the writer plunges into a world of cultural and topographical difference. Sprung loose from sustained projects, the travel writer exchanges his imagined worlds for the real world of people and places. He travels light, with or without a notebook, and his powers of observation are quickened by the changing scene in front of him. Travel writing is obliquely or openly self-expressive: although Lawrence's magnetized attention to objects approaches clairvoyance at times, he also foregrounds strongly felt personal responses. In *Sea and Sardinia*, the tone of a speaking voice—lyrical, reckless, rapturous, cavorting, hortatory, denunciatory, scathing—is encoded in the rhetoric. Lawrence's concentrated use of informal language shows his linguistic verve, in comic scenes, dialogue, *skaz* (Bakhtin's term for stylized speech), or invective.[10]

In *Sea and Sardinia* and the early essays of *Mornings in Mexico*, Lawrence dramatizes his irascibly sensitive persona. Momentaneous interactions with people and places put the writer in the picture, adding personal and critical dimensions to his travels. A notable example of ironic self-dramatization is his outrage at the filth of Sorgono, in which he ridicules his own overreaction and buttonholes the reader: "I cursed the degenerate aborigines, the dirty-breasted host. . . . All my praise of the long stocking-cap— you remember?—vanished from my mouth. I cursed them all, and the q-b for an interfering female" (*SS* 96). In dialogic style, Lawrence features his own short-fused personality in a face-to-face diatribe against the innkeeper, in which aggressive questions and insistent repetition reflect the Italian idiom: "Why do you have the impudence to take in travelers? What does it mean, that this is an inn? . . . Say then—what does it mean?" [*Dica—che significa?*] (112). The shrill, scolding tone of the sociolect is well adapted to the traveler's persona, as he turns the tables on his host. Lawrence excels at parodic imitation, as does Loerke with the Cologne dialect in *Women in Love* (406). His irritation with "dumb-bells" comes through less appealingly in "Walk to Huayapa," where he self-consciously (if facetiously) portrays himself as an imperialist bully: "But we don't belong to the ruling race for nothing. Into the yard we march" (*MM* 46). Lawrence, like Robert Louis Stevenson flogging his donkey in the Cevennes, was a sick man, who found it impossible to control his exasperation at times. But given the vicissitudes of travel (derived from "travail"), it is not surprising that exasperation is a keynote of the genre.

Lawrence uses synecdoche flippantly or satirically to reduce those who annoy him to grotesque traits. Examples abound in *Sea and Sardinia*, reflecting the narrator's irritability. The objects of his satire are reduced to isolated parts or metaphoric functions, signifying fixed attitudes that do not cohere to form a whole human being—"The tall lean alpaca jacket, with a face of yellow stone and a big black moustache," for instance (33). The advantage of such Dickensian caricature is that it deploys the visual spotlight economically, encoding temperamental reactions in the object[11] and so controlling the reader's responses. Codewords like the metaphoric "bluebottles" and metonymic (or synecdochic) "alpaca jackets" imply satiric dehumanization of the ship's waiters. When the queasy passengers decline a meal, "the blue-bottles . . . dart in a black-alpaca bunch to the tin altar, and there loudly buzz, wildly, above the sallow cakes"; when the narrator finishes a glass of wine, "the voracious blow-flies buzz derisively and excited" (46). Such satiric spleen provides comic relief and, through rapid shifts of tone, contrasts with Lawrence's exultation in non-human nature. The alchemy of sunrise at sea, "the sky all golden, all a joyous, fire-heated gold" (47), transforms his mood, underlining the baseness of bourgeois humanity and the volatility of his own inspiration.

Lawrence's sensitivity to the quality of living makes his travels a form of on-the-spot research. His vitalism, allied with a streak of puritanism, makes him abrasively thin-skinned. He combines the prickly gifts of a satirist with ironic observation of men and manners.[12] Metonymy serves in various ways to pinpoint his *bêtes noires*, such as the popular submergence of individuals in national identities: "You become—if you are English—*l'Inghilterra*, *il carbone*, and *il cambio*: and as England, coal and exchange you are treated" (*SS* 50). But Lawrence himself practices a similar trick, labeling people "black cap[s]" or "red-caps" after single items of dress or uniform (77). The slovenly innkeeper at Sorgono, who provokes his ire, is demolished with the sobriquet, "spotty-breast" (95). Tired and hungry, he dislikes the inn at Siniscola, with its "long table" and "foully blotched table-cloth" and its "young sludge-queen" of a waitress, and hilariously mimics "the sucking chorus" of soup-drinkers (154). But if he ridicules country manners, he is even more satirical of pretentious, *nouveau-riche* behavior. Jealous exasperation colors his portrait of "the bounder," a traveling salesman on the steamer to Palermo, who fancies himself a ladies' man, "splash[ing] out noise on the piano in splashes, like water splashing out of a pail" and "wriggl[ing] his large bounder's back [and well-filled haunches] upon the piano-stool" (184).

In a more genial mood, Lawrence produces some sharply etched comic characters and episodes, employing a narrative style, similar to that of stories such as "Tickets Please," on the raw material of life. The taciturn but masterly bus-driver takes on a mythic aura, "wrapped in his gloom like a young bus-driving Hamlet" or "a sort of ginger-haired, young, mechanic Mr. Rochester" (*SS* 143). This anti-romantic hero "darted the bus at the curves; then softly padded round like an angel: then off again for the next parabola" (144). Comic episodes abound—an old peasant for the first time thinks the bus is going because the door is shut; a man with a piglet under each arm wants to get aboard without paying for his pigs; a fat, perspiring businessman is desperately late (144, 145, 146–48). This last episode is a comic masterpiece in miniature:

> Thunder came into the gloomy dark eyes of the Rochester. . . . Click! went his face into a look of almost seraphic peace, as he pulled off the brakes. . . . The fat woman shoved Beppin' in, gasping farewells, the brother-in-law handed in the ox-blood-red suit-case, tottering behind, and the bus surged savagely out of Orosei. (*SS* 147–48)

The literary traveler is alternately a masochist with a sense of humor or a satirist with high blood-pressure. On the Sardinian trip, Lawrence experiences pestiferous stewards and fellow-travelers, national prejudice, sordid inns and befouled lanes, surly innkeepers, cold, hunger, and fatigue. Yet there are moments of surprise, wonder, or exhilaration and even the occasional triumph, as when (on the return trip) he enters the fray for steamer tickets at Naples, "like a screw biting into a bit of wood," and emerges "[c]lutching paper change and the green slips" of two first-class tickets (*SS* 178).

If we dismantle the canonical notion of a hierarchy of genres, the uniqueness of Lawrence's travel writing, and the visual acuity and linguistic verve that interrelate it with letters, essays, novels, and short stories, will appear more clearly. All his writing is charged with intuitive responses and ethical or aesthetic values.[13] He is never restricted by preconceived notions of form: his travel books follow the sensory and intellectual graphs of his experience. The experimental, provisional nature of travel writing allows for impulsive digressions, which may be the sunshine or the shadow of the work[14]; they express the rhythm of the writer's temperament, the fluctuating play of his senses and intellect. Lawrence's responses are eclectic: he can move, without batting an eyelid, from the mechanics of a door-hinge to Renaissance painting and the Last Judgment (*TI* 114–16).

*Twilight in Italy* and *Mornings in Mexico* began as collections of essays; *Sketches of Etruscan Places* was a series of field studies. Of the four travel books, only that roller-coaster *Sea and Sardinia* has the narrative continuity and picaresque form of traditional travel literature. Yet here too, as Fussell notes, "Lawrence's prose is attractively loose . . . alive with comic apostrophe and interjection. . . . He aspires to no consistency of vision. . . . In Lawrence's travels . . . each place fills his whole awareness, displacing others" (157). The movement of his writing, in short, is metonymic. If we take each book as a chapter of Lawrence's creative autobiography,[15] the eclectic brilliance and variety of his travel writings come to the fore. The verve is stunning, the vitality untrammeled. As well as "acts of attention" to the "circumambient universe" (*Hardy* 172), these exuberant investigations are seismograms of discovery in the writer himself and in his art.

## NOTES

1. In his review of H. M. Tomlinson's *Gifts of Fortune*, Lawrence writes:

We travel, perhaps, with a secret and absurd hope of setting foot on the Hesperides, of running our boat up a little creek and landing in the Garden of Eden. . . . Yet, in our very search for them, we touch the coasts of illusion, and come into contact with other worlds. (*P* 343)

2. Weiner observes that Lawrence, in his travel books, "clearly conceived of his artistic role as prophetic and homiletic" (230).

3. Fussell speaks of "the joyous power of [Lawrence's] creative memory" (156) and Burgess of his "seeing everything, making no notes, achieving something like total recall" (109).

4. See Franks, "Il Duro and Lawrence: The Reflecting Stone."

5. See Porteous, *Landscapes of the Mind*, chapters 2, 3, 4 (21–85).

6. Sabin argues that "[the] motive of escape attaches the travel memoir to Romantic conventions"—yet she concedes that "[by] the end of the book, Lawrence's holiday trip represents a distinctive form of imaginative freedom" (85). For Theroux, escape, departure, and the freedom to come and go at will are prime travel motives (*Kingdom* 131). Theroux is a looser, more detached traveler than Lawrence: "What I liked most was having space and time . . . setting off for a destination which at any moment . . . I could abandon" (*Pillars* 471–72).

7. Cf. Fussell on Lawrence's "prepositional perception" (161).

8. Jakobson analyzes "synecdochic 'close-ups' and metonymic 'set-ups'" in the cinematic art of D. W. Griffith and Sergei Eisenstein (92). Metonymy, film, and travel writing employ similar techniques of spatial fragmentation, signifying continuity among separate items in a series.

9. See the famous opening paragraph of *A Farewell to Arms* (3). Hemingway's image of the dust raised by the troops bears some resemblance to Lawrence's animated image of the column of dust in *Mornings in Mexico* (quoted above). Lawrence reviewed Hemingway's *In Our Time* in 1927, the year that *Mornings in Mexico* was published and two years before *A Farewell to Arms* appeared.

10. Sabin observes: "In Lawrence's strong voice, discomfort and even indignation are carried aloft by the comic and celebratory verve of the language. Delight is the dominant tone . . . [depending] on Lawrence's own indefatigable alertness to every ragged bit of life as it goes momentaneously by" (90). Burgess also appreciates the aural qualities of Lawrence's prose: "There is a sense of reading a private notebook; there is also a sense of hearing actual speech, com-

plete with fractured syntax, repetition, slang, facetiousness, buttonholing, even bullying" (110). Instead of being "irritating," the personal style "charm[s] and disarm[s]," because of its freshness and candor.

11. When it comes to observing people, Burgess notes that "[the] sharpness of Lawrence's eye is incredible, and his judgments are madly sane" (111). According to Gray, "[the] felicitous combination in the book of delicacy and force stems from the author's ability to render . . . the 'quickness' of experience in rapid emotional turns and passionate ventings of attraction and distaste" (42).

12. It is only fair to add that he also shows appreciation. He admires a dignified peasant in costume as "handsome," "beautifully male," "indomitable," and "superb" and praises the men of Nuovo for their extraordinary generosity and natural good breeding (*SS* 62, 126).

13. Sabin comments that "the achievement of style in *Sea and Sardinia* implicitly connects Lawrence's exhilaration in travel with the spirit of a certain kind of art." His travel memoirs leave "the pervasive impression of a sensibility which makes, and remakes, experience through brilliant forms of language" (86).

14. See Sterne, *Tristram Shandy,* 1:xxii:73.

15. Regarding the "autobiographical" element, Kowalewski observes that "[at] the heart of [travel writing as a literary form] . . . is a self-revealing figure" (8). Fussell maintains that, "because [Lawrence] lived with such intensity of perception and such shrewdness of imagination, his four travel books seem to sketch the stages of his own life" (163–64). More justifiably, Kalnins maintains that "Lawrence's travel writings . . . can be seen as a metaphor for his inner development and his growing understanding of the human psyche" (68).

## WORKS CITED

Bakhtin, M. M. *The Dialogic Imagination: Four Essays.* Edited by Michael Holquist. Translated by Caryl Emerson and Michael Holquist. Austin: University of Texas Press, 1981.

Burgess, Anthony. *Flame into Being: The Life and Work of D. H.Lawrence.* London: Heinemann, 1985.

Chatwin, Bruce. *Anatomy of Restlessness: Uncollected Writings.* Edited by Jan Born and Matthew Graves. London: Picador-Macmillan, 1997.

———. *The Songlines.* New York: Penguin, 1988.

Douglas, Norman. *Old Calabria.* 1915. Reprint, London: Secker, 1955.

Durrell, Lawrence. "Landscape and Character." In *Spirit of Place: Letters and Essays on Travel,* edited by Alan G. Thomas. New York: Dutton, 1969.

Franks, Jill. "Il Duro and Lawrence: The Reflecting Stone." *DHLR* 26 (1995–96): 109–20.

Fussell, Paul. *Abroad: British Literary Traveling Between the Wars.* Oxford: Oxford University Press, 1980.

Gray, Rockwell. "Travel." In *Temperamental Journeys: Essays on the Modern Literature of Travel,* edited by Michael Kowalewski. Athens: University of Georgia Press, 1992.

Hemingway, Ernest. *A Farewell to Arms.* New York: Scribner's, 1929.

Jakobson, Roman and Morris Halle. *Fundamentals of Language.* 4th ed. The Hague: Mouton, 1980.

Kalnins, Mara. "'Terra Incognita': Lawrence's Travel Writings." *Renaissance and Modern Studies* 29 (1985): 66–77.

Kinkead-Weekes, Mark. *D. H. Lawrence: Triumph to Exile 1912–1922.* Cambridge: Cambridge University Press, 1996.

Kowalewski, Michael, ed. "Introduction: The Modern Literature of Travel." *Temperamental Journeys: Essays on the Modern Literature of Travel.* Edited by Kowalewski. Athens: University of Georgia Press, 1992.

Little, Kenneth. "On Safari: The Visual Politics of a Tourist Representation." In *The Varieties of Sensory Experience: A Sourcebook in the Anthropology of the Senses*, edited by David Howes. Toronto: University of Toronto Press, 1991.

Porteous, J. Douglas. *Landscapes of the Mind: Worlds of Sense and Metaphor.* Toronto: University of Toronto Press, 1990.

Rossman, Charles. "D. H. Lawrence and Mexico." In *D. H. Lawrence: A Centenary Consideration*, edited by Peter Balbert and Phillip L. Marcus. Ithaca: Cornell University Press, 1985.

Sabin, Margery. "The Spectacle of Reality in *Sea and Sardinia*." In *The Art of Travel: Essays on Travel Writing*, edited by Philip Dodd. London: Cass, 1982.

Sterne, Laurence. *The Life and Opinions of Tristram Shandy, Gentleman.* 1759–67. Edited by James A. Work. New York: Odyssey, 1940.

———. *A Sentimental Journey Through France and Italy.* 1768. Reprint, New York: Capricorn, 1964.

Stevenson, Robert Louis. *Travels with a Donkey in the Cevennes and Selected Travel Writings.* Edited by Emma Letley. Oxford: Oxford University Press, 1992.

Templeton, Wayne. "'Indians and an Englishman': Lawrence in the American Southwest." *DHLR* 25 (1993–94): 14–34.

Theroux, Paul. *Kingdom by the Sea: A Journey Around the Coast of Great Britain.* London: Penguin, 1984.

———. *The Pillars of Hercules: A Grand Tour of the Mediterranean.* London: Penguin, 1996.

Weiner, S. Ronald. "The Rhetoric of Travel: The Example of *Sea and Sardinia*." *DHLR* 2 (1969): 230–44.

Wichmann, Siegfried. *Japonisme: The Japanese Influence on Western Art in the 19th and 20th Centuries.* Translated by Mary Whittall, James Ramsay, Helen Watanabe, Cornelius Cardew, and Susan Bruni. New York: Harmony, 1981.

Wordsworth, William. "Lines Composed a Few Miles above Tintern Abbey." In *The Prelude, with a Selection from the Shorter Poems, the Sonnets, The Recluse, and The Excursion*, edited by Carlos Baker. New York: Holt, 1964.

# Metaphor in *Women in Love*

Kyoko Kay Kondo

ALTHOUGH NIETZSCHE'S REMARK, "WHAT THEN IS TRUTH? A MOVABLE host of metaphors, metonymies, and anthropomorphisms" (84), had a deconstructive intent, it also anticipated an immense potential for tropological creativeness over the century that followed. Paul Ricoeur has defined a late twentieth-century awareness of the positive, creative function of metaphor. He writes in *The Rule of Metaphor:* "Metaphor is living by virtue of the fact that it introduces the spark of imagination into a 'thinking more' at the conceptual level" (303). In my view, D. H. Lawrence realized this Ricoeurian function of metaphor to the full in his writing, not through overt theoretical analysis but through an attentiveness to language and sensitivity to metaphor. This essay argues that, for Lawrence in *Women in Love,* metaphor is a vehicle of understanding, discovery, and revelation.

Roman Jakobson's essay, "Two Aspects of Language and Two Types of Aphasic Disturbances" (1956), following the observations by semioticians and Russian formalists, became the source of a late twentieth-century focus on metaphor and metonymy. His dyadic tropology, together with further studies by structuralists like Claude Lévi-Strauss and post-structuralists like Jacques Lacan, and more recently, deconstructionists, has brought about fruitful and influential insights. However, the tetradic tropologists and phenomenologists of language, including Vico, Foucault, Husserl, Ricoeur, James Edie, Hayden White, and James Mellard, and especially those with a cyclical view of tropic development, are more profoundly relevant to what Lawrence had striven to manifest in his narrative form. Their basically anti-Cartesian view, a belief in the close relationship between words and concrete human experience, and emphasis on *parole* rather than *langue* in the abstract, are all akin to Lawrence, and particularly to the world of *Women in Love.*

Lawrence's use of metaphor is distinctively modernist. A comparison will help clarify the point. The Victorian novelist George Eliot, famously a creator of metaphors, says in *Middlemarch* (1872), "for we all of us, grave or light, get our thoughts entangled in metaphors, and act fatally on the strength of them" (111). Eliot, the omniscient narrator of a classic nineteenth-century realist novel, delineates authorially the process in which her characters become mentally entangled in metaphors. However, as narrator, she is apparently not herself entangled. Lawrence uses pervasive metaphorical language in *Women in Love,* but in a radically innovative way, he lets his characters join in his own struggle with metaphors. That is why metaphor becomes a dramatic action in this novel. Each character sees the world through the prism of his or her own metaphorical interpretation, either expanding or limiting the awareness of what it contains. What is unique with Lawrence is that the characters' entanglement with metaphor is also a vehicle for the book's exploration and discovery. He partly shares their condition and must find his own way through metaphor.

While George Eliot's metaphors are conscious products of the subliminal level, the reader feels Lawrence's total immersion in language. Lawrence says in "The State of Funk": "My field is to know the feelings inside a man, and to make new feelings conscious" (*P II* 567). In "Morality and the Novel" he says, "As mankind is always struggling in the toils of old relationships, art is always ahead of the times" (*Hardy* 171). Neuroses often develop, he believes, when certain "disturbances" in our psyche are no longer comfortably felt in conventional feeling-patterns and therefore find no way to be acknowledged and understood. Lawrence regards it as an artist's role to articulate this "new feeling," which he does by creating new metaphors: he thinks metaphorically. Or rather, he thinks and feels at once in metaphors. At its best, metaphor plays a significant role in determining "what is real for us" (Lakoff 146). Here Lawrence's metaphor is "a condition of finding something out," as Fiona Becket argues. It is "a medium of knowledge" (Becket 197), knowledge not of "things concluded, in the past" (*WL* 86), but of things to come.

One metaphor that appears and reappears in *Women in Love*—that of "opening"—excellently demonstrates that Lawrence's radically heuristic use of metaphor in the novel is one of his most distinctive features. As can be expected, the word is often used literally: flowers open, windows open, eyes open and close—and thus the word exists without attracting any special attention, buried in the literal context, until it starts emanating a special aura, supported by the network and layers of networks of other related metaphors and develops a deeper resonance. In the end we find that "opening" plays a central role among the cluster of metaphors that encompass the main themes of the novel: dark river of dissolution, silver river of life, star-equilibrium, and finally the promise of the New World. Ursula says about Gudrun, "She likes to look through the wrong end of the opera glasses, and see the world that way" (39). Gudrun has "a vivid, subtle, critical consciousness, that saw the world distorted, horrific" (451). How one sees the world determines one's world view. One creates one's own network of metaphors drawn from a particular world view. For example, in contrast to Birkin, who uses cosmic metaphors, and Ursula, who uses metaphors based on nature and natural processes, "a curious sort of mechanical motion intoxicated [Loerke], a confusion in nature" (448), and the mechanical "struggle with the natural conditions" gives Gerald a sense of "pure fulfilment" (223–24). Ursula's hostility towards Gerald's treatment of a mare at the railway crossing reflects their profoundly contrasting world views: for Ursula a mare is an independent being, while the horse has to be "useful" for Gerald.

When Birkin says, "We've got to bust [this life] completely, or shrivel inside it, as in a tight skin. For it won't expand any more" (54), Gerald tries to accommodate this into his own instrumental discourse, and says, "I suppose you mean, reform the whole order of society?" (54). When Birkin tells Gerald that Gerald's aphorisms bore him, Gerald reminds him that actually Birkin wants all the aphorisms his "own way." When Birkin says, "Anybody who is anything can just be himself and do as he likes," Gerald wonders if it is an "aphorism or a cliché" (32). Although the characters are all modern, well-educated, worldly, and articulate, they often speak in different, mutually uncomprehending discourses. The characters' sensitivity toward metaphor, or the capacity to understand metaphor, differentiates them. Aphorism states a general doctrine, which originally could have been a creative metaphor. Having been widely assimilated and accepted in society, it has lost its freshness. Cliché is a hackneyed phrase. Both can be seen as dead metaphors, and Gerald's difficulty lies in his incapacity to understand real metaphor.

The difference between Birkin and Gerald, noted above, corresponds to a cultural difference in layers of modernity, in Michel Foucault's and Hayden White's terms. Foucault in *The Order of Things* traces the progress of knowledge toward an objectivity in science, and divides the successive historical epochs into what he calls four "epistemes": the "Renaissance," the "Classical," the "Modern," and the "Postmodern" or "Contemporary." White relates his study of tropes to these epistemes, and maintains that the tropes corresponding to each episteme—metaphor, metonymy, synecdoche, and irony—represent modes of consciousness in each episteme. Metaphor, based on similarity, is used to map or encode the world of experience; metonymy, highly contextual, is based on contiguity, and explains operations through analogies to mechanisms. With synecdoche, a part represents a whole, and therefore has temporal, organic orientation. As for the last mode, irony, Foucault asserts that Mallarmé, if asked, would say, "What is speaking [there] is . . . the word itself" (305). Here humanity disappears into a verbal universe.

Looking at the language of the characters in *Women in Love* through these tropological lenses, we can see that, while Birkin's question above is metaphorical, Gerald's answer is metonymical. To Birkin's further question, "[W]herein does life centre, for you?" Gerald replies, "It is artificially held together by the social mechanism" (58). It can be said that in managing the mine, he has achieved the eighteenth-century ideal, putting the Newtonian mechanistic nature of thought into practice. Here the universe is a machine, a cosmic mechanism. In the highly organized system of his mine, each part is indispensable for supporting the whole, an idea often reflected in his synecdochic expressions. He believes that the roles assigned to each individual to be the actual identity of the person. Society's need defines an individual. Metonymy and synecdoche are considered more refined and sophisticated than metaphor (Mellard 15), and hence Gerald's confidence that "he, himself, Gerald, had harder and more durable truths than any [Birkin] knew. He felt himself older, more knowing" (59). Gudrun fatally identifies with the synecdochic and mechanical view of the universe in her long interior monologue: "Oh God, the wheels within wheels of people—it makes one's head tick like a clock, with a very madness of dead mechanical monotony and meaninglessness. How I *hate* life, how I hate it" (464). She tries to escape and to find a new world in Loerke. She also creates a comfortable world to inhabit in irony and satire.

Ursula feels that "No flowers grow upon busy machinery, there is no sky to a routine, there is no space to a rotary motion" (193). She attacks and rejects the mechanical world, using metaphors from nature: nature gives life, while industry suffocates it. Foucault's four epistemes are the equivalent in *Women in Love* of the differently multilayered psychology of *The Rainbow*. In *Women in Love* these different modes coexist in one generation, within modernity. Each character lives in each mode: of either growing or deteriorating. At the same time, one direction toward which the age is heading is clearly discernible.

*Women in Love* explores how far each character can go through these psychic and internalized modes. Gerald says that Gudrun seems "like the end" (439) to him. At first, she thinks that Gerald is "the final approximation of life" (181), but later she sees further possibilities in Loerke, beyond whom there is "no going" (427). In White's terms, the mechanical world they live in is now sliding down toward the ironical and satirical. Gudrun and Loerke's shared world is at the bottom. Birkin refers to this fatal descent using the metaphor of the "dark river of dissolution" as opposed to the "silver river of life" (172). Although there can be no natural "silver river" now, he pessimistically explains, he nevertheless directs his efforts toward regaining the "silver river of life."

Birkin uses extreme metaphors when he refers to life and humanity: "[People] are apples of Sodom . . . Dead Sea Fruit, gall-apples" (126). He wishes that humanity would be "swept away," so that "The real tree of life would then be rid of the most ghastly heavy crop of Dead Sea Fruit" (127). This startling utterance can be understood both in its negative and positive aspects. He feels antipathy toward present circumstances: how life is and how people are. He also feels a strong sense of isolation, which seems to be second nature to him. At the same time, though, he talks about the possibility of "the real tree of life." He focuses his hatred on the idea of the supremacy of human beings. For him mankind is just one living thing among all the others, "just one expression of the incomprehensible" (59) in the universe, where everything should coexist, relating to each other organically. Birkin's strong metaphors, which pull in two directions (toward isolation and toward unity), can be understood as mirroring the contrast between science and myth. Science tends to specialize and divide itself further and further, whereas myth moves toward unification.

According to Mary Douglas, the so-called "primitive" worldview is closely integrated, for it embraces the universe in a single, symbolic whole. The opposing world-view of scientific culture tends toward specialization and compartmentalization (201). Birkin and Hermione, for instance, respond to stars differently: Birkin creates a metaphor, "star-equilibrium" (319) while Hermione is fascinated by scientific knowledge about the stars; she is delighted that she has "really understood something about the stars. One feels so *uplifted,* so *unbounded.*" She talks about the pleasure of knowing, which is "*so* great, so *wonderful*" (85). Their contrasting attitudes reflect their respective world views.[1]

All the characters in *Women in Love* feel isolated, one result of fragmentation. Gudrun believes in the "purest form of accident" (49) and ignores the line of cause and effect. She can switch her consciousness on and off mechanically (287). She regains "her will with a click" (402), and things "snap in her" (418). She believes that "outwardly was all that mattered, for inwardly was a bad joke" (418). Breadalby conversation is "like a rattle of some artillery" with "the continual crackling of a witticism, the continual spatter of verbal jest" (84). Loerke is "isolated in his own complete envelope" (450); he is "a pure, unconnected will," making "not the slightest attempt to be at one with anything" (427). Hermione likes to depart first, "leaving the other behind," to give herself a spurious "sense of strength" (44). The characters protect their isolated selves in a shell, a hard cover. Each longs to be "impervious, self-completed, a thing isolated" (445). The characters are social beings protected by the frame of society.

Birkin strives throughout to overcome this sense of isolation, by breaking free from the shell and becoming truly self-sufficient, establishing "free proud singleness" (254), the pre-condition of achieving communion with others. "Communion" is Birkin's terminology for the state embodying mythical and metaphoric sensibility. It is the sign that one can overcome the fragmented self. Personally, his goal is set on "perfect union with a woman—sort of ultimate marriage" (58), but with his genuinely historical understanding and perspective, this does not stop at being merely personal. With his metaphor, "star- equilibrium," he attempts to change the consciousness of people, thereby "trying to save the world" (128).[2] Birkin's concern echoes what Emerson says in

"Nature": "Why should we too not enjoy an original relation to the universe?" (7). Cassirer expresses the same sentiment:

> Have we been led into a fatal mistake by venturing on this course into the new world of symbols? Is it *possible* that by so doing man has torn himself loose from nature and estranged himself from the reality and immediacy of natural existence? Are the things he has exchanged for this really good? Or are they not the gravest threat to life? (Cassirer *The Logic of the Humanities* 76)

Hayden White, following the line of *ricorso* (cyclic return) in Vico, insists that after the phase of irony, the tropic process returns to metaphor: when language itself becomes an object of reflection in irony, it becomes apparent that language has become inadequate to represent the object fully, and consciousness tries to return to the original state, that is, to the "naming function" in metaphor (White 204). Mellard sums up: "[A]s consciousness moves through the tropic moments it becomes exhausted, but there exists the potential for reinvigoration in the *ricorso*, the cyclic return to the source of energy provided by metaphor" (143). Birkin also talks about "a new cycle of creation after—but not for us" (173). He attempts through his metaphors to stop the age's fatal descent by changing people's consciousnesses back to mythological perception. It is possible "to become aware of one's episteme, to understand its features, the ways in which it determines or delimits knowledge, and its potentialities for transformation into another episteme" (Mellard 73).

The ongoing metaphor of "opening" individuates the characters: from isolation toward singleness and finally the attainment of communion. Only when they are "open" can a "flow"—one of Lawrence's positive metaphors—wash them and thereby enable them to gain a view of the universe as a symbolic unity, and make them ready for the final ascent toward star-equilibrium, a true communion. I would stress at this point that in my view the workings of the metaphor, like this "opening," create the novel's sense of urgency; and star-equilibrium is clearly in the domain of metaphor.[3]

At the beginning, the characters' sense of dissatisfaction takes the form of being unable to open themselves. Gudrun feels that "Everything withers in the bud . . . everything—oneself—things in general" (8). Ursula is also frustrated: "The only window was death. . . . [T]he soul was a prisoner within this sordid vast edifice of life, and there was no escape, save in death. . . . Everything was gone, walled in, with spikes on top of the walls (193). Birkin cannot get his flower to blossom: "Either it is blighted in the bud, or has got the smother-fly, or it isn't nourished. . . . It is a contravened knot" (125–26). In Birkin's eyes, Gerald has "a clog," and "could never fly away from himself" (207). All the characters are living in an enclosure. Birkin says rather cruelly to Hermione, who suffers from "a terrible void, a lack, a deficiency of being within her" (16): "You want it all in that loathsome little skull of yours, that ought to be cracked like a nut. For you'll be the same till it *is* cracked, like an insect in its skin.—If one cracked your skull perhaps one might get a spontaneous, passionate woman out of you, with real sensuality" (42).

A change, however, comes over Birkin: Hermione, feeling the presence of Birkin as a "wall" which she must "break down" (104), attacks him with a lapis lazuli paperweight. When she crashes the ball on his head, he feels "smashed to atoms"; he "was all fragments, smashed to bits" (106). Later, lying naked on the soft, delicate vegetation that is "travelling into [his] blood," he feels "fulfilled" and "enrichened." Birkin "would put away the old ethic, he would be free in his new state" (107–8). Hermione's attack brings to mind Birkin's assertion that "a man who is murderable is a man who in a profound if hidden lust desires to be murdered" (33). Birkin needed his head "cracked" to be really free, free from his own binding sense of isolation. For anything new to happen, "prison walls" must be "broken," "coverings" and the "veil" must be "torn," "skin" must be "cast off," "life" "bust," and "nut" "cracked" and "crushed." "Ideas" and "illusions" can be a tight "confinement." "Fixed will," "deliberate voluntary consciousness" (42), and "self-righteous self-opinionated self-will" (44) create this situation. Therefore Birkin entreats Ursula: "I want you to drop your assertive *will*, your frightened apprehensive self-insistence. . . . I want you to trust yourself so implicitly, that you can let yourself go" (250–51). "Opening" is possible for Gerald only when he finds "a flaw in his will" (445).

This stage of "letting oneself go," "lapsing out" (178), "release" (313, 446, 467), and the experience of "real sensuality" (42) are presented by water images and metaphors, "melting," "flow," and "flood." One is "drowned in darkness," in the "deluge" (43). "Excurse" makes heavy use of water metaphors: the river of strange dark fluid richness carries away Ursula's mind and sweeps away everything (313–14). Locked inside a hard shell, one is partial and isolated but can believe oneself self-completed, protected by the walls. However, self-knowledge is "death to one self" (43); now one cannot help realizing one's own limitation. No wonder some characters feel this opening as a wound.

Through Gerald, Lawrence provides one of the most striking examples of his use of tropes to distinguish types of consciousness. When Gerald finally completes the mechanization of the mine, he feels that he has become a "void" (325). The process of his struggle to regain himself suddenly is expressed in metaphor: he feels himself "on the point of caving in," unable to stand "holding the roof up" (325). He "must seek reinforcements" (337) before a "collapse" (325) occurs. These metaphors are highly metonymical, deriving from mines, machinery, and industry. Gerald, with his life and sense of purpose wholly dependent on his daily working context and living mainly in the world of metonymy, understandably becomes totally empty and feels "nothingness" (266). He had been "so guarded, all his life," but meeting Gudrun he "lapsed out for the first time in his life" (178). Here was a chance for him to open up. A character like Gerald understandably feels this opening as a "wound" (446), all the more so because Gudrun cruelly rejects him. But here we notice that his interior monologue is truly poetic and metaphorical and full of similes for the first time:

> A strange rent had been torn in him; like a victim that is torn open and given to the heavens, so he had been torn apart and given to Gudrun. How should he close again? This wound, this strange, infinitely-sensitive opening of his soul, where he was exposed, like an open flower, to all the universe, and in which he was given to his complement, the other, the unknown, this wound, this disclosure, this unfolding of his own covering, leaving him incomplete, limited, unfinished, like an open flower under the sky, this was his cruelest joy. . . . Why should he close up and become impervious, immune, like a partial thing in a sheath, when he had broken forth, like a seed that has germinated, to issue forth in being, embracing the unrealised heavens.
>
> He would keep the unfinished bliss of his own yearning even through the torture she inflicted upon him. . . . [I]n being near her, even, he felt the quickening, the going forth in him, the release, the knowledge of his own limitation and the magic of the promise, as well as the mystery of his own destruction and annihilation. (445–46)

All through the novel, Gerald's chance to open takes the form of an inflicted wound. In "Man to Man" Birkin tentatively invites Gerald to "swear a Blutbrüderschaft," the old tradition of the Teutonic knights of making a "little wound in their arms, and rub[bing] each other's blood into the cut" (206). In another scene, Bismarck the rabbit badly scratches the arms of Gerald and Gudrun. Gerald's "hard forearm" is "torn in red gashes," and Gudrun's arm has a "deep red score down the silken white flesh" (242). The scream of the rabbit tears "the veil of her consciousness" (241), and "the long, shallow red rip [on her arm] seemed torn across his own brain, tearing the surface of his ultimate consciousness, letting through the forever unconscious, unthinkable red ether of the beyond" (242). He feels as if Gudrun has "hit him across the face—or rather, as if she had torn him across the breast" (243). And Gudrun feels "revealed" (241). She protects herself with "multiple defences" (377), and she shares with Gerald "the subterranean desire to let go, to fling away everything, and lapse into a sheer unrestraint" (287).

The stage after the opening, then, is like limbo, a time of suspension, promise, and apprehension. For Gerald to have attained this stage is in itself an achievement, a kind of personal growth, and therefore a cruel joy. Having grown out of the metonymic and synecdochic in White's tropological terms, Gerald can finally incorporate the metaphorical world within himself. He has seen beyond and embraced the "unrealised heavens" (446). To reach the "new universe" (312), however, one must be able to fly up to a higher plane. Gerald cannot go beyond this stage to establish a real sense of singleness: "his joints were turned to water . . . and [he] went drifting away" (472). In death, he is frozen—the solid, static state of "water" and stabilized. His rejection by Gudrun— "divorced, debarred, a soul shut out" (403)—is partly the cause. Gerald's death causes Birkin bitter regret at the end as well: *Blutbrüderschaft*—rubbing one another's wounds to mix blood—if only Gerald had accepted it, would have been a symbolic mutual act, a commitment, another possibility which was open for Gerald.

The idea of a New World is totally irrelevant to Gudrun for whom "All possibility" is "pure illusion" (468), and to Loerke, who "never talk[s] of the future" (453). The "river of dissolution" is a comfortable home for Loerke, the "wizard rat" (428). Here Gudrun joins him in "silvery isolation and interplay" (469), a degraded parody of star-equilibrium. The truly new state sought by Birkin and Ursula, a "new planet" (438), is no longer described with water metaphors. The experience in "Excurse" leaves Ursula an "essential new being, . . . free in complete ease, her complete self" (314). Even in her most difficult period, she had hope, feeling that "something was coming to pass. If only she could break through the last integuments!" (9). She has kept faith in "the unknown forces" (264). Ursula at this stage has become "beautiful as a new marvellous flower opened at his knees, a paradisal flower she was, . . . a flower of luminousness" (313); "a radiant, shining flower that moment unfolded in primal blessedness" (368). A seed is germinated, producing buds which blossom to be flowers. And the flower is linked with the "morning sun," "the sun that has just opened above clouds" (407). "New eyes were opened in her soul" (312).

Birkin likewise feels "born out of the cramp of a womb" (311). He describes this new birth: "One is delivered over like a naked infant from the womb, all the old defences and the old body gone, a new air around one, that has never been breathed before" (186). But he is aware of the limitation of "his own metaphors" (40) and "weary of having a telling way of putting things" (189). Ursula says to Birkin, "You always seem to think you can *force* the flowers to come out. . . . [Y]ou can't *make* them" (363). There is "always confusion in speech. Yet it must be spoken" (186). He talks about this necessity using the same metaphor of opening:

> [I]f one were to move forwards, one must break a way through. And to know, to give utterance, was to break a way through the walls of the prison, as the infant in labour strives through the walls of the womb. There is no new movement now, without the breaking through of the old body, deliberately, in knowledge, in the struggle to get out. (186)

Language, the "struggle for verbal consciousness" ("Foreword to *WL*" 486) opens the way to the new world. Gerald Doherty points out that the "utterance" above is "the Lawrentian term for apocalyptic annunciations," and maintains that it entails "the leap from the known into the unknown" (57). Birkin's self-consciousness about metaphor expresses Lawrence's own creative perspective. In his review of *Chariot of the Sun* Lawrence asserts that "the essential quality of poetry is that it makes a new effort of attention, and 'discovers' a new world within the known world" (*P* 255). Lawrence seems to be seeking to "open" himself, to escape mental and emotional entrapments, as do his characters in *Women in Love*: "In his terror of chaos [man] begins by putting up an umbrella between himself and the everlasting whirl. . . . Then comes a poet, enemy of convention, and makes a slit in the umbrella; and lo! the glimpse of chaos is a vision, a window to the sun" (*P* 255). This opening, and this alone, is the essential act of attention, the essential poetic and vital act (261).

The characters' development could be viewed as a Jungian initiation or rite of passage: life (consciousness), through a kind of dying (unconsciousness), to a rebirth on a new plane. In Birkin's terms, this is an attainment of true communion, which is the state of star-equilibrium. Although one cannot escape the "dark river of dissolution," one must resolutely choose "the silver river of life, rolling on and quickening all the world to a brightness, on and on to heaven, flowing into a bright eternal sea" (172).

Significantly this river flows to heaven. Lawrence presents and illustrates the way toward star-equilibrium with bird metaphors: Birkin is "like a bird when it comes out of an egg, into a new universe" (312). The egg is cracked, a bird "hop[s] off" "fl[ies] off" (438), and rises "free on the wings of her new condition" (410). The elusive relationship Birkin seeks is a "paradisal bird that could never be netted, it must fly by itself to the heart" (250). Finally a bird is linked to the stars when Ursula "imagined distinctly she could hear the celestial, musical motion of the stars . . . like a bird flying amongst their harmonious motion" (408). She is now "her complete self" (314), ready for a communion. Star-equilibrium—"free proud singleness" and "a definite communion" (254)—signifies "a pure balance of two single beings" (148).

What words seem to achieve may slip away in an instant. But even if words are "but a gesture we make, a dumb show," Ursula is able to feel Birkin's "gesture through her blood" (186). Living relationship "must happen beyond the sound of words." The "paradisal bird" must indeed "fly by itself to the heart" (250). Lawrence's vision of a new world thus potentially embraces star-equilibrium at its center. Mellard argues that the " 'grand images' of the world (as Dufrenne calls them) are out there in the phenomenological universe, but only our language, our figures, our tropes, can capture them for human use" (163).

This metaphysical structure of *Women in Love* is supported, sustained, and reinforced by networks of associated metaphors, concrete and often literal, and also by parallel scenes and parodies. These define the direction and prepare the way toward the central metaphor, star-equilibrium. David Lodge partly explains the necessity of careful preparation and process: "The greater the distance (existentially, conceptually, affectively) between the tenor . . . and vehicle of the metaphor, the more powerful will be the semantic effect of the metaphor, but the greater, also, will be the disturbance to the relationships of contiguity between items in the discourse and therefore the realistic illusion" (112). Lawrence places star-equilibrium in a supportive network. The repeated use of "opening" figures significantly in giving the direction. Characters look up at real stars. Birkin often uses astral metaphors. In the "Mino" chapter, Mino and a female cat play its parody.

A strong sense of self-criticism is also at work as part of the internal creative process of metaphorical thought. Ursula becomes suspicious of Birkin's insistent use of stars as metaphor. Birkin maintains that his ideal of star-equilibrium includes no element of "meeting and mingling" (148), "merging . . . clutching" (200), or "fusion" (309). Ultimately Ursula knows that "she belonged only to the *oneness* with Birkin" (409; my emphasis). Birkin's "Flux of Corruption" letter (383), mockingly read aloud by Halliday in "Gudrun in the Pompadour," expresses Birkin's genuine view of life. As Lawrence says in "Morality and the Novel," "Morality in the novel is the trembling instability of the balance" (*Hardy* 172).

Fiona Becket argues that Lawrence's metaphors and metaphysics are inseparable (67–86). The creation of metaphors is the creation not just of a new conceptual system, but also of new qualities of feeling, a vision that constitutes and prophesies the coming of a New World.

*all*

## NOTES

1. "Star-equilibrium" is a powerful metaphor. The essential feature of metaphor, according to Stephen Ullmann, is that although metaphor is generated by the process of substitution based on similarity, the awareness of difference should not be suppressed. "Similarity must be accompanied by a feeling of disparity; [tenor and vehicle] must belong to different spheres of thought" (214).

Relationship in the human environment and the configuration of the stars are on separate planes. The feeling of wonder and surprise in the linkage makes this a creative metaphor. Humanity looks up at the sky as a model, and the two are bridged. The human mind incorporates the cosmological.

2. Cassirer remarks that "for the mythical imagination there is no separation of a total complex into its elements, but that only a single undivided totality is represented—a totality in which there has been no 'dissociation' of the separate factors of objective perception and subjective feeling" (*The Philosophy of Symbolic Forms* 2:45–46).

3. Mikel Dufrenne argues that a phenomenological apprehension of languages can reverse man's relation to the world: "[T]he world speaks to us; it comes and lets itself be caught in the snare of words; the words that [the world's] grand images wrench from us are full of its presence. And here perhaps we are at the very source that we sought to regain, at that point where the world reveals itself to us, where what is spoken is itself speaking" (96).

## WORKS CITED

Becket, Fiona. *D. H. Lawrence: The Thinker as Poet*. London: Macmillan, 1997.

Cassirer, Ernst. *The Logic of the Humanities*. Translated by Clarence S. Howe. New Haven: Yale University Press, 1961.

———. *The Philosophy of Symbolic Forms*. Translated by Ralph Manheim. Vol. 2 of *Mythical Thought*. New Haven: Yale University Press, 1953.

Doherty, Gerald. "The Art of Leaping: Metaphor Unbound in D. H. Lawrence's *Women in Love*." *Style* 26 (1992): 50–65.

Douglas, Mary. "Pollution." In *Reader in Comparative Religion: An Anthropological Approach*, edited by William A. Lessa and Evon Z. Vogt. New York: Harper & Row, 1972.

Dufrenne, Mikel. *Language and Philosophy*. Translated by Henry B. Veatch. Bloomington: Indiana University Press, 1963.

Edie, James M. *Speaking and Meaning: The Phenomenology of Language*. Bloomington: Indiana University Press, 1976.

Eliot, George. *Middlemarch*. 1872. Reprint, Harmondsworth: Penguin, 1979.

Emerson, Ralph Waldo. *The Collected Works of Ralph Waldo Emerson*. Vol. 1. Edited by Alfred R. Ferguson and Jean Ferguson Carr. Cambridge: Harvard University Press, 1971.

Foucault, Michel. *The Order of Things: An Archaeology of Human Sciences*. New York: Vintage, 1973.

Jakobson, Roman and Morris Halle. "Two Aspects of Language and Two Types of Aphasic Disturbances." *Fundamentals of Language*. The Hague: Mouton, 1956.

Lakoff, George and Mark Johnson. *Metaphors We Live By*. Chicago: University of Chicago Press, 1980.

Lodge, David. *The Modes of Modern Writing: Metaphor, Metonymy, and the Typology of Modern Literature*. Ithaca: Cornell University Press, 1977.

Mellard, James M. *Doing Tropology: Analysis of Narrative Discourse*. Urbana: Illinois University Press, 1987.

Nietzsche, Friedrich. *Philosophy and Truth: Selections from Nietzsche's Notebooks of the Early 1870's*. Translated by Daniel Breazale. Atlantic Highlands, N.J.: Humanities Press, 1990.

Ricoeur, Paul. *The Rule of Metaphor: Multi-disciplinary Studies of the Creation of Meaning in Language*. Translated by Robert Czerny with Kathleen McLaughlin and John Costello. London: Routledge & Kegan Paul, 1986.

Ullmann, Stephen. *Style in the French Novel*. Cambridge: Cambridge University Press, 1957.

White, Hayden V. *Tropics of Discourse: Essays in Cultural Criticism*. Baltimore: Johns Hopkins University Press, 1978.

# *Kangaroo* and the Narrative of Contingency

## Neil Roberts

MOST OF THE NARRATIVES THAT LAWRENCE WROTE BETWEEN 1921 and 1925 are, not surprisingly, dominated by motifs of travel. Having settled (in so far as he ever settled anywhere) in Sicily in 1920 he made a brief but creatively fruitful journey to Sardinia in 1921, traveled to New Mexico via Ceylon and Australia in 1922, visited Mexico twice in 1923 before joining Frieda in England, and returned to New Mexico, Mexico, and New Mexico again in 1924–25. In the course of these travels he wrote *Sea and Sardinia, Kangaroo, Quetzalcoatl, The Boy in the Bush, Mornings in Mexico,* "St. Mawr," "The Princess," "The Woman Who Rode Away," and *The Plumed Serpent.*

Travel functions in these works not only as a theme, but as a structuring principle, and in them Lawrence thinks of travel, and accordingly structures his narratives, in contrasting and perhaps conflicting ways. The experience of travel takes many different forms. When we set off on a journey we may be embarking on no more than a holiday, inspired by random curiosity. On the other hand, our travel may take a more serious form: emigration, quest, or even conquest. These different kinds of travel will generate different narrative structures. A particularly important contrast for this essay is between the kind of narrative, usually purporting to be factual, which tells us what "happens to happen," which in this essay I call the narrative of contingency, and the kind in which events form a coherent, meaningful, and even teleological pattern. I shall be illustrating this contrast with reference to *Sea and Sardinia* and "The Woman Who Rode Away."

*Sea and Sardinia,* written in February 1921, begins with the abrupt statement, "Comes over one an absolute necessity to move," followed by an attempt to account for this experience, and the re-creation of a remarkably subjective process of decision-making:

> Tunis? Africa? Not yet, not yet. Not the Arabs, not yet. Naples,
> Rome, Florence? No good at all. Where then?
> Where then? Spain or Sardinia. Spain or Sardinia. Sardinia, which
> is like nowhere. Sardinia, which has no history, no date, no race, no
> offering. Let it be Sardinia. (*SS* 9)

The impression given is one of the utmost freedom, openness of
horizons, and obedience to the impulse of the moment. Biographical evidence suggests that this is not a gross exaggeration of the
processes by which Lawrence actually made decisions about
travel in the next few years, including the series of decisions
which sent him successively to Ceylon, Australia, New Mexico,
and Mexico. For example, on 11 April 1923, after three weeks in
Mexico City, he wrote to his sister, "I like Mexico better the
longer I stay." Ten days later, from Orizaba, he wrote eight letters and postcards to the effect that he had "had enough" of Mexico and would return to England; on the evening of the same day,
back in Mexico City, he wrote to Amy Lowell, "Here we are, cir-
cling uneasily round, wondering whether we shall settle for a
time, or not," to Edward Marsh, "I suppose I must stay a little
longer over here," and to Kai Götzsche and Knud Merrild, "I'm
*still* going to look for a place here" (*L* iv. 423–30).[1]
In 1922, writing to Thomas Seltzer about his desire to visit
America, Lawrence implies a more considered, historically determined process of decision-making:

> I believe in America one can catch up some kind of emotional impetus
> from the aboriginal Indian and from the aboriginal air and land, that
> will carry one over this crisis of the world's soul depression, into a
> new epoch. (*L* iv. 157)

There is some continuity between the apparently free, impulsive
decision to go to Sardinia and the more settled, reasoned plan to
visit America: they are both expressions of Lawrence's preoccupation with finding an alternative to the Christian, idealistic civilization of Europe. They are also examples of a peculiarly
European attitude to the rest of the world, an attitude that can
be described as imperialist in the sense implied by Terry Goldie
when he writes in "The Representation of the Indigene" that
"imperialist discourse valorizes the colonized according to its
own needs for reflection" (Goldie 233–34)—the dynamic of self
and Other which is perhaps inescapable in such writing. The "aboriginal," whether person or land (and especially when the per-

son is assimilated to the land) is plainly the "Other" of European consciousness in Lawrence's letter, and a less obvious dialectic of Otherness is also at work in the *Sea and Sardinia* passage. Africa represents an extreme of Otherness for which Lawrence is "not yet" ready; the Italian cities, the already known European civilization; Sardinia offers the promise of a European location which is, however, "outside the circuit of civilisation" (*SS* 9). Lawrence does not question that the world, including the various "indigenes" or "aboriginals" that inhabit it, is available for his purposes. However, the narratives that this travel produced, taken as a whole and in all their variety, constitute a much more searching investigation of this attitude.

I want to frame my discussion of *Kangaroo* with a consideration of two contrasting models of travel narrative which I will call "adventure" and "quest." This rather simplified opposition helps illustrate the significance of the contrast between, at one extreme, *Sea and Sardinia* and at the other, "The Woman Who Rode Away." Why compare these texts at all? The obedience to the impulse of the moment that sends Lawrence to Sardinia is quite different from the woman's settled feeling that it is her "destiny to wander into the secret haunts of these timeless, mysterious, marvellous Indians of the mountains" (*WWRA* 42). However, as we have seen, they are linked by the relation they both bear to Lawrence's looking elsewhere in the world for an alternative to European consciousness.

Although Lawrence wrote in a letter shortly before his trip to Sardinia that he was thinking of moving there, little trace of this possibility is discernible in the text of the book. Retrospectively he represents his journey as free and aimless, almost a holiday. No outcome is determined by the shape of the narrative or the nature of the contacts that the traveling protagonist makes. In one respect it is an example of the kind of narrative time that Bakhtin calls "adventure time," which "lies outside biographical time; it changes nothing in the life of the heroes, and introduces nothing into their life. It is, precisely, an extratemporal hiatus between two moments of biographical time" (Bakhtin 90). The characters whom the narrator meets, the incidents that occur and even the landscapes that he passes through are individualized, detailed and above all contingent: they do not contribute to any overarching narrative or symbolic structure. His meetings with the *"girovago"* or the bus driver whom he calls "Mr. Rochester" leave a vivid impression on his imagination but none on his life: he observes and passes on. In "The Woman Who Rode Away," by contrast, the heroine subjects herself, from the beginning, to a fate unknown to her but known to the narrative. She surrenders her freedom in the act of, apparently, asserting it. The landscape through which she passes maps a journey from the "white" world to that of the Chilchuis, which is a journey from one cosmos to another. Nothing is contingent about her meeting with the Indians, and they are not individualized. They are distinguished from one another in accordance with their role in the narrative: the remote, impersonal cacique; the young man who has been to America, speaks Spanish, and interprets between the woman and the cacique with dubious accuracy. Once she has met the Indians her life is changed in the most extreme way.

On the one hand, we have a Western consciousness which moves through the world of the Other, observing and engaging with sympathy and insight but always free to withdraw or move on. On the other hand, a different Western consciousness's commitment to the quest for the Other draws her irretrievably out of her known world, and subjects her to a "destiny" that is determined by the consciousness and historical needs of the indigenes themselves, their desperate attempt to win back the "mastery" (71) that the whites have taken from them. These are the narrative poles that I have called adventure and quest, and the two major novels of the period, *Kangaroo* and *The Plumed Serpent*, enact the conflict between these poles, resolving it, always provisionally, in significantly different ways. Even between *Quetzalcoatl* and *The Plumed Serpent* the balance changes. The early version literally ends with Kate packing a suitcase, more deeply affected than Somers or the Lawrence of *Sea and Sardinia* by her traveling experiences, but ready to move on (*Q* 326). Significantly, in both short story and novel the consciousness that finds itself, to a more or less unambiguous degree, drawn into the quest, is that of a woman. For Lawrence the paradigmatic racial and cultural Other is male, from his celebration of the manliness of the Sardinian peasant to the apotheosis of Cipriano Viedma in *The Plumed Serpent*. The central white protagonist of all his New World narratives is female, and these narratives approach—and *The Plumed Serpent* finally commits itself to—the sexual union of the European and the Other which Lawrence initially found so disturbing.[2] With the exception of *The Escaped Cock, Kangaroo* is the last major Lawrentian narrative with a male protagonist and the last of a series of semi-autobiographical "thought-adventures" that includes *Sons and Lovers*, *Women in Love*, *Aaron's Rod*, and *Mr Noon*.

Most readers of *Sea and Sardinia* would concur with Mark Kinkead-Weekes that it is "one of the most delightful of Lawrence's books" (622). Its humorous self-portrayal, surrender to contingency, and comparative detachment from Lawrence's obsessions make it a book that corresponds very closely to the most enchanted accounts of Lawrence as a person. For the same reasons *Kangaroo*, despite its odd reputation as a blood-dimmed fascist polemic, is one of Lawrence's most delightful novels. The book shares many of the characteristics of the travel narrative, particularly the sense of humor, the even-handed portrayal of the marriage of Somers and Harriett, and the absorption in the passing scene that makes for what I am calling the narrative of contingency. Consider, for example, the way Chapter 10, "Diggers," breaks off from the summary of Jack's account of the political movement:

> They were interrupted by Harriett calling for Somers to come and rescue the tea-towel from the horns of a cow who had calmly scrambled through the fence on to their grass. Somers was used to the cow: she had scrambled through the *Coo-ee* fence long before the Somers had ever walked through the gate, so she looked on them as mild intruders. He was quite friendly with her, she ate the pumpkin rind and apple parings from his hand. Now she looked at him half guiltily out of one eye, the kitchen towel hanging over the other eye. She took it quite calmly, but had a disreputable appearance.
>
> "Come here," said he. "Come here and have it taken off. Of course you had to poke your head through the bush if you thought there was a towel on it." (188)[3]

Consider also the pair of fishing birds, the "parson-looking weed" (189) carrying a gun, the local library, the war memorial, and more details of this kind. Such passages do not function merely as illustrative detail, or even as reality-effect; they do not occupy the background to the "thematic" political or metaphysical discussions. They assert themselves as thematically significant in themselves, they constitute a pressure *against* other tendencies in the novel. This is partly a consequence of the novel's "travel" character; because everything is literally unfamiliar to Lawrence, the smallest, most contingent detail is defamiliarized and fore-grounded. Everything is, he writes, "so clear, so very distinct, and yet so marvellously aloof," and he goes on to specify details whose meaning is their very unfamiliarity:

> And all the miles alongside the road, tin bungalows in their paling fences: and a man on a pony, in a long black overcoat and a cold nose, driving three happy, fleecy cows: long men in jerseys and white ker-chiefs round their necks, à la Buffalo Bill, riding nice slim horses; a woman riding astride top speed on the roadside grass. (275)

The significance of these observations is very different from that of details in Lawrence's English fiction, such as the clothes of the boy in "Odour of Chrysanthemums" made from "cloth that was too thick and hard for the size of his garments" because they were "evidently cut down from a man's clothes" (*PO* 182), or the school windows in *Women in Love* "all open for the holiday" (13), beneath which there is a depth of intimate knowledge and under-standing. The narrators and protagonists of these texts are not traveling observers but men and women who have been formed by the world they describe and inhabit.

This characteristic of *Kangaroo* may also reflect the extraordi-nary rapidity of the novel's composition, and the immediacy of its relation to the Australian experience that prompted it, so that in David Ellis's words it is written "without the benefit of hind-sight" and creates "the illusion that what his protagonists expe-rience is being recorded as it occurs" (42). These passages also function, and partly because of these peculiarities of composition, as resistance to those elements in the novel that do show evidence of forethought and plotting. If Somers's involvement with Jack and Kangaroo seems willed and inauthentic, it is partly because this absorption in the passing scene, and irresponsible delight in it, seem to come so much more naturally to him and to the nar-rator.

Because *Kangaroo* is a novel and not an autobiographical travel narrative like *Sea and Sardinia*, there are of course elements of designed plot structure that are *disguised* as contingent incident. Such is the opening episode when the Somerses are observed on their arrival in New South Wales by a group of men including Jack Calcott, who turns out to be their neighbor and is responsi-ble for drawing Somers into involvement with the Diggers movement. Jack says to Somers, "Your instinct brought you here—and brought you straight up against me. Now that I call fate—" (56). In other words, he represents Somers's journey as akin to the "destiny"-driven quest of "The Woman Who Rode Away." Somers, however, does not find his destiny in Australia; he is free to move on, as we see him doing at the end of the novel despite the threats of Jack and Kangaroo. The whole political plot remains strangely contingent. Somers may be more affected by his "adventures" in Australia than the Lawrence-protagonist by Sardinia, but not greatly: the end effect is of a parenthesis in the protagonist's life, not unlike Bakhtin's "adventure time." The plot that Jack would like to think is Somers's "fate" leads him not to a new discovery but to another version of the Christian-idealistic metaphysic of love that he is in retreat from. Moreover, the political plot has little weight independently of Somers's spasmodic involvement in it: few readers, I imagine, are left at the end wondering about the fate of the Diggers movement after the death of its leader.

At the same time, Somers insistently refers to the dark gods, the symbols of what Australia doesn't satisfy in him, and of what eventually drives him on to America:

> "Now it is time for the spirit to leave us again; it is time for the Son of Man to depart, and leave us dark, in front of the unspoken god: who is just below the dark threshold of the lower self, my lower self." (135)

These references are constant reminders of the search for the Other that will lead to "The Woman Who Rode Away" and *The Plumed Serpent*. Note that "it is time for the Son of Man to depart" anticipates the departure of Christ in favor of Quetzalcoatl. The object of the quest is thematically represented in the novel, but remains separate from the plot: this is one of the many peculiarities of *Kangaroo* as a fictional construct.

Lawrence explicitly foregrounds contingency, and its disintegration of predetermined notions of plot, in the notorious opening of chapter 16:

> To be brief, there was a Harriett, a Kangaroo, a Jack and a Jaz and a Vicky, let alone a number of mere Australians. But you know as well as I do that Harriett is quite happy rubbing her hair with hair-wash and brushing it over her forehead in the sun and looking at the

threads of gold and gun-metal, and the few threads, alas, of silver and tin, with admiration. And Kangaroo has just got a very serious brief, with thousands and thousands of pounds at stake in it. . . . And Jack and Vicky have gone down to her father's for the week-end, and he's out fishing, and has already landed a rock-cod, a leather-jacket, a large schnapper, a rainbow-fish, seven black-fish, and a cuttle fish. So what's wrong with him? While she is trotting over on a pony to have a look at an old sweetheart who is much too young to be neglected. And Jaz is arguing with a man about the freight-rates. And all the scattered Australians are just having a bet on something or other. (284)

The passage goes on—as some readers of *Women in Love* do, for example—to complain that "We can't be at a stretch of tension *all* the time" and, in the aggressively self-conscious manner developed in *Mr Noon*, "If you don't like the novel, don't read it." David Ellis is probably right to refuse to get excited about the apparently "modernist" character of passages such as this, but I would not agree with him that this is "an aberration in the work as a whole" (40–41). Lawrence's willingness to be explicit about the breakdown of the novel's plot and his inability to drive the characters through a structured narrative is an extreme case of the thematic importance of contingency. Note that his apparent pretense that the characters are real people obstinately going their own ways is only playful. What is really at issue, as the reference to novel-writing makes plain, is his imaginative tendency in this novel to privilege contingency and his inability to keep up an interest in the plot. This device is comparable to the break at the beginning of chapter 4 of *Fantasia of the Unconscious*, where Lawrence exclaims, "Oh, damn the miserable baby with its complicated ping-pong table of an unconscious" (*FU* 37), and focuses his attention on the trees among which he is writing.

In Somers's view Australian life is temporally inconsecutive and geographically unintegrated with the land on which it takes place. He likes the *Sydney Bulletin*'s "Bits" because "It was the momentaneous life of the continent. There was no consecutive thread. Only the laconic courage of experience" (272). He sees Sydney itself as unreal, "sprinkled on the surface of a darkness into which it never penetrated" (13). This is echoed in his first American essay, "Indians and an Englishman," in which he describes the American West as "like a stage to me, and not like the proper world" (*P* 92). In America, however, he is not charmed by this superficiality, perhaps because he had more invested in his visit to that country.

Harriett, in a remark with which neither Somers nor Lawrence seems to disagree, thinks Australia "feels as if no-one had ever loved it" (77). Somers asserts in the same conversation that "somebody will have to water Australia with their blood before it is a real man's country" (78)—a cliché that Lawrence himself utters, in a letter from Thirroul, the "Mullumbimby" of the novel: "generation after generation must people it with ghosts, and catastrophes water it with blood, before it will come alive with a new day of its own" (*L* iv. 273). Near the end of the novel the narrator maintains that Australia "is the land that as yet has made no great mistake, humanly" (347). Nothing in the novel contradicts this view of Australia as a land without history, or more strictly without a human past, the most extreme of colonialist illusions. It suggests that Lawrence was unaware of the genocidal history of contact between whites and blacks.[4] Contrast this with his assertion in "America, Listen to Your Own," two years before he visited America, that its inhabitants must "catch the pulse of the life which Cortés and Columbus murdered" (*P* 90). We have seen that he described Sardinia as a land with "no history." There, however, he meant that the country had resisted the forces—essentially imperialist—that had shaped "the circuit of [European] civilisation": "They say neither Romans nor Phoenicians, Greeks nor Arabs ever subdued Sardinia" (*SS* 9). After all, as Derek Walcott has argued, history itself may be a problematic concept for the colonized subject.[5] Lawrence is not saying that Sardinia does not have an indigenous people with a past. But that appears to be exactly what he is saying about Australia.

In the letter to Seltzer quoted earlier, about his projected visit to America, Lawrence spoke of "the aboriginal Indian" and "the aboriginal air and land." This phrasing tends to assimilate Aboriginal people to the land, rather than represent them as subjects who have a culturally specific relationship with it. This is more strongly marked in most of the uses of the word "aboriginal" and its cognates in *Kangaroo*. In the novel Lawrence describes "tree-trunks like naked pale aborigines" (14) and cliffs that "looked as silent and as aboriginal as if white men had never come" (60); Somers imagines being "alone with a long, wide shore and land, heartless, soulless. As alone and as absent and as present as an aboriginal dark on the sand in the sun" (332). The only point at which an individual Aborigine emerges from this identification with the landscape is, ironically, in the archly narrated anecdote from the *Sydney Bulletin* about a mixed marriage (271). In the most interesting of these passages, Lawrence appears momentarily to acknowledge that Australia has been experienced by people other than white settlers:

> The strange, as it were *invisible* beauty of Australia, which is undeniably there, but which seems to lurk just beyond the range of our white vision. You feel you can't *see*—as if your eyes hadn't the vision in them to correspond with the outside landscape. For the landscape is so unimpressive, like a face with little or no features, a dark face. It is so aboriginal, out of our ken, and it hangs back so aloof. Somers always felt he looked at it through a cleft in the atmosphere; as one looks at one of the ugly faced, distorted aborigines with his wonderful dark eyes that have such an incomprehensible ancient shine in them, across gulfs of unbridged centuries. (77)

The phrase "beyond the range of our white vision" implies another vision that might be able to see this "invisible" beauty. This possibility recedes when the landscape is yet again *identified* with the Aborigine, especially when it is described as a *featureless* "dark face." In the last sentence, which is the most substantial evocation of an Aboriginal person in Lawrence's own words, the featureless Aborigine suddenly has "wonderful dark eyes," the very eyes, one might think, for seeing beyond "our white vision." However, these are not represented as eyes that someone looks through or with: they are eyes "*one looks at*," objects of the very "white vision" that fails to see Australia.

Sartre, in his discussion of Otherness in *Being and Nothingness*, sets out to theorize the Other not merely as an object but as another subject. Central to this concern is "my permanent possibility of *being seen* by the Other" (Sartre 256). So important is this point that he goes as far as to say that "If I apprehend the look, I cease to perceive the eyes" (258). Apprehension of the Other as subject is incompatible with seeing his eyes as objects. In Sardinia Lawrence claimed to see "eyes of soft, blank darkness, all velvet, with no imp looking out of them" (*SS* 67). Sardinians, individually and collectively, feature infinitely more strongly in Lawrence's writing than Aborigines, but one can see here a common predisposition to see the eyes of the Other as objects.

Aborigines are invariably, if predictably, associated with darkness, and therefore might be said to occupy the same symbolic space as Somers's "dark Gods." But these two darknesses are never brought into explicit relation to each other. The scattered references to the "aboriginal" on which I have dwelt really signify an absence in the text. The role of the aboriginal Other, that is taken by the Sardinian peasants in *Sea and Sardinia*, is in this text displaced onto the Celts and particularly the Cornish. In the analeptic "Nightmare" chapter Lawrence writes, "The old Celtic countries have never had our Latin-teutonic consciousness, never will have." Only in Cornwall is Somers able to "drift into a sort of blood-darkness, to feel in his blood the thrills and presences of the old moorland dusk, to take up in his veins again the savage vibrations that still lingered round the secret rocks, the place of the pre-christian human sacrifice" (238). He calls on the Tuatha De Danaan (226), which a few years earlier, in the poem "Mutilation" he had identified with the dark Gods—"Night folk, Tuatha De Danaan, dark Gods, govern her sleep" (*Poems* 213)—the first instance, according to L. D. Clark, of "dark Gods" in Lawrence's writing (Clark 45).

This absence, moreover, is necessary to the text's very existence. If Lawrence, looking for "an emotional impetus from the aboriginal Indian" of America, had become interested in native Australians, can we imagine him wanting to write about Kangaroo and Jack Calcott? This is not an attack on the novel or its author; the circumstances of Lawrence's life in Australia sufficiently account for his ignorance of Aborigine culture, though not perhaps for the apparent unconsciousness with which he reveals it. More relevantly, the very pleasures of the narrative of contingency, the novel's freedom of spirit and delight in the passing scene, may also depend on this absence. In *The Plumed Serpent* we see these qualities fighting a losing battle against a quest narrative in which the history, religion, and dark vision of a native people assert themselves with a vengeance. These alternative visions, and his hesitations between them, are his unique contribution to the literature of imperialism.

## NOTES

1. See Bynner 37–39 for Lawrence's extraordinary reaction to Orizaba, declaring on the station platform that it was an evil place, which presumably has a bearing on these changes.

2. See Ellis, *Dying Game* 60, for Lawrence's "hostility to miscegenation" and his discomfort on meeting Mabel Sterne and Tony Luhan.

3. Consider also the conversation between Somers and Jack in chapter 5, "Coo-ee" (88 ff.), where Somers is forced by the sound of the waves to "yell" his replies, reinforcing the sense of something willed in his involvement. Conversations in *The Rainbow* or *Women in Love* are never ironized by contingency in this way.

4. "The estimated number of persons of predominantly Aboriginal descent declined from about 180,000 in 1861 to less than 95,000 in 1901. In accordance with contemporary ideas of racial superiority, many Europeans believed that the Aborigines must die out, and they acted in such a way as to ensure that outcome" (*Encyclopedia Britannica CD 98 Multimedia Edition*: "Australia: HISTORY: Australia to 1900: SEVERAL SMALL DEMOCRACIES: 1860 to 1900: The Aborigines").

5. "In the New World servitude to the muse of history has produced a literature of recrimination and despair, a literature of revenge written by the descendants of slaves or a literature of remorse written by the descendants of masters. . . . The truly tough aesthetic of the New World neither explains nor forgives history. It refuses to recognize it as a creative or culpable force" (37).

## WORKS CITED

Bakhtin, M. M. "Forms of Time and of the Chronotope in the Novel."In *The Dialogic Imagination: Four Essays*. Edited by Michael Holquist, translated by Caryl Emerson and Michael Holquist. Austin: University of Texas Press, 1981.

Bynner, Witter. *Journey With Genius: Recollections and Reflections Concerning the D. H. Lawrences*. New York: John Day, 1951.

Clark, L. D. *The Minoan Distance: The Symbolism of Travel in D. H. Lawrence*. Tucson: University of Arizona Press, 1980.

Ellis, David. *D. H. Lawrence: Dying Game 1922–1930*. Cambridge: Cambridge University Press, 1998.

Goldie, Terry. "The Representation of the Indigene." In *The Post-Colonial Studies Reader*, edited by Bill Ashcroft, Gareth Griffiths, and Helen Tiffin. London: Routledge, 1995.

Kinkead-Weekes, Mark. *D. H. Lawrence: Triumph to Exile 1912–1922*. Cambridge: Cambridge University Press, 1996.

Sartre, Jean-Paul. *Being and Nothingness: An Essay on Phenomenological Ontology*. Translated by Hazel E. Barnes. 1943. Reprint, London: Methuen, 1958.

Walcott, Derek. *What the Twilight Says: Essays*. London: Faber, 1998.

# Mexican Cypresses: Multiculturalism in Lawrence's "Novel of America"

## Virginia Hyde

They say the fit survive,
But I invoke the spirits of the lost.
Those that have not survived, the darkly lost,
To bring their meaning back into life again
Which they have taken away
And wrapt inviolable in soft cypress-trees,
Etruscan cypresses.

Evil, what is evil?
There is only one evil, to deny life
As Rome denied Etruria
And mechanical America Montezuma still.

"Cypresses," *Poems* 298

## I

THIS QUOTATION FROM "CYPRESSES" (WRITTEN IN ITALY IN 1920) DEM-
onstrates that, even before coming to America in 1922, D. H.
Lawrence thought of the Mexican people, as he did of the Etruscans, as a "colonized" populace—in this case, dominated by a
powerful American neighbor. Spain's literal colonization was also
in his mind. These associations emerge again in *The Plumed Serpent* (1926), perhaps especially the first version *Quetzalcoatl*,
which was published for the first time in 1995 (edited by Louis L.
Martz).[1] A deep recognition of the "lost" is part of Lawrence's
more general theme of the subjection of native America by all en-
croaching forces; it counterpoints the novel's more famous
themes of hierarchy and dominance. This "underside" of the
text, although little recognized in criticism of *The Plumed Ser-*

*pent*, echoes a longstanding idea in his work. In 1919, for example, Lawrence states, "The Aztec lives unappeased and destructive within the Mexican, the Red Indian lives unappeased and inwardly destructive in the American," adding that "a new race" can arise only when "the soul of the dead red man will be at one with the soul of the living white man" (*TSM* 80–81). Continuing this theme with a female protagonist is his "real novel of America" (*L* iv. 457)—as he called the book that became *The Plumed Serpent*.

In this text, views of rebirth and reconciliation are embodied in tree imagery, which, asserting perennial plant growth in the face of monolithic power, links both versions of the novel with the earlier "Cypresses" and the later *Etruscan Places* (1932). In the latter, Lawrence again implies a comparison between Etruscans and ancient Americans, and he employs a similar motif of vegetation for the tender life that will always "rise again" despite "brute force" (*SEP* 36). It is a matter, he adds, of "the endless patience of life," that is "always putting forth a flower," in contest with "the endless triumph of force" (129). Etruscans (like the people of "aboriginal America" and other primordial cultures) had a sense of the "myriad vitalities" of the cosmos (57); they were incorporate with the "tree of life," receiving "quick powers" that "run up the feet and legs" from the earth (165).

In *The Plumed Serpent*, the plant image even delineates the "human family" on the "Tree of Life," which can communicate within an atemporal dimension, a repository for "the soul" of the human race;[2] here "even the trees come and go" in cycles of recurrence, serving as emblems of diverse peoples (*PS* 126). The novel's Mexican cypresses form a case in point. As Sandra Gilbert points out in her discussion of the poem "Cypresses," the cypress is "traditionally the death tree," thus "dark" but "immortal" (343). The name of Cipriano, the Indian general who is a main character in both *Quetzalcoatl* and *The Plumed Serpent*, may owe something, linguistically and even conceptually, to the word cypress (a sprig of greenery used in mourning to suggest rebirth). When Cipriano assumes his role as Huitzilopochtli—both a war god and a tribal guardian to the Aztec people—he is said to hold "the black leaves of death mingled with the green leaves of life renewed" (*Q* 266). Lawrence knew, too, that some Pueblo Indian dances feature evergreen sprigs, used like cypress to betoken fertility and resurrection of the plants,[3] and the eventual characterization of Cipriano may draw upon this mythology just as the final novel incorporates recurrent elements of North American dances. His nature is greatly complicated by instances of *machismo*, but in the broadest sense he represents the resurgence of an old race, older even than the Aztec.

While editing D. H. Lawrence's *Mornings in Mexico* and his essays on Native Americans,[4] with the rich evolution of multicultural themes they contain, I have been continually reminded how much American Studies—and the contemporary classroom with its emphasis on diversity—should gain from Lawrence. Mark Kinkead-Weekes, writing about one of the short American fictions, states that Lawrence is the only major English novelist of his time "who tries seriously to imagine under the skin" of indigenous culture and religion (254).[5] Yet *The Plumed Serpent*—which might be expected to contribute most to such a study—has been dogged for many years by charges of authoritarianism, even proto-fascism, and misogyny. It was a particular casualty of the inevitable revulsion from European fascism in the 1930s and 1940s—although Lawrence firmly condemned fascism—and of criticism in the first wave of the women's movement in the 1970s. As L. D. Clark has said, "one has to make such damaging admissions" about Lawrence "as would convict a lesser man" (*Dark Night* 3), and this is especially true on the subjects of race, class, and gender.

Nonetheless, the publication of *Quetzalcoatl*, more than seventy years after its creation, brings new readers with fresh eyes to this version. It should also lead us to revisit the finished novel, for the two go best hand in hand, serving as complements to each other. *Quetzalcoatl* is unambiguously outspoken against fascism. Despite Cipriano's own military position, he calls fascism a "great bully movement," stating, "Fascism won't hold against the lust for anarchy which is at the bottom of the Fascisti themselves" (*Q* 248). *Quetzalcoatl* also presents one of the least dominated female characters in Lawrence; unfortunately, it leaves her with strong feelings that she can never accept "the gulf of race, of colour" separating her from Cipriano (*Q* 312). *The Plumed Serpent* follows her in her acceptance of the racial "other," marrying Cipriano, and furthers her significant confrontation with classes outside her own. Each version contains, therefore, important attitudes that few contemporary readers will want to relinquish.

In fact, postmodern, postcolonial, and multicultural readings promise to do justice at last to this controversial novel in one or more versions. Joyce Wexler finds that, "when postmodern criteria are applied, . . . works such as . . . *The Plumed Serpent* acquire new eminence in a Lawrence canon" (61), and Gerald Doherty finds this novel fertile for his contemporary approach to Lawrence's "one vast hermeneutic sentence" (1139–41).[6] The relation of Lawrence's postmodern touch to his multiculturalism is particularly significant. Fiona Becket notes that he challenges the *status quo* by adverting to "non-European" figures and situations: "The extent of that challenge, and its relation to Lawrence's thinking on complex kinds of otherness, can only usefully be ascertained by examining the representations of European and non-European identities in the fiction and discursive writing post-*Women in Love* (perhaps *The Plumed Serpent*)" (201). Non-European readings of *The Plumed Serpent* are especially noteworthy, particularly Nak-chung Paik's discussion of its pertinence to indigenous "Third World revolutions in our time" (204).[7] David Ellis, in the third volume of the Cambridge Lawrence biography, *Dying Game* (1998), uses both versions when pointing to new interpretations, stating that this work is "firmly anti-colonial in its attitude to the effects on the Indian population of the Spanish Conquest," and, as such, is a beneficiary of today's interest in colonial and postcolonial studies (219). And feminist criticism of *The Plumed Serpent* has shifted in many cases—for example, from Kate Millett's scathing interpretation in 1969 to Marianna Torgovnick's more recent judgment that "we can modify the anger in Millett's critique to a new understanding of . . . Lawrence" (168).

Particularly helpful is the expanding recognition that Lawrence's important theoretical statements on dialogical functions of the novel as a genre belong to the months when he was revising *The Plumed Serpent*, that the Mexican novel is more polyphonic than we have supposed—not simply monophonic as David Lodge once suggested (100)—and that its multiple stances represent not just a formal device but an approach to multiculturism (Hyde and Clark 140–44; Hyde, Introduction to *PS* xxx).[8] Plural viewpoints, and plural versions of his texts, are part of Lawrence's dynamic method of thought and dialogue throughout his career, but it is in 1925 that he most directly voices the critical view that has some affinities with Bakhtin's. Thus Lawrence's impulse to include the "lost" and unrepresented is, not surprisingly, evident in some fiction of the American period.

Lawrence's commitment is proclaimed in the very name *Quetzalcoatl*, now the title of the first version but also Lawrence's preference for his final Mexican novel: in 1925 he argued with the publisher Alfred A. Knopf against the anglicized title *The Plumed Serpent* (*L* v. 250, 254, 320). The novel brings together the early Mesoamerican god and culture-hero Quetzalcoatl, the Aztec tutelary deity Huitzilopochtli, and the Tabascan-Aztec Malintzi, combining Marina the mistress of Hernán Cortés with divinities like Malinalxochitl and Chalchiuhtlicue (Clark and Hyde, appendix 1 of *PS* 447–48; Hyde, "Kate and the Goddess"). This Mexican pantheon is to manifest itself through three characters, Ramón, Cipriano, and Kate. The central use of such mythology was unusual in its time, and Lawrence's critics have often continued to find it exotic and even bizarre. In fact, however, Arnold Odio has shown that *The Plumed Serpent* was a forerunner in the Spanish American novel's shift from an *"indianista"* tradition—dominated by European styles and worldview—to a new vehicle that valorizes indigenous myth (172).[9]

*Quetzalcoatl* (written in 1923), can be seen as the wellspring of several important directions that Lawrence's work took increasingly in America and later. It departs from the previous "leadership" works by introducing a woman, Kate, as the principal "viewpoint" character, and she continues as such into *The Plumed Serpent* (written in 1924 and early 1925). *Quetzalcoatl* begins Lawrence's return to his old theme of romance and courtship, which will be furthered (and greatly complicated) in *The Plumed Serpent* and *Lady Chatterley's Lover* (1928). It also introduces Mexican and Indian characters who are not simply incidental figures. Kate is a delightfully individual creation, being placed in both versions in a dialogical pattern, countering and modulating the views of her male companions as surely as Ursula does Birkin's in *Women in Love* (1920). It is quite possible to see the first Kate as a more independent woman than the second because she retains her freedom, rejecting sex and marriage altogether and lacking a binding commitment to Mexico. The second Kate is often seen as submissive, yet she has also been called the stronger of the two women for welcoming diversity and for taking an active part in the Mexican movement (VanHoosier-Carey 104–18). Margaret Storch, while acknowledging the "anti-colonialism" by which Lawrence privileges the "dark non-dominant culture," believes that this theme is, however, linked to one of dominance by the "non-Western male" (54). Linda Ruth Williams states, too, that Lawrence's "racial redistribution of power" becomes "sexually weighted" when Kate, as representative of Europe, accepts the new Mexican dispensation (104). I have made the case myself for a strictly patriarchal aspect of *The Plumed Serpent* (*The Risen Adam* 173–206),[10] but the long-standing concern with sexual patterns in this novel should not deflect us from observing Lawrence's achievement in re-imaging race relations.

It should go without saying that he had none of what we call "political correctness." But he had the gift of writing beyond himself; of transcending, in his best fiction, his own biases; of being a good candidate for his own advice: "Never trust the artist. Trust the tale" (*SCAL* 2). His ten-year preoccupation with native America went through an unsteady arc from idealization to disillusionment with real-life conditions—the old culture eroded by modernization—and back again to the visionary evocation of a New World Atlantis in the final pages not of *Quetzalcoatl* but of *The Plumed Serpent*.

## II

In the second chapter of both versions of the novel, Kate visits an elderly American archaeologist, Mrs. Norris, who has lived for many years in a house dating back to the Spanish Conquest. This building, full of dusty and inert archaeological objects, is described as a "tomb of dead Conquistadores" with "the Aztec cypresses rearing dark and enormous above it" (*Q* 16). From Lawrence's poem "Cypresses" we know that the spirits of Etruscans waited in those Italian cypresses despite their defeat by the Romans, ready to rear up in the face of seemingly prevailing materialism and insentience. They bespeak a "great secret," a message from "a dead, dead race," still seeking articulation though the "tongues are dead" (*Poems* 296–97). In *Aaron's Rod* (1922), in the same Tuscan countryside, Aaron Sisson too finds Etruscan cypresses "communicating" with mysterious "inflection" and, "like ghosts," recalling "lost races, lost language, lost human ways of feeling and of knowing" (265). He even sees the trees "as it were walking," echoing a Biblical description of "men as trees, walking" (Mark 8:24). The passage in the Bible presents the perception of a blind man who, upon regaining his sight, sees people moving about; and Lawrence, too, is referring to the return of a lost faculty—a lost way of consciousness—that may put a new world in motion. In the essay "America, Listen to Your Own," written in Italy in precisely the same period as the poem "Cypresses" and the *Aaron's Rod* passage, Lawrence hails not "mechanical" America but the still viable native America, urging Americans to "pick up the life-thread" from "the Red Indian, the Aztec, the Maya, the Incas" (*P* 90). In the Foreword to *Fantasia of the Unconscious* (1922), too, he names "Amerindians" with Etruscans and others as adepts in ancient ways of communicating wisdom through "ritual, gesture, and myth-story" (55). The voices for Americans to "listen to" are thus linked through a network of texts to the phantom speech from the Etruscan cypresses.

Similarly, then, the cypresses beside Mrs. Norris's home harbor the surviving spirits of the Aztecs. Likened to a museum, her house is based on the historic home of "one of the boldest of the conquistadores" with Cortés, Pedro de Alvarado (Clark, *Dark Night* 28); in this chapter, the house is like a model of the Mexican power structure, suspended through the ages. Mrs. Norris, having "rooted among Aztec remains so long" (*Q* 16, 17), is further described as looking "like one of the Conquistadores followed by a quiet, mocking Indian chief" (*Q* 20). In *The Plumed Serpent*, the visit to Mrs. Norris is preceded by a look at the lost Aztecs' living avatars in the streets: downtrodden men with "blackened faces" and "bare, blackened legs," women with "strong, dark-brown arms," a horseman, vendors selling fruit (*PS* 31–32). Kate has just been thinking how poorly the leaders of countries, even in post-revolutionary time, "save the people, in Mexico and elsewhere" (*PS* 31). Lawrence is conflating all the conquerors together, condemning famous patriots and tyrants alike in his opposition to merely political solutions. At the same time, he juxtaposes the living Mexican people with their dead ancestors. No doubt this method is part of what Peter Scheckner means when he says that, even in the "leadership" works, we overhear "the great background sounds of the multitudes" along with a sense of "warning to the ruling classes" (136).

Lawrence is well aware that history is created by conquerors. In "Cypresses," the "evil-yclept Etruscan" is known to history by the claims of the dominant Romans (*Poems* 297); and in *Etruscan*

*Places*, too, Lawrence associates these Roman masters with "brute force and overbearing" (*SEP* 36). Writing in opposition to Mussolini, he finds "the Roman salute unbecoming, and the Roman Imperium unmentionable" in a place where Etruscans had so long resisted Rome (*SEP* 158). Although Ramón's neo-Aztec "salute" moves the Mexican people to national pride in *The Plumed Serpent*, Lawrence is not without a sense of the irony and danger attending such a revival. He had generally idealized Montezuma before coming to America (*TSM* 23; "America, Listen to Your Own"), but he came to dislike what he heard about his human sacrifices and preferred "the older Indians, who knew [Quetzalcoatl] before the Aztecs raised their deities to heights of horror and vindictiveness" (*PS* 58). In final excisions from the text, Lawrence had even commented that "the life-hope was dead, there was an instinct of death-worship in the Aztecs" when they sacrificed at the temple of Huitzilopochtli (*PS* 509–10). Ambivalently, however, he still liked the image of delicate nobility he had originally attached to Montezuma and even considered writing a play about him while working on the final *Plumed Serpent* (*L* v. 174). Thus the novel's adaptation of the Aztec motif is conflicted and far from simplistic, but this in itself turns out to increase its eclecticism.

Lawrence's shifting attitude toward Montezuma does not mean a rejection of ancient Indian cultures. In "The Hopi Snake Dance," for instance, he praises a primordial tradition he attributes to the Pueblos: "In Mexico, men fell into horror of the crude, pristine gods, the dragons. But to the pueblo Indian, the most terrible dragon is still somewhat gentle-hearted" (*MM* 145). He soon broadens Cipriano's ethnic significance in *The Plumed Serpent*, making him a Zapotec Indian, from a tribe whose culture dates back before Christ (and before Aztec dominance). Lawrence further relates how Cipriano has learned to dance among the Indian villages of the American Southwest. Teaching his troops this form of ceremony—"the dance which has meaning"—Cipriano becomes something of a spokesman for the "old Indians of the north" who, as Lawrence puts it, still possess an age-old "secret" of animistic ritual, of physical and spiritual discipline (*PS* 364). Lawrence had not seen the dances in the state of Oaxaca (the Zapotec home), which might have served quite well as sources, for they were suspended in his time (Parmenter 222)[11]; and the text therefore depends on the presentations he knew in New Mexico and Arizona. Nonetheless, he enlarges the provenance of such meaningful performance in *The Plumed Serpent* by asserting that it is actually "the dance of the Aztecs and Zapotecs and the Huicholes, just the same in essence, indigenous to America" (*PS* 348).

The *Plumed Serpent* Cipriano once expresses national pride in the name Montezuma (*PS* 361), but he has already been warned in *Quetzalcoatl* to avoid the mistakes of the Aztec gods and to be a new Huitzilopochtli who "has learned a great deal" (*Q* 127). It is therefore the more surprising that *The Plumed Serpent* goes too far for most readers with a parallel to past violence—an execution by Cipriano. Even though the plot seems to grope for some newly innocuous form of sacrifice—the victims are condemned criminals—it fails to naturalize this scene into the novel's larger fabric and only raises troubling issues that are never resolved. It is intriguing to realize that Lawrence was creating two Zapotec characters in the same period—one a militant figure and the other—the Lawrences' servant in "The Mozo"—a peace-loving boy who had fled military conscription by the revolutionary forces that had overrun his real-life village. In the essay, written in 1924 and early 1925, Lawrence clearly identifies with the boy in his "blank kind of horror" at seeing soldiers take a "blanched prisoner"; and behind the horror is his people's recollection of capture when—and even before—"Montezuma marched his prisoners to sacrifice" (*MM* 76). Thus Lawrence names Montezuma himself as one of the conquerors of the tender shoots of life. But he sides firmly against the Spanish conquerors and the American entrepreneurs.

As Ramón tells Kate in *Quetzalcoatl*, the Indians of America are "lying low" but form "a tree" that still lives (like the cypresses), and "from the roots we grow up, up, as far as the sap will carry us" (*Q* 48). Later hymns in both versions do not simply consist of meaningless repetition (as is often charged) but take up this important motif, among others. "We are like trees, the tall and rustling / Mexican men," says one song in the first version (*Q* 238), and *The Plumed Serpent* gives more detail: "Quetzalcoatl loves the shade of trees. / . . . Call back the trees! / We are like trees, tall and rustling. / *Quetzalcoatl is among the trees*" (*PS* 349–50; Lawrence's emphasis). Indeed, Ramón has already explained the full import of this growth of trees:

"And to me, the men in Mexico are like trees, forests that the white men felled in their coming. . . . And each new shoot that comes up overthrows a Spanish church or an American factory. And soon the dark forest will rise again, and shake the Spanish buildings from the face of America." (*PS* 80)

In one of the "written hymns," the god Quetzalcoatl is represented looking down at Mexico: "There are dead that sit under the trees," he says, "watching with ash-grey eyes" (*PS* 258).[12]

As agents of potential "earthquake" as well as growth, the roots represent change that comes from below, upward from the populace and not simply downward from a hierarchical source. The further value of an "upwards" force is indicated in *Quetzalcoatl* when Ramón refers to vital existence in terms of a tree: "Life is still a tree, Señora," he tells Kate, and "will rise from the roots only," not "descend from above, out of words or aeroplanes . . . or thin air" because "the human blood sends up the tree of life" whereas the mind is "only a flowering on the tree" (*Q* 48). One way of viewing this concept is as an aspect of "spirit of place," which becomes incarnate in its people, linking them with the dead ancestors who have shared their particular geography. Thus race can be seen as part of a populist stance in Lawrence, as Williams recognizes when she states that *The Plumed Serpent* and other works of this period show the "strong relationship" between subject, land, and culture, "which Lawrence saw as most authentically lived by the Indian civilizations of southwest America and Mexico" (104). In "Cypresses," the tree roots probe "the deeps," where they merge with frankincense and myrrh (*Poems* 298), both suggesting not only the grave but also nativity; and in funerary art in *Etruscan Places*, the underearth, paradoxically, yields life-force by expressing a "pulse" that continues in Italian art and lifestyle (*SEP* 36, 129, 166). Similarly, the Mexican future needs its own deep-rootedness. When Ramón acknowledges Kate's charge that the Mexican "people pull you down like a great weight," he defends them, suggesting that they do so "as the earth draws down the roots of a tree," preparing for a flourishing of renewed growth "back to the sky" (*PS* 80).

Martz finds the novel's local or popular aspect more pronounced in the first version, partly because its Quetzalcoatl songs seem to arise spontaneously from workers rather than from Don Ramón as national artist ("Two Versions" 163–70; *Q* xiii–xix).

This may be true of the songs, but other aspects of the movement have bases among the common people in both versions. For example, a man (in one case a stranger, in one a boatman) gives Kate "ollicitas" (or "ollita[s]") from under the water where these prehistoric potteries—"cooking-pot[s]" of the gods—have been part of local myth and discovery over the centuries (*Q* 58–61; *PS* 94–95), representing an "underground" heritage. *The Plumed Serpent* actually proliferates the number of common people in its expanded cast of characters. Despite Kate's aristocratic lineage, her strong sense of self-worth, and even her "godhood" in the later novel, she is affected progressively by claims of kinship from the servant Juana (Felipa in *Quetzalcoatl*), from the boatmen with whom she shares a "communion of grace" (*PS* 107), from the unnamed man who dances with her in the plaza, from the aguador, from the masses who insist, "*Blood is one blood. We are all of one blood-stream*" (*PS* 416; Lawrence's emphasis). Sandra Gilbert, too, has seen this plea as one to "our common humanity, the great, sacred community in which we have an existence" beyond ourselves (198). Kate thinks of it as a "primeval oneness" (*PS* 417).[13]

## III

Such passages as the one I have quoted about the Mexican cypresses show why *The Plumed Serpent* profits from today's interest in post-colonial studies, as Ellis says. Although some of its views seem far removed from such ideology, some are not at all removed—and may have caused the finished novel to suffer not only for its illiberal side but also for the opposite, for its pioneering probe, for example, of interracial marriage. In other contexts, *Quetzalcoatl* contains some of Lawrence's most effective statements against oppression. No postcolonialist could wish to alter much in this assertion: "Mexico the treasure-house of the world, and the peons [were] used as nothing more than spades to dig the treasure out, for four centuries" (*Q* 113–14). In the white man's endeavor "to overwhelm and convert the dark man" to the white way of life, "the white man has lost his own soul, collapsed upon himself" (*Q* 44). While repeating some of these expressions, *The Plumed Serpent* also originates some barbs, often in Kate's mind, about "nasty whiteness" and states that "the white man, let him bluster as he may, is hollow with misgiving about his own supremacy" (*PS* 47, 148).

Lawrence's Mexican novel reveals its interest in race in many subtle references to color. In both versions, Mrs. Norris, even though she has spent her life on cross-cultural studies, proves to oppose the mixing of colors—in her flowers. She pushes the magenta blossoms of one plant "away from the rust-scarlet bell-flower," lamenting, "I have such a time trying to keep these [reds] apart" (*PS* 39; *Q* 18–19). Another speaker, insisting that jade must always be green, is displeased to hear that "there's jade of every imaginable tint," including white, rose, lavender, green, and black (*Q* 25). In *The Plumed Serpent*, an additional conversation centers explicitly on racial intermarriage, the characters representing different points of view. When one speaker deplores this practice and blames Mexico's problems on it, Kate speaks up: "Some people believe in the mixed blood" and think it is "better," she tells him (*PS* 66). (In *Quetzalcoatl* it is Kate herself who "understood why half-breeds were usually all half souled and half unnatural" [*Q* 215].) Ramón and his men form a rainbow when they meet together: "Some were of a dark, ruddy coffee-brown, two were white, Ramón was of a soft creamy brown" (*PS* 175). Then there is the parable which Kate tells, attributing it to the local people: when the Lord was creating humans, he didn't bake his first clay figures long enough and they turned out white and doughy; he burned the next batch, which emerged quite dark; but the third was his favorite, a deep brown color: "*They're just right!* said the Lord" (*PS* 47; Lawrence's emphasis). This parable, which compliments the appearance of many Mexicans, appears only in the novel's final version.

But so does Ramón's expanded discussion of the tree of life as a structure with exclusionary characteristics, casting each nationality onto a rather skewed paradigm of the tree metaphor already mentioned. This is one of the most controversial passages in *The Plumed Serpent*. Although "the Tree of Life is one tree," he pontificates, "the races of the earth are like trees, in the end they neither mix nor mingle" except in their utmost flowers, as "Natural Aristocrats" meet (*PS* 249, 248). We are all well aware that Ramón himself assumes such supposed ascendancy, and this is one reason why *The Plumed Serpent* has incurred a charge of proto-fascism—which Ellis, however, calls "inaccurate and unfair" (218). Although Ramón's claim of the singularity of the branches is one of the rationales for a neo-Aztec religion in Mexico, instead of a European one, the passage is generally glossed for its more problematic leadership implications. But Ramón's elitist theory of this tree of life is not quite the same as Kate's ultimate experience of it (or even his). She is not identical with him in the dialogical pattern, and her story moves her toward "an immediate contact" not only with Cipriano but also with "all these men and all these women," including the servants and people in the street (*PS* 417). Since such passages often come late in *The Plumed Serpent*, readers can easily fail to notice them.

Already in the first version of the novel, Kate is drawn to a "strange soft flame of life-courage" in the Mexican Indians (*Q* 44), and, in *The Plumed Serpent*, she shares her author's increased knowledge of them. Early in her visit to Mexico City, she refuses to admire mural art that depicts the people in caricatures. In fact, she charges the guide, "*You* aren't Mexico" because he is "full of European ideas" (*PS* 54; Lawrence's emphasis). In a line that expands upon an earlier counterpart in *Quetzalcoatl*, Kate thinks, "Mexico meant the dark-faced men in cotton clothes and big hats: the peasants, peons, pelados, Indians, call them what you will" (*PS* 75). This insight is shifted from Ramón's tutelage in *Quetzalcoatl* to Kate's independent consciousness in *The Plumed Serpent*. Another passage that was partly rewritten to show Kate's broadening awareness reflects, in its additions, Lawrence's own trek alone in 1923 (after writing *Quetzalcoatl*) through rugged western Mexico, then to Guadalajara and the sea:

> The wild, sombre, erect men of the north! . . . The big men in Tlaxcala . . . ! The quick little [Zapotec] Indians . . . down in Oaxaca! The queer-looking half-Chinese natives towards Veracruz! The dark faces and the big black eyes on the coast of Sinaloa! The handsome men of Jalisco, with a scarlet blanket folded on one shoulder! (*PS* 75–76)

While they are from diverse tribes and languages, and "far more alien to one another than Frenchmen, English, and Germans are," they are "a people" with "some Indian quality which pervades the whole" (*PS* 76).

Lawrence turns increasingly in *The Plumed Serpent* to details he considers "aboriginal" in a deliberate effort to de-familiarize his text, to estrange it, to strip the old Spanish veneer from his setting and revise the *status quo*. While this places the novel in line with certain postmodern trends, it also puts off many readers who, thinking of Mexico in more familiar Latinate terms, may therefore prefer the linguistic texture—and different aura—of the first version. Major additions in the later text—songs, homilies, and rituals—often contain more autochthonous motifs. This shift shows in the way time is ultimately marked, not by clocks and bells but by the drums "heard at the Hours" and arranged into "watches" of day and night (*PS* 359) reminiscent of the ancient Mesoamerican day-signs (with animal and other nature symbols) and the *Quecholli* (with bird signs) (Brotherston 226): Lawrence's "watches" take on the names of the rabbit, deer, turkey-buzzard, hawk, and so forth; and elsewhere he refers to the coyote, hummingbird, parrot, jaguar, and she-bear that all have special significance in various Indian mythologies (*PS* 126, 226, 360–61). If such aspects of the text seem more archaistic than postmodern, they must nevertheless be seen in the context of radical dissent from the continuing imposition of colonial European or Euro-American norms—and they help to explain why Lawrence has been seen as a precursor of today's Mexican "novel of magic realism" with its fusion of past and present in mythic patterns (Odio 188).

The process of estrangement is perhaps most obvious in the cosmological vision of the afterlife as it changes from one version of the novel to the next. In the first, Quetzalcoatl's otherworld sounds almost orthodox, being "heaven where the angels are, and the sons of God" (*Q* 237); and the god states, in even more Biblical terms: "In my Father's house are many mansions" (*Q* 232). The goal of enlightenment is termed "a Canaan of tomorrow" (*Q* 309), and Ramón offers to take Easter Mass from the priests under certain conditions: "I will still kneel, at Easter," he says, for "the old mass of Redemption" of the "Risen Adam" (*Q* 298). In *The Plumed Serpent*, however, the otherworld is chiefly figured in terms of the "four dark arms" of a "dark sun" (*PS* 123), a term shared with "The Hopi Snake Dance." This essay also refers to "the dark, lurking, intense sun at the centre of the earth," a "vast dark protoplasmic sun," and "the nameless Sun . . . which we call sun because the other name is too fearful" (*MM* 147, 163). In *The Plumed Serpent* the ultimate god-force seems modeled, at least at times, after the dual-sexed Mesoamerican deity Ometeotl—so that this being is even said to possess a womb (*PS* 125).

Yet Ramón is very conscious of his own mythmaking when he speaks of heaven to his own son: "It is very far—and very empty." (*PS* 355).

Curiously enough, *The Plumed Serpent* seems to contain at least two different mythic perceptions of the otherworld, one as presumably seen by white Christians and another as by Quetzalcoatl or his followers. Both share in the tree metaphor already traced. The Virgin Mary presides over "the Paradise of God" with its "scentless rose-trees" (*PS* 124), in accord with her traditional rose symbolism. These trees, defined by their lack of appeal to the senses, seem static and lifeless. In the same mythic account, however, Quetzalcoatl makes his reappearance from a dark cave, "far behind the sun," in the form of an anthropomorphic tree: "The cup of my flowering is unfolded. . . . My stem is in the air, my roots are in all the dark" (*PS* 226). This dynamic imagery, suggesting vigorous organic growth, contrasts with the wan serenity of the rose-trees. Yet both belong to the same cycle of recurrence. Inside the "axis of our worldly space" is said to be a site where, as observed earlier, even trees know death and renewal, along with the peoples associated with them (*PS* 126); this realm has been associated with Peter Ouspensky's "Fourth Dimension" (Young 30–44). It is the matrix "where alone can the human family assemble in immediate contact" (*PS* 126). These extraordinary passages conclude with a reference to the tree of life: "We are the Tree with the fruit forever upon it," for "we are faith forever" (*PS* 127). Lawrence is referring to an eternal "now," whether in the everyday or the more metaphysical sense. Evidently, according to the novel's first version, even the most hateful criminals are not left out of the great round of becoming. At least, after the execution of Ramón's would-be assassins, one of Huitzilopochtli's songs tells how their wretched souls and bodies will be obliterated, smelted down in the brown earth, and (unexpectedly) recycled again: "trees will rise" from them, they will eventually aspire upwards and "flower, hoping again towards Almighty God" when "Almighty God will give them again the hearts of men" (*Q* 266).

Some of this mystical rebirth myth joins with Etruscan influences to reemerge in the "longest journey" theme of the posthumous *Last Poems* (1932). In fact, Quetzalcoatl's journey to the otherworld is described in terms that suggest "The Ship of Death." The projected trip has both cosmic and mundane sides.

For the journey, the ancient Mexicans have had their "cooking-pot[s]," some of which are presented to Kate as utensils of the gods (*PS* 95); the Etruscans have taken their "small dishes" with them (*SEP* 17); and Lawrence's "soul" is to have its "little cooking pans" (*Poems* 719). The Mexican route through the "plains of darkness" is, surprisingly, a landscape with a kind of vegetation: "the stars spread out like trees, like trees and bushes" (*PS* 225). Similarly, "Invocation to the Moon," with its "long, long street of the stars," refers to the cosmology in terms of plant growth—for the "silver bells" of flowers surround the moon (*Poems* 696). "Shadows," also from *Last Poems*, states that the dying soul knows "the pain of falling leaves, and stems that break in storms," but is at the same time forming its "new, strange flowers" (*Poems* 727). Even in "The Ship of Death," the soul is discovered "cowering in the last branches of the tree of our life" before reemerging (*Poems* 718). Ultimately such images take their quintessential form in the talisman of life in death, "the blue, forked torch" of a gentian in "Bavarian Gentians" (*Poems* 697). This imagery develops from Lawrence's earlier flower tropes, identified by Michael Black with sequences of passionate blossoming followed by eventual withering and death (65–72); in the process I am describing, the sequence proceeds to rebirth.

Such themes remind us anew that Lawrence, before coming to America, had posited the survival in Mexico and Central and South America of an old religious vision from the Atlantean world. The early version of "The Spirit of Place," published in the *English Review* in 1918 (later rewritten in America for *Studies in Classic American Literature* [1923]) speaks of "mystic" Mayan and Aztec cultures that may have been allied with Atlantis in a united world (*TSM* 18, 23–24), and a vestige of this myth reasserts itself in *The Plumed Serpent* (*PS* 414). The same idea appears in the Foreword to *Fantasia of the Unconscious* (54–55) and in *Etruscan Places* (*SEP* 57–58, 129); and *Aaron's Rod*, too, refers to the pre-Flood era (110). Not *Quetzalcoatl* but *The Plumed Serpent* alludes again to "the world before the Flood" (415). This finished novel looks for a new epoch that moves quite beyond binaries: there will be "a new germ, a new conception of human life, that will arise from the fusion of the old blood-and-vertebrate consciousness with the white man's present mental-spiritual consciousness," and this will be "the marriage which is the only step to the new world of man" (*PS* 415–16). Of course, the marriage between Cipriano and Kate is intended as the example of this achievement, resolving the racial issue in more human terms than any essentializing formula could do. This is true despite Kate's provisional bid to visit England again near the end of the novel and despite the couple's controversial sexual relations. It is entirely typical of Lawrence that the racial resolution should come in the flesh, in marriage, and not in abstract argumentation. In *Quetzalcoatl*'s apocalyptic scheme, the races are to face each other in a confrontation: "We are the masters of the new gates," Ramón tells Kate. "The rider on the white [horse] has passed by down the road of tombs, and the rider on the black horse is knocking with thunder at the gate" (*Q* 305, 306). In *The Plumed Serpent*, however, Kate thinks in ways that rule out such conquest: "Not the rider on the white horse: nor the rider on the red" (*PS* 418).

In Lawrence's time, the vast Indian population of Mexico was strangely invisible to many visitors, who remarked, instead, upon the country's elite Europeanized church and secular culture. But Lawrence, looking for that which was left out of this picture, wanted to find the indigenous foundation. It is true this strain in his work is only one strain—and hard-won and precarious—but it is one we should seek out. Including the interracial theme, it may account for some of the past case against his Mexican novel. But it will sound less frightening to people today who know postcolonial and multicultural discourse. Why, then, can we not more readily discern it in *The Plumed Serpent*? For one thing, some of the clues exist in its early version, being elided in revisions in the later one. Both would have been in Lawrence's mind as part of the debate of ideas he was unfolding.

As I have indicated before, his exploratory method is articulated in the essays of literary theory that closely follow his last Mexican trip. When he outlines a concept of multiple forces in "Why the Novel Matters" (probably written in 1925), he could be anticipating the critical opposition to Ramón's sermonizing: "[L]et us have done with the ugly imperialism of any absolute." In the same essay he defines a novel as "a strange assembly of apparently incongruous parts, slipping past one another" (*Hardy* 196). In "The Novel," another 1925 essay, he asserts that a character "must have a quick relatedness to all the other things in the novel"; what the character "says and does must be relative to them all" (*Hardy* 183). Again, in *Etruscan Places*, he states that we must rejoice in "an infinite number of different starts to an infinite number of different goals" (*SEP* 176), a far cry from a monophonic or even dualistic philosophy. In her study of *The Plumed Serpent*, Torgovnick suggests that Lawrence chafes at the binary and hierarchical constraints of our inherited languages, striving beyond these toward a vision of new relationships; she believes that contemporary feminist vocabulary could have helped him in this endeavor (167–70). In this essay, I have added that he moves, too, toward some of the insights of postmodern and multicultural discourse. It seems surprising that views of this kind should be illustrated in *The Plumed Serpent*, often considered one of his least subtle texts. But the idea that the Mexican novel is an arena of multiplicity is strongly supported and opened up by a consideration of both versions, especially as they recall the voices of the "lost."

## NOTES

1. See Martz, "Two Versions, Two Novels," 159–82, and his "*Quetzalcoatl*: The First Version," 287–98; Clark, Introduction to *The Plumed Serpent* xxiv–xxxii; Hyde and Clark 140–48; and Hyde, Introduction to *The Plumed Serpent* xv–xxxv. Clark states that *Quetzalcoatl* "differs from *The Plumed Serpent* much as the three versions of *Lady Chatterley's Lover* differ," amounting to a separate creative effort (*PS* xxv).

2. In "Reflections on the Death of a Porcupine," Lawrence even defines the "fourth dimension" as that which "the old people called heaven" (*RDP* 363).

3. See Lawrence's drawing of corn dancers (*New Mexico* 33). The dancers wave evergreen sprigs (though of pine, not cypress), illustrating "Dance of the Sprouting Corn" (1924), in which he compares the dancers to a waving forest and their singing to "the booming and tearing of a wind deep inside a forest" (*MM* 123). See also a second Lawrence drawing in which a dancer wears such a sprig (Huxley *Letters*, opposite 596). And see Clark, "American Indian" 305–74.

4. *Mornings in Mexico and Other Essays*, ed. Hyde, will be issued in the Cambridge Edition of the Works of D. H. Lawrence.

5. Kinkead-Weekes makes an exception of Kipling "at his best" but not of E. M. Forster, who reveals "the precise limits of his ability to take what he encounters with full seriousness" (254).

6. See also Pinkney 147–62.

7. See also Yoshimura 7–71 and Tabei 335–60.

8. On dialogism elsewhere in Lawrence, see, for example, Lodge 92–108; Eggert, Introduction 11–13; Eggert, "Comedy and Provisionality" 134–37; Fleishman, "Lawrence and Bakhtin" 109–19; and Fleishman, "He Do the Polis" 162–79.

9. As Odio puts it, "Lawrence's conception of the Mexican Indian became the predominant view of several novelists of the Boom Period [for the Spanish

American novel] who started incorporating Indian mythologies into the narrative universe of their novels as an ontological answer to man's problems" (172). Carlos Fuentes, for one, acknowledged Lawrence's influence (176–77).

10. But see also my essays "Kate and the Goddess" and "Picking Up 'Life-Threads'" as well as Carpenter's compelling look at strong women in *The Plumed Serpent* (119–29).

11. Lawrence reported from Mexico, "There's never a dance down here. They're terribly un-dancy, these Zapotec and Miztec Indians" (*L* v. 195).

12. The relation between tree-spirits and the dead is significant elsewhere in Lawrence, as in the foreword to *Fantasia of the Unconscious* and in "The Border-Line" (1924), in which a powerful ghost returns from the dead with aspects of a tree.

13. Although Lawrence has been criticized for courting a form of "mass movement" in *The Plumed Serpent*, Templeton seems to state, on the contrary, that he had no concept of communal experience, totally rejecting "collective will" or "tribalism" (25). Both positions are hard to understand in light of some of Lawrence's actual passages.

# WORKS CITED

Becket, Fiona. *D. H. Lawrence: The Thinker as Poet*. New York: St. Martin's, 1997.

Black, Michael. *D. H. Lawrence: The Early Philosophical Works*. Cambridge: Cambridge University Press, 1992.

Brotherston, Gordon. *Book of the Fourth World: Reading the Native Americans Through Their Literatures*. Cambridge: Cambridge University Press, 1992.

Carpenter, Rebecca. "'Bottom-Dog Insolence' and 'The Harem Mentality.'" *DHLR* 25 (1993–94): 119–29.

Clark, L. D. *Dark Night of the Body: D. H. Lawrence's "The Plumed Serpent."* Austin: University of Texas Press, 1964.

———. "D. H. Lawrence and the American Indian." *DHLR* 9 (1976), 305–74. (Cited as "American Indian").

———. Introduction to *The Plumed Serpent*, by D. H. Lawrence, edited by L. D. Clark. Cambridge: Cambridge University Press, 1987.

Clark, L. D. and Virginia Hyde. Appendix 1 of *The Plumed Serpent* by D. H. Lawrence. Harmondsworth: Penguin, 1995.

Doherty, Gerald. "One Vast Hermeneutic Sentence: The Total Lawrentian Text." *PMLA* 106 (1991): 1134–45.

Eggert, Paul. "Comedy and Provisionality." In *Lawrence and Comedy*, edited by Paul Eggert and John Worthen. Cambridge: Cambridge University Press, 1996.

———. Introduction to *Lawrence and Comedy*, edited by Paul Eggert and John Worthen. Cambridge: Cambridge University Press, 1996.

Ellis, David. *D. H. Lawrence: Dying Game, 1922–1930*. Cambridge: Cambridge University Press, 1998.

Fleishman, Avrom. "'He Do the Polis in Different Voices': Lawrence's Later

Style." In *D. H. Lawrence: A Centenary Consideration*, edited by Peter Balbert and Phillip L. Marcus. Ithaca: Cornell University Press, 1985.

———. "Lawrence and Bakhtin: where pluralism ends and dialogism begins." In *Rethinking Lawrence*, edited by Keith Brown. Milton Keynes, England: Open University Press, 1990.

Gilbert, Sandra M. *Acts of Attention: The Poems of D. H. Lawrence*. 2d ed. Carbondale: Southern Illinois University Press, 1990.

Hyde, Virginia. Introduction to *The Plumed Serpent*, by D. H. Lawrence, edited by L. D. Clark and Virginia Hyde. Harmondsworth: Penguin, 1995.

———. "Kate and the Goddess: Subtexts in *The Plumed Serpent*." *DHLR* 26 (1995–96): 249–74.

———. "Picking Up 'Life-Threads' in D. H. Lawrence's Mexico." In *Approaches to Teaching D. H. Lawrence*, edited by M. Elizabeth Sargent, and Garry Watson. New York: MLA, 2001.

———. *The Risen Adam: D. H. Lawrence's Revisionist Typology*. University Park: Pennsylvania State University Press, 1992.

Hyde, Virginia and L. D. Clark. "The Sense of an Ending in *The Plumed Serpent*." *DHLR* 25: (1993–94): 140–48.

Kinkead-Weekes, Mark. "The Gringo Señora Who Rode Away." *DHLR* 22 (1990): 251–65.

Lodge, David. "Lawrence, Dostoevsky, Bakhtin: Lawrence and Dialogic Fiction." In *Rethinking Lawrence*, edited by Keith Brown. Milton Keynes, England: Open University Press, 1990.

Martz, Louis L. "D. H. Lawrence, *The Plumed Serpent (Quetzalcoatl)*: Two Versions, Two Novels." In *Many Gods and Many Voices: The Role of the Prophet in English and American Modernism*. Columbia: University of Missouri Press, 1998. (Cited as "Two Versions, Two Novels.")

———. Introduction to *Quetzalcoatl: The First Version of "The Plumed Serpent."* Edited by Louis L. Martz. Redding Ridge, Conn.: Black Swan Books, 1995.

Odio, Arnold. "D. H. Lawrence Among the Mexicans." In *The Reception of D. H. Lawrence Around the World*, edited by Takeo Iida. Fukuoka: Kurume University Press, 1999.

Paik, Nak-chung. "Reflections on *The Plumed Serpent*." *D. H. Lawrence Studies* (D. H. Lawrence Society of Korea) 1 (1991): 184–210.

Parmenter, Ross. *Lawrence in Oaxaca: A Quest for the Novelist in Mexico*. Salt Lake City: Peregrine Smith Books, 1984.

Pinkney, Tony. *D. H. Lawrence and Modernism*. Iowa City: University of Iowa Press, 1990.

Scheckner, Peter. *Class, Politics, and the Individual: A Study of the Major Works of D. H. Lawrence*. Rutherford, N.J.: Fairleigh Dickinson University Press, 1985.

Storch, Margaret. "'But Not the America of the Whites': Lawrence's Pursuit of the True Primitive." *DHLR* 25 (1993–94): 48–60.

Tabei, Yoshiko. "The Plumed Serpent That Cannot Fly: Another Meaning of the Title." *D. H. Lawrence Studies* [of Kyoto]. *Plumed Serpent* Number (1994): 335–60.

Templeton, Wayne. "'Indians and an Englishman': Lawrence in the American Southwest." *DHLR* 25 (1993–94): 14–34.

Torgovnick, Marianna. *Gone Primitive: Savage Intellects, Modern Lives*. Chicago: University of Chicago Press 1990.

Van Hoosier-Carey, Kimberley. "Struggling with the Master: The Position of Kate and the Reader in Lawrence's 'Quetzalcoatl' and *The Plumed Serpent*." *DHLR* 25 (1993–94): 104–18.

Wexler, Joyce. "D. H. Lawrence Through a Postmodernist Lens." *DHLR* 27 (1997–98): 47–64.

Williams, Linda Ruth. *D. H. Lawrence*. Plymouth: Northcote House and the British Council, 1997.

Yoshimura, Hirokazu. "Fascism, Leadership and *The Plumed Serpent*." *D. H. Lawrence Studies* [of Kyoto]. *Plumed Serpent* Number (1994): 7–71.

Young, Richard O. "'Where Even the Trees Come and Go': D. H. Lawrence and the Fourth Dimension." *DHLR* (1980): 30–44.

# "Demonish Maturity": Identity, Consumption, and the Discourse of Species in *The Plumed Serpent*

Carrie Rohman

Recent studies of primitivism in the modernist aesthetic have privileged the categories of race and gender in an effort to rearticulate our understanding of imperialist binaries. Such studies show that modernist writers juxtapose Western subjectivity with that of racialized and sexualized "others," who are considered less technologically and ideologically advanced, in an anxious attempt to shore up imperialist identity. The animal "other"—though fundamental to modernist ideologies of difference—is usually omitted from these critical discussions of modernism's implicit "power relations" (166), as Marjorie Perloff has called them. In fact, the human/animal binary recurs frequently in modernist literary conventions and registers anxiety about Western identity in a post-Darwinian age.

Among such conventions, D. H. Lawrence's ongoing interrogation of the boundary between "human" and "animal" is especially compelling. Lawrence repeatedly deploys the discourse of species to explore the contours of the human, with results that can be wildly divergent. At times his exploration of the species problem unsettles conventional definitions of the human, but at other times his work recapitulates the traditional humanist subject position through violence against animals. Lawrence's various literary investigations resonate with the recent theoretical interests of thinkers like Jacques Derrida, who argues that animality figures as humanism's constitutive outside.

Animality operates as humanism's "other" because the autonomy of the human subject is dependent upon the disavowal of the animal. That is, we define our humanness through our difference from animals. But the human and animal cannot be entirely sep-

216

arated. Indeed the human being is constituted as both a primate body linked to basic physical necessity and a "human" mind capable of abstracting itself from those connections. Derrida points to the asymmetrical valuation of this intersection of carnality and concept when he speaks of the dominant schema of Western subjectivity as "carno-phallogocentrism" (113). Derrida adds the prefix "carno" to indicate his further delineation of the patriarchal subject. Just as that subject is identified with phallic power (phallocentrism) and with the metaphysics of presence (logocentrism), so too it is associated with carnivorous virility. Thus Derrida explains, "The subject does not want just to master and possess nature actively. In our cultures, he accepts sacrifice and eats flesh" (114). For this reason, Derrida concludes that in Western cultures the head of state could never be a vegetarian since "the *chef* must be an eater of flesh" (114). This sacrifice of the animal is necessary, in deconstructive terms, to enact the disavowal of the other precisely because that "other" already infects the subject itself.

Lawrence's *The Plumed Serpent* (1926) provides a studied meditation on the discourse of animality and its relationship to consumption. Specifically, this work contains a complex species economy that maintains *and* resists the distinction between human and animal by foregrounding connections between eating and power. Lawrence represents the unspeakable confrontation with animality as Kate's fear of cannibalistic incorporation by the Mexican "other," which is figured as an animal other throughout the novel. By registering this fear of the dissolution of self, Lawrence thematizes the modernist anxiety that Darwin set in motion, that we are, in short, more similar to non-human animals than we are different from them. In fact, the species boundary rivals the racial one in Lawrence's imagination and emerges as one of his fundamental axes of thought.

Recent postcolonial criticism has illuminated the dialectic between Western self and non-Western "other" that served to stabilize European identity in the modernist era. Work by such scholars as Marianna Torgovnick and Anne McClintock identifies Western anxiety about the racialized "savage" and notes the gendering of such identity binaries. Torgovnick, like Edward Said in his work on imperialism, gives primacy to the sexualized and racialized dichotomies that are prominent in modernist uses of the primitive. While the elaboration of discursive relationships between races and genders is crucial to our understanding of modernism, critical work on species distinctions in primitivism remains incomplete.

The human/animal binary is not only a recurring theme in primitivist literature; in some ways it also underlies racial and sexual distinctions. Since notions of the primitive almost always imply the possibility of evolutionary regression, it is necessary to explore the ways in which modernist authors have figured the animal in relation to the primitive and the civilized. Like modernism, its theoretical progenitor, primitivism often engages conflicting oppositions. In *Gone Primitive: Savage Intellects, Modern Lives*, Torgovnick begins her discussion by noting the modernist predilection for imagining primitives within a "cherished series of dichotomies" (3). As objects of study and comparison for Western subjectivity, primitive peoples are defined alternately as "gentle, in tune with nature, paradisal, ideal—or violent, in need of control" (3). The "primitive," then, has been marshaled by modernist writers to represent both the excessively desirable and the excessively feared, the sublime and the abject. As Torgovnick explains, this is a self-serving paradigm: "the primitive can be—has been, will be (?)—whatever Euro-Americans want it to be. It tells us what we want it to tell us" (9).

This self-reflexivity is grounded in the Western conviction and fear that humans are all fundamentally primitives, an anxiety that has obsessed modern culture since the popularization of Darwin's work. On some level, then, the question of the primitive is always a question of the civilized. According to Torgovnick, this "conceived link between us and them often depends on evolutionist premises" (8). She quotes Freud's claim in *Totem and Taboo* (1913) that the primitive is "a necessary stage of development through which every race has passed" (8). While this quotation implies some historical connection between past and present, it also insists that the primitive is extinct since it merely represents a stage passed through by civilized cultures. More to the point is Freud's argument that there exists "a collective mind, in which mental processes occur just as they do in the mind of an individual" (*Totem* 195). Within this supra-historical mind, an original, presumably singular sensibility can have "persisted for many thousands of years and has remained operative in generations which can have had no knowledge of that [sensibility]" (195). This is certainly the more frightening prospect for modernity, that some savage vestige is operative in the very minds of the civilized. Thus, the unavoidable implication surfaces: the civilized could actually be savage.

Most threatening about the modern evolutionary view of the primitive is not simply that the civilized might be intimately connected to the primitive, but that the civilized are organically linked to the animal. This more profound by-product of the evolutionary reasoning linked to primitivism—one which Torgovnick fails to address—is itself registered in the human/animal binary, which is often integral to primitivist ideology and metaphor. And while this dichotomy sometimes overlaps with other primitivist distinctions, it requires focused consideration for our further comprehension of the modernist relationship to otherness.

Modernist ideology about the relationship between human and animal has partial roots in the philosophical and social scientific discourses of the late-nineteenth and early-twentieth centuries. The works of Friedrich Nietzsche, for instance, are filled with implications about species boundaries. In *The Birth of Tragedy* (1872), his earliest book, Nietzsche outlines the polar, aesthetic categories "Apollonian" and "Dionysian," which frame his analysis. In many ways, the *Ur*-binary of primitivism is already operational here since Apollo and Dionysus represent the reason/instinct dichotomy which saturates modernist literature. On one side of the divide, the Apollonian position is characterized by symbolism and reason or "philosophical calmness" (25). On the other side, the Dionysian partakes of "self-forgetfulness" as man is reunited with nature (26). Nietzsche's description of a Dionysian revelry is telling:

> In song and dance man exhibits himself as a member of a higher community: he has forgotten how to walk and speak, and is on the point of taking a dancing flight into the air. His gestures bespeak enchantment. Even as the animals now talk, and as the earth yields milk and honey, so also something supernatural sounds forth from him. (27)

Ironically, Nietzsche figures this return to the animal as something beyond nature (supernatural). Dionysian reunification with nature seems to set men apart from and above the Apollonian thinkers who "do not divine what a cadaverous-looking and ghastly aspect" they present (26). The value judgment implicit in Nietzsche's dichotomy favors the Dionysian, for Apollo breeds a deterioration that Nietzsche will name later.

The sickness that haunts *The Birth of Tragedy* is exorcised in Nietzsche's *Genealogy of Morality* (1887). At the outset of his second essay, "Guilt, Bad Conscience and Related Matters," he delineates the required developmental steps that humans must have taken in order to become conscionable: "That is precisely what constitutes the long history of the origins of *responsibility*. That particular task of breeding an animal which has the right to make a promise includes . . . first *making* a man to a certain degree undeviating [*notwendig*], uniform, a peer amongst peers, orderly and consequently predictable" (39). Most important here is what brings humanity to its orderly state, the process of "sickly mollycoddling and sermonizing, by means of which the animal 'man' is finally taught to be ashamed of all his instincts" (47). At this point, Nietzsche has no qualms about claiming humanity as primarily animal. His placing of the word "man" in quotation marks is particularly radical, for it indicates a linguistic and cultural constructedness that separates humans from other living creatures.

Nietzsche later argues that responsibility was ushered in after a fundamental shift in human history which resulted in man's "forcible breach with his animal past" (62). Consequently, the responsible person is the person estranged from his "real and irredeemable animal instincts," which have become suppressed (68). Ultimately, then, Nietzsche opposes the civilized to a naturalized humanity that supposedly came before it. Accordingly, what modern people have embraced are "all those other-worldly aspirations, alien to the senses, the instincts, to nature, to animals" (70).

Lawrence explores the potential rekindling of "real animal instincts" throughout his oeuvre, but especially in *The Plumed Serpent*. The novel's opening chapter introduces animality as a compelling trope as the Irish protagonist, Kate, dares to experience the last bull-fight of the season in Mexico City. She considers her own dread of the event to be justified when the bloody spectacle registers as a "half-hearted ceremonial rape" (Clark 52). To Kate's chagrin, a bull continually pushes "his sharp, flourishing horns in the horse's belly, working them up and down inside there with a sort of vague satisfaction" (16). In Kate's estimation, this display reveals more about humans than animals: she is shocked by "[h]uman cowardice and *beastliness*, a smell of blood, a nauseous whiff of bursten bowels!" (16; my emphasis). For

Kate, the Mexicans' abuse of animals reveals a lack of humanity which is metaphorized through abject corporeality, in blood and excrement. She is overcome by the animal nature of human "civilization."

By contrast, her American friend Owen delights in the scene. He insists that viewing the bullfight is viewing "Life" (26). Owen figures as the voyeuristic European primitivist who, according to Torgovnick, takes pleasure in observing the primitive with "a scientific eye" (4). Owen is guilty of exoticism, because he seeks to be enticed by otherness. Lawrence's anti-American sentiment surfaces here as Owen is representatively "cold and abstract" (12). He is like the mechanical gadgets that American capitalism produces. But Lawrence also repeatedly figures Owen as "primitive" and "bird-like" (12), and thus the American appears to embody both the civilized *and* the ancient, the mechanistic and the natural.

While Kate is contrasted to bird-like Owen, her own desire to become a bull just "for five minutes" (26) to seek revenge against sadistic bullfighters signals another dissolution of species boundaries. Her cross-species identification subtly but clearly registers a desire to "become-animal" in Deleuze and Guattari's sense (238). Becoming-animal, according to Deleuze and Guattari, involves a de-individuation or loss of selfhood that surfaces as Kate's primary internal conflict in the novel. Anxieties about incorporation begin to emerge alongside questions of species as this scene progresses. Kate appears to recognize the violence inherent in Derrida's carnophallogocentric schema as she staunchly disapproves of her friends' enjoyment and decides that the two Americans are veritable vultures, "picking over the garbage of sensations, and gobbling it up like carrion birds. At the moment, both Owen and Villiers seemed to her like carrion birds, repulsive" (27–28).

In the novel's opening chapters, then, Kate's relationship to Mexico and Mexicans remains primarily abstracted. The bullfight causes her to perceive an uncivilized, abject Mexican affinity with death and decay. While this spectacular physicality is beastly to her, American voyeurism also has cannibalistic implications. Thus, both the European and its other seem equally primitive at the outset of *The Plumed Serpent* because they participate, to varying degrees, in unclean forms of consumption.

Not surprisingly eating is a prevalent metaphor in Lawrence's species rubric. In "Reflections on the Death of a Porcupine" (1925), Lawrence outlines a hierarchy of power based on species lines. He insists that "the life-species is the highest which can devour, or destroy, or subjugate every other life-species against which it is pitted" (*RDP* 358). Lawrence places European men at the top of this gastro-political hierarchy, descends through various races, and ends by classifying non-human animals. Such systems, which were used to justify Social Darwinism in the late-nineteenth century, stratify a certain slippage between non-whites and non-human animals.

The discourses of race and species are sometimes mutually deployed, therefore, in Lawrence's work. In *The Plumed Serpent*, non-Europeans are often animalized, or represented as closer in evolutionary terms to non-human animals, further down on the evolutionary chain than Westerners. For instance, when Cipriano, the Indian general who becomes Kate's husband late in the novel, joins a tea party after the bullfight, the two peruse a collection of "Aztec things, obsidian knives, grimacing, squatting idols in black lava" (39). These pieces disturb Kate, who admits that the centerless nature of Mexico oppresses her. Having said so, she looks into Cipriano's "black, slanting, watchful, calculating eyes" and sees something childish but "at the same time something obstinate and mature, a demonish maturity, opposing her in an animal way" (40). Here Kate's imagination conflates the primitive, the Mexican, and the animal.

As the novel unfolds, the dark other is more clearly represented as the animal force in Lawrence's world. For Kate, Mexico itself is the dark antithesis of Western culture. When she looks out across the Valley of Mexico, her impressions are unsettling:

> Superficially Mexico might be all right. . . . Until you were alone with it. And then the undertone was like the low angry, snarling purring of some jaguar spotted with night. . . . And on the bright sunshine was a dark stream of an angry, impotent blood, and the flowers seemed to have their roots in spilt blood. The spirit of place was cruel, down-dragging, destructive. (49, 50)

Mexico is metaphorized as a bloodthirsty, threatening jaguar waiting to pounce upon Kate and presumably to consume her. Even a nearby church, the symbolic seat of charity and welcome, appears with "its barrel roof humping up like some crouching animal" (50). The fear of being devoured is apparently all too familiar for Kate, who, as she confronts these frightening impressions, remembers why she had come to this "high plateau of death" in the first place (50). Ironically, she was propelled by another kind of death: "Over in England, in Ireland, in Europe, she had heard the *consummatum est* of her own spirit" (50). In Mexico, however, death and consumption are material, rather than spiritual, concerns.

Kate experiences Mexicans as nothing more than creatures. Many "eat food so hot with chile it burns holes in their insides. . . . They live in houses that a dog would be ashamed of" (65). "Insignificant looking" Mexican men harbor a "cold, mud-like antagonism as they stepped cattishly past" and are poisonous "like scorpions" (76). The drunks of Mexico City register even further down on Kate's chain of being with their "faces of pure brutish evil, cold and insect-like" (76).

Mexican women fare just as poorly in Kate's assessment. They present "images of wild submissiveness, the primitive womanliness of the world," and they are also "somewhat reptilian" with the "dark eyes of half-created women" (77). It is clearly the undifferentiated identity or self in these women that repels Kate, for she repeatedly notes their "queer void insolence! Something lurking, where the womanly centre should have been: lurking snake-like" (77). Ironically, Kate is frightened by the kind of consciousness she seeks in Mexico. She has fled Europe and its individuated humanism, but she cannot yet accept the "void" that she considers her primitive, animal alternative.

Kate's growing intimacy with Cipriano, her future husband, allows her to study him with a certain intensity, and she spies this same racialized animality in him:

[T]he movement of his hand was so odd, quick, light, as he ate, so easily a movement of shooting, or of flashing a knife into the body of some adversary, and his dark-coloured lips were so helplessly savage . . . that her heart stood still. There was something undeveloped and intense in him, the intensity and the crudity of the semi-savage. She could well understand the potency of the snake upon the Aztec and Maya imagination. Something smooth, undeveloped, yet vital in this man suggested the heavy-ebbing blood of powerful reptiles, the dragon of Mexico. (67)

Once again, an emphasis on incorporation emerges. Kate watches Cipriano eat, focusing first on his hand, which exhibits an instinctual tendency to kill, and then on his mouth and "savage" lips. In keeping with the conflation of the primitive and the animal, Kate compares Cipriano to a snake that is ready to strike. His glittering eyes threaten her just as the crouching Mexico has, and she feels "as the bird feels when the snake is watching it" (67). Rather than figuring as a rapacious predator, the bird becomes quarry in Kate's imagination as she finishes her dinner.

Lawrence's animalizing characterizations seem at first to rehearse a familiar theme: humans have a developed sense of self that other animals lack, or Europeans have a more demarcated identity which elevates them above non-whites. But Lawrence is ambivalent about his caricatures. For instance, this seeming regression to animality in Cipriano is both threatening and precocious; his animal way is characterized as a "demonish maturity" (40). On some level, then, Cipriano is more civilized than Kate; he sees through the ruse of Western individuality and spies some primal multiplicity or intersubjectivity that Kate cannot perceive.

Indeed, Lawrence's novel, like his earlier works of long fiction, troubles Western notions of individuality. As Jürgen Habermas explains, the philosophical discourse of modernity "turns centrally on the critique of subjectivistic rationalism" (McCarthy viii). That is, absolute self-consciousness, inherent in the "atomistic and autonomous, disengaged and disembodied" subject, is under attack in the late-nineteenth and early-twentieth centuries (ix). Lawrence is clearly skeptical of this Western legacy of a reason-centered identity. When juxtaposed to Kate, in fact, a character like Cipriano seems to figure outside the economy of Western individuality.

His literary resistance to a rigid notion of self allows Dolores La Chapelle to entitle her book on Lawrence *Future Primitive*. According to La Chapelle, Lawrence longs for a time beyond industrialized modernity that will once more recognize humanity's connection to nature and disallow rationalistic notions of self. In Thomas Lyon's introduction to *Future Primitive*, he notes that La Chapelle and Lawrence both long for a less fragmented subjectivity:

[They grieve] over the loss of place brought about by the economics of the industrial growth society. The world in which a mountain stood wild and had its full being, was trembling with sacred potential: a human being could realize that mountain, could transcend the limited sense of self through whose perceptual filters the mountain had seemed likewise separate and alone. (xvi)

For La Chapelle, Lawrence desires this intersubjective connectedness to the natural world since he himself was able to feel the "old ways" of animistic culture in which all natural entities contained a spiritual charge (32). In the passage at hand, for instance, a mountain is not utterly other than a human being; they share some basic ontology. In Cipriano, then, this intersubjective awareness is animal-like and yet sophisticated. Unlike Kate, he is able to see beyond the subjectivistic rationalism that Horkheimer and Adorno call "a new kind of barbarism" (xi). We will see, however, that Lawrence's allegiance to individuality is not so easily relinquished as La Chapelle would have it.

The problem of the self becomes exponentially exacerbated for Kate as the novel continues, and her dilemma points out the connection between individuation and incorporation. Thinking about her fear of the "centreless" Mexicans, Kate undergoes an epiphany about human subjectivity. She recognizes her illusion about the "I": "She had thought that each individual had a complete self, a complete soul, an accomplished I. And now she realised as plainly as if she had turned into a new being, that this was not so. Men and women had incomplete selves, made up of bits assembled together loosely and somewhat haphazard" (105). Kate recognizes individuality as a kind of fiction and believes the self to be multiple and fragmentary. In recognizing this multiplicity, Kate relinquishes a founding Western premise, but in doing so, she is immediately plagued by fears of incorporation:

> In the great seething light of the lake, with the terrible blue-ribbed mountains of Mexico beyond, she seemed *swallowed* by some grisly skeleton, in the cage of his death-anatomy. She was afraid, mystically, of the man crouching there in the bows with his smooth thighs and supple loins like a snake, and his black eyes watching. (106; my emphasis)

The loss of autonomous selfhood renders Kate susceptible to a kind of identity imperialism. If her own borders of self are not distinct and encompassing, she feels absorbed by others against her will. This absorption is almost always figured in terms of animal predation. Thus Lawrence implies that the crossing of ego

boundaries is instinctual but dangerous. Indeed such crossings
are particularly dangerous for Westerners who cling to Cartesian
notions of identity which privilege a transparent and absolute
self-consciousness.

On the other hand, Lawrence questions the possibility of intersubjectivity, of overcoming the boundaries of identity. He is particularly skeptical when the problem of selfhood is scrutinized
through the lens of sexuality, one of Lawrence's recurring consid-
erations. Kate has noticed that Ramón and Cipriano share a kind
of passion that includes "the recognition of each other's eternal
and abiding loneliness" (252), and she begins to consider the passion between men and women. Then, rather than envisioning her
own engulfment by another, she theorizes unbreachable selves:

> Men and women should know that they cannot, absolutely, meet
> on earth. In the closest kiss, the dearest touch, there is the small gulf
> which is none the less complete. . . . They must bow and submit in
> reverence, to the gulf. Even though I eat the body and drink the blood
> of Christ, Christ is Christ and I am I, and the gulf is impassable. (252)

Here Lawrence seems to posit an essential, individual identity.
Even eating the "flesh of my flesh," as evidenced by the reference
to consuming the body of Christ, cannot bridge the impassable
gap between two persons. Only one process can bridge the gulf
between selves, but in explaining this phenomenon, Lawrence
waxes ambiguous. To "meet in the quick," he explains, "we must
give up the assembled self, the daily I, and . . . meet unconscious
in the Morning Star. . . . But without transfiguration we shall
never get there" (253). Such passages make Lawrence's ambiguity more evident. He both confirms and resists the sovereign individual; he believes and disbelieves in the melding of identities.
Thus, Don Ramón's pronouncement on the indecipherability of
sexual relationships reflects this paradox. He tells Kate, "in these
matters, one never knows what is half way, nor where it is. A
woman who just wants to be taken, and then to cling on, is a para-
site. And a man who wants just to take, without giving, is a creature of prey" (271).

Lawrence follows this theory to the letter, and his conclusions
have long since commanded the outrage of feminist critics. As it
turns out, the parasitic engulfment of men occurs primarily at
the moment of female orgasm, when "the great cat, with its

spasms of voluptuousness and its lifelong lustful enjoyment of its own isolated, isolated individuality," takes without giving (438). Kate knows "many women" who "played with love and intimacy as a cat with a mouse. In the end, they quickly ate up the love-mouse, then trotted off with a full belly and a voluptuous sense of power" (438). Here the anxiety about selfhood translates into castration anxiety. The discourses of gender and species are mutually deployed as feminine sexuality is animalized and the woman is tritely figured as the *vagina dentata*.

When confronted with the possibility of becoming a goddess in the new Aztec pantheon orchestrated by Cipriano and Ramón, Kate unfailingly returns to the dilemma of self and other, of distinction and incorporation. Cipriano begins to call her by the Aztec goddess's name, "Malintzi." Since naming is always central to identity, Kate revolts against this perceived usurpation. Resisting Cipriano's proposal to become his bride, Kate insists, "You treat me as if I had no life of my own. . . . But I have" (370). When she is unable to fully answer Cipriano's query about who gave her this life, she simply retorts, "I don't know. But I have got it. And I must live it. I can't be just swallowed up" (370).

For Ramón and Cipriano, the plumed serpent, Quetzalcoatl, appears to resolve the tension that Kate cannot put to rest. Quetzalcoatl is the god of both ways: mind and body, self and loss of self, earth and sky. This god makes manifest the overlap of species, both bird and snake, and Lawrence's characters, who "become" Aztec gods in the novel, also become non-human animals.

In many ways, Quetzalcoatl embodies the binaries or paradoxes that primitivism itself rehearses. John Humma has noted that the eagle and snake serve "one [as] our higher, the other our lower consciousness" (201). What is perhaps most profound for this analysis is the way in which a bizarrely cross-bred animal being is elevated to a spiritual level. Most animal manifestations in the novel remain only on the physical level. But the great bird-snake is the chief of gods, and such transgressing deification implies a fundamental tainting of Western abstraction. In other words, the spiritual is never purely spirit; it is always connected to the snake, to the grounded materiality of the body. One is reminded here of Lawrence's poem "Snake," in which a serpent drinking at the narrator's water-trough is experienced as both god-like and repugnant, as an inspiration and a horror.

Despite its frequently posited status as Lawrence's most ambitious failure, then, *The Plumed Serpent* is an unusual and complex text for the consideration of species ideology in the modernist imagination. While Lawrence appears to rely upon an outmoded, imperialistic equation of racial and animal otherness in the novel, his European and Mexican characters are depicted in a complicated ideological framework that troubles the distinction between human and animal consciousness. Moreover, Lawrence's somewhat fantastic use of the Quetzalcoatl myth places his characters in a liminal reality beyond Western individualism where animality becomes the privileged mode of being. As a result, the interrogation of rationalist humanism in *The Plumed Serpent* can be read as a post-humanist critique deployed through the discourse of species. Though this critique is ambivalent at times, Lawrence's use of the animal as a symbol of salvation from Western culture is exceptional because it destabilizes the West's traditional hierarchizing of human over animal as a matter of course. Thus, as the novel ends with Kate's unresolved dilemma between remaining in the consciously mythologized world of Quetzalcoatl and returning to the individuated life of the West, it seems clear that Lawrence's contradictions bespeak a refusal to choose between the spirit and body, the rational and instinctual, the human and animal.

## WORKS CITED

Clark, L. D. *Dark Night of the Body: D. H. Lawrence's "The Plumed Serpent."* Austin: University of Texas Press, 1964.

Deleuze, Gilles and Félix Guattari. *A Thousand Plateaus: Capitalism and Schizophrenia*. Translated by Brian Massumi. Minneapolis: University of Minnesota Press, 1987.

Derrida, Jacques. " 'Eating Well,' or The Calculation of the Subject." An Interview with Jacques Derrida." In *Who Comes After the Subject?* edited by Eduardo Cadava, Peter Connor, and Jean-Luc Nancy. New York: Routledge, 1991.

Freud, Sigmund. *Totem and Taboo*. 1913. Reprint, New York: Norton, 1950.

Horkheimer, Max and Theodor W. Adorno. *The Dialectic of Enlightenment*. New York: Continuum, 1944.

Humma, John. "The Imagery of *The Plumed Serpent*: The Going-under of Organicism." *DHLR* 15 (1982): 197–218.

La Chapelle, Dolores. *D. H. Lawrence: Future Primitive*. Denton: University of North Texas Press, 1996.

McCarthy, Thomas. Introduction to *The Philosophical Discourse of Modernity*, by Jürgen Habermas. Cambridge: MIT Press, 1987.

McClintock, Anne. *Imperial Leather: Race, Gender, and Sexuality in the Colonial Conquest*. New York: Routledge, 1995.

Nietzsche, Friedrich. *The Birth of Tragedy*. 1872. Reprint, New York: Russell and Russell, 1964.

———. *On the Genealogy of Morality*. 1887. Reprint, Cambridge: Cambridge University Press, 1994.

Perloff, Marjorie. "Modernist Studies." In *Redrawing the Boundaries: The Transformation of English and American Literary Studies*, edited by Stephen Greenblatt and Giles Gunn. New York: MLA, 1992.

Torgovnick, Marianna. *Gone Primitive: Savage Intellects, Modern Lives*. Chicago: University of Chicago Press, 1990.

# Ritual Sacrifice in "The Woman Who Rode Away": A Girardian Reading

## Laurie McCollum

D. H. LAWRENCE'S OBSESSION WITH THE TROPE OF SACRIFICE BEGINS in his earliest works but is enacted most directly in "The Woman Who Rode Away." In this short story, where the crisis of sexuality doubles as the crisis of civilization, Lawrence focuses on related concerns: the figure of the modern woman that is apparent in so much of his work, and sacrifice as an integral part of cultural regeneration. These concepts are particularly important as they impinge on Lawrence's views of women. In "The Woman Who Rode Away" Lawrence envisions the end of the modern malaise as tied to the removal or regeneration of the modern woman. Here he engages in a fiction of emergent possibility based on the most ancient models of ritual sacrifice. The female enacts cultural salvation, and the sacrifice of the Woman is ultimately empowering as it places women at the nexus of culture formation.

This reading of the story emerges from an application of the theories of René Girard to Lawrence's work. Girard is Andrew B. Hammond Professor Emeritus of French Language, Literature, and Civilization at Stanford University. He began his career as a psychoanalytic critic with *Deceit, Desire, and the Novel: Self and Other in Literary Structure* (1961), which examines the nature of desire, sexuality, and violence in the works of Stendhal, Proust, and Dostoevsky. Girard subsequently turned to cultural anthropology, and he explores the phenomenon of persecution in *Violence and the Sacred* (1977), *The Scapegoat* (1984), and *Things Hidden Since the Foundation of the World* (1987). Girard finds evidence in cultural myths, ethnography, and literature to argue that ritual murder is at the foundation of cultural order and civilization. Violence enacted at these times is not related to any "cult of violence," but is instead regenerative and sacred. Sacrifice sometimes even saves cultures from extinction. Girard's theories about the mimetic dimension of cultural crisis, the different categories of sacrificial victim, and the connections between sacrifice, prestige, and potential power are particularly applicable to "The Woman Who Rode Away."

Girardian analysis not only illuminates the story, but also helps clarify the polarized critical response it has generated. "The Woman Who Rode Away" is a site of contestation in Lawrence studies where critics hostile to Lawrence find him particularly vulnerable to attack. The story's detractors, especially feminist critics, view it solely as a product of Lawrence's alleged misogyny. This interpretation has held currency since the publication of Kate Millett's *Sexual Politics* in 1970, which described the story's sacrificial ending as a "death fuck" (292). Other critics have followed suit. Lois Rudnick, for example, characterizes the story as a "revenge fantasy" where Lawrence symbolically kills his patron, Mabel Dodge Luhan, and Laurence Steven claims that Lawrence transfers his own feelings of hostility toward women onto the Indians. More recently the story has also been interpreted as imperialistic and bigoted. Sheila Contreras charges that Lawrence reveals conventional assumptions about third world peoples in the story that "fundamentally link Indians with violence" (93) and ethnocentrically portray them as "dirty, misogynist, and intent on overthrowing the master race" (96).

The sacrifice at the conclusion of the story is often judged harshly and used to discredit either Lawrence or his Indian characters. Steven compares the cave scene to the type of writing done by H. Rider Haggard, and Contreras argues it is part of a Western erotic fantasy that evidences a European notion of sacrifice. Rudnick perceives the scene as horribly perverted: "That the death of the Woman is eroticized as the ultimate religio-sexual experience is the most horrible of all" (99). While a few critics see the Indians as sincere and religious in their performance of the sacrifice, most critics who defend Lawrence do so by differentiating between his feelings and those of his fictional Indians. Mark Kinkead-Weekes writes that the reader should recognize the duplicity and vengefulness of the Indians (260), and Peter Balbert argues that Lawrence leaves textual clues in the story to "chart his horror of a tribe's passion that has gone wild" (123). Of course these readings emphasize Lawrence's negative feelings about Native American culture at the expense of his positive ones.

However, a Girardian explication of the text, set against the background of Lawrence's own knowledge of anthropology, shows that both critics and defenders of the work have focused on one aspect of the text at the expense of synthesis. Sheila Mac-Leod, James C. Cowan, and Peter Balbert have come closest to understanding the story when they focus on its ritual elements, note the ways in which the Woman is a sacrificial Christ-figure, and characterize the Woman as "victim." They err only in their explanation of the type of victim she is: Girardian theory clearly postulates the Woman as sacralized victim rather than *pharmakos*. Moreover, with the exception of MacLeod's brief treatment of the story, these readings do not reveal the significance of her gender in Lawrence's vision.

In light of Girard's theories, it is crucial to examine the reading Lawrence had been engaged in just prior to writing "The Woman Who Rode Away" in 1924. It is possible that Lawrence had read an edition of Frazer's *The Golden Bough* as early as 1911, but undoubtedly he was familiar with the work by 1915 (Marcus 232). Around this time he also read Jane Harrison's *Art and Ritual*. Moreover, Lawrence read Frazer again in 1924, when he borrowed the book from Mabel Dodge Luhan in New Mexico (Ellis 187). The descriptions of ritual Lawrence encountered in these texts would no doubt have been reinforced by his visits with Luhan to Native American ritual dances and ceremonies, as well as her extensive collection of religious icons from the American Southwest, featuring gory, bleeding Christ figures. Lawrence's visit to the San Geronimo Chapel at Taos Pueblo is also striking in this regard. The rear of the sanctuary features a towering icon of the Virgin Mary in the center, with other Mary icons descending to the left and right dressed in vivid blues. This was almost certainly the arrangement when Lawrence visited. Anthropologist Elsie Parsons described it in this way when she attended the Procession of Our Blessed Mother on 24 December 1932: "The large image of the Virgin stands on a table in the middle of the church, surrounded by the smaller images, seven or eight" (86). Only one Christ icon is present in the church, and it is smaller than the central Mary and located on the viewer's far right. Parsons also noted that in 1932 the church featured a painting of Christ on the side wall: "Christ stands on a crescent moon and at the side of his right leg emerges the sun" (86). The iconography parallels the mythical sun and moon employed in the short story, with the Woman as the intermediary figure. This almost total absence of the male figure and predominance of the female in the European-derived Catholic chapel is jarring, and very possibly stimulated imaginative possibilities in Lawrence concerning female presence in religion and culture that find expression in his short story.

In *The Golden Bough*, Lawrence would have read material more descriptive than theoretical that indicates the commonality of the sacrifice of kings in various parts of the world. These descriptions would have included prohibitions against these rulers touching members of the opposite sex, leaving their temples or houses, or even being allowed to touch the ground by walking, thus necessitating their being carried on litters. He would have read of a Pawnee sacrifice of a Sioux girl in 1837, where the captive had been held for six months, given gifts and good treatment, and finally had her heart eaten before her body and blood were sprinkled over the fields to ensure the fertility of the harvest (501). Undoubtedly, he would have been most intrigued by Frazer's chapter called "Killing the God in Mexico," which opens with this sentence: "By no people does the custom of sacrificing the human representative of a god appear to have been observed so commonly and with so much solemnity as by the Aztecs of ancient Mexico" (680). Here Lawrence would have read in even more ritualistic detail about Aztec practices and the distinctions they made between their victims. For example, during the Mexican harvest festival it was common for a criminal, with little ado, to be crushed between two stones. This treatment of the *pharmakos* was quite different from the treatment of other types of victims. Some sacrificial victims were not only esteemed as gods but worshiped as idols. They generally were held for six months to a year before being sacrificed, and in the days before the ceremony they were part of public festivals where people came to be cured and blessed by them. These victims, mostly men, were attended by a retinue of priests on the chance they might flee (681). The only Aztec sacrifice of a female delineated by Frazer is the yearly ritual of the maize goddess, where a young slave girl was fumigated by censers, paraded during public ceremonies on a frame, and sacrificed the next day (682–84). This included laying her body on a stone and stabbing her with a flint knife while she was held by four priests, a scenario familiar to readers of "The Woman Who Rode Away."

Lawrence also makes explicit the connection between the

Aztecs and the Chilchui Indians in his story. The Chilchui "were the sacred tribe of all the Indians. The descendants of Monte-zuma and of the old Aztec or Tontonac kings still lived among them, and the old priests still kept up the ancient religion, and offered human sacrifices" (42). Two points should be made about these descriptions. One is that Lawrence drew the particulars of the sacrificial rituals from scholarly sources. This should be enough to call into question the idea of the Woman's sacrifice as evidence of Lawrence's perverted misogyny, or the portrayal of the tribal rites as a product of his prejudiced European imagina-tion.

As for my own argument in light of Girardian analysis, we should note the two types of victims portrayed here: the criminal victim and the sacral victim. We should also recognize the limited status afforded to the few female victims Frazer notes. The Sioux girl was afforded high status by the Pawnees but not treated as the incarnation of a goddess. The Aztec victim was a slave, and while she was treated as a goddess, the time that elapsed between her captivity and death was very short, only a matter of days. In both cases, the female victims died in order to ensure a good har-vest, a sacrifice of some importance but one made to achieve a relatively short-term goal. This is in contrast to the Woman in Lawrence's story. Her sacrifice is expected to yield vastly signifi-cant results that will lead to the survival of an entire culture. The maize goddess is a marginalized insider, while the Woman is an outsider of status in her culture. She is treated as an incarnated goddess *and* endures a lengthy captivity. The importance of these characteristics will soon be evident.

Girard's theory postulates that mythological structures, as well as ethnological data, indicate that actual murder is at the founda-tion of cultural order and civilization. "The objective of ritual is the proper re-enactment of the surrogate victimage mechanism," which perpetuates whatever benefits the culture may have ac-crued by an original murder (Girard *Violence* 92). "The rite is therefore a repetition of the original, spontaneous lynching that restored order in the community" (Girard *Violence* 95). Thus, sacrifice is a culturally conditioned reaction to crisis designed for purposes of restoration or self-preservation. This crisis often has a mimetic dimension; in this case it is the crisis of acquisitive mi-mesis. That is, a contested object within a group or between two groups may instigate violence and lead to the extinction of one faction or group. The Woman senses the cultural crisis that affects the Chilchui because, as they believe, the white man has stolen the sun: a "shadow . . . was on the Indians of the valley, a deep, stoical disconsolation, almost religious in its depth" (63). One of the closing paragraphs of the story also underlines the crisis, as the word "anxious" is used three times to describe the Indians' state of mind (71). When this is the case, the sacrificial victim often in some ways embodies the crisis: "In myth, below the level of sacralization, it is easy to uncover the accusation of which the victim was the object. The accusation makes the victim responsible for the disorder and catastrophe, in other words for the crisis, that afflicts the community" (Girard *Things Hidden* 38). Thus, Lawrence accurately understands the sacrificial mechanism in "The Woman Who Rode Away" when the Indians believe the sacrifice of a white woman is necessary to reclaim the sun the white man has stolen and (let us not forget, as have some critics) also to reclaim the moon the white woman has hidden in her cave and return her to the Chilchui women (62).

While Lawrence wedded his own concerns—the disintegration of Western culture and the inauguration of a new era contingent on restored sexual relations between women and men—to the myths of the Chilchui, he did not create the allegory the young cacique relates without reference to Aztec myth. As Girard explains, "There would be no sun or moon without victims; the world would be plunged in obscurity and chaos. This is the basis of the whole Aztec religion" (*Scapegoat* 61). At this point it would be helpful to paraphrase a myth of the Aztec gods Girard relates. A group of gods gathers to decide which ones should light the world by immolating themselves and reemerging as the sun and moon. Tecuciztecatl volunteers to be immolated, but no one else will. When the gods "suggest" to a pock-marked god named Nanuatzin that he volunteer, he abruptly agrees. During the second critical episode, Nanuatzin casts himself into the fire but Tecuciztecatl loses his nerve. Only after the other gods' "encouragement" does the initial volunteer screw up his courage and cast himself onto the flames. Because of his hesitation, he becomes the moon, which is less bright (*Scapegoat* 57–58).

Girard suggests that the myth reveals several things about the Aztec culture and victims. First, the myth tries to assure the sacrificers that death is voluntary and that no murder is involved. Despite the presentation of the self-sacrifice of the gods, a subtle element of constraint reveals itself, suggesting persecution. Paradoxically, there is also "some truth in the myth of the consenting victims": at different times the victims want to sacrifice themselves (*Scapegoat* 63). These same structures are present repeatedly in "The Woman Who Rode Away." The Chilchui myth emphasizes the voluntary agency of the Woman, saying that "when a white woman *give herself* to our gods, then our gods will begin to make the world again" (61; my emphasis). The Woman participates in the Indians' myth-making by her evasive and misleading answers to their questions. When asked where she comes from, she replies, "I come from far away" (46), and says the reason for her journey is to "visit the Chilchui Indians—to see their houses and to know their Gods" (47). Thus, the Woman enhances the mystery about her presence and feeds her captors' suspicion that her arrival may fulfill a prophecy (46). When the Woman is brought into the presence of the old cacique, she confirms that she has brought her heart to the god of the Chilchui (54), and when she, "fatally," as Lawrence writes, tells the young cacique she hopes the Chilchui will regain the sun, he is ecstatic (63). The aged cacique also sees the Woman's willing participation in the ceremony as vital.

Nevertheless, the Chilchui also make sure that the Woman is in some sense a prisoner, and, as she recognizes, the drug she imbibes not only increases her consciousness but also keeps her tractable. Periodically the Woman consents to her sacrifice. At one point "the Indians, with their heavily religious natures, had made her succumb to their vision" (64). Again, near the end of the story, the Woman "knew she was a victim: that all this elaborate work upon her was the work of victimising her. But she did not mind. She wanted it" (67). Steven claims that with these lines Lawrence "absolves the victimizers of any responsibility and characterizes the woman as a masochistic thrill-seeker" (214), but nothing could be further from the truth. Lawrence not only portrays the doublethink of the persecutors in the story, but also offers a vivid description of the ritual from the victim's point of view—including her conflicting feelings and drugged perceptions.

I would now like to examine the Woman's status as sacral victim in more detail. Earlier, I described the mimetic dimension of the sacrificial crisis, which the Woman embodies as a member of white culture. Her status as foreigner has another dimension. According to Girard, "Foreigners are considered something less and more than human. . . . They may appear very maleficent or very beneficent, but in either case they are deeply imbued with the sacred" (*Violence* 267). Lawrence accentuates the Woman's otherness when, moments before the sacrifice, she is turned away from the Indians and they see her long, newly washed blonde hair. Lawrence devotes even more attention, however, to the privileges the Woman receives and the rituals she undergoes; these descriptions comprise nearly half the story. Clearly, the Woman is not a victim of marginal or criminal status, but a sacralized victim. She is housed in a part of the temple and continually waited on by priests and the young cacique, who "watched over her and cared for her like women" (66). Her ritual murder does not take place immediately but is postponed for months while she lives among the tribe. She is given a garden, delicacies to eat although the tribe is starving, special clothing, and a pet dog. Not only do the young cacique and other Indians spend hours in her presence, hoping to attain religious benefit from her, but they also believe she has the power to bless. The old cacique wants her blessing and asks her to make the sign of peace to him. When the Woman asks the significance of the color of her clothing, she is told blue is the color that "look[s] at us from the distance" (64). This indicates the Indians' belief that she is to live with the gods and watch over the tribe. It is important that she not come too near, as they fear as well as worship her power. Girard explains that "the original victim is endowed with superhuman, terrifying prestige because it is seen as the source of all order and disorder. Subsequent victims inherit some of this prestige" (*Things Hidden* 53).

This may lead us to ask whom the Woman represents. James Cowan suggests that the Woman may be an incarnation of the earth sun Tezcatlicapa (78), and, according to Girard's relation of Aztec myth, she may be an incarnation of the moon god. In both cases, the origin of the incarnation is of fundamental importance to the culture, thereby indicating her own stature. The Woman will have cosmic effect. Significantly, Lawrence chose to change the gender of the victim, representing the male moon god as female, incarnated in the Woman.

If the sacrifice of the Woman proved beneficial to the tribe, that would lead to two implications that must be examined here. The first is her potential status as a goddess of the Chilchui. As incarnated goddess, the woman will become a mythological figure rep-

resenting female power and influence in the culture. The second
is the potential political power for female rulers who come after
her, as Girard argues that ritual sacrifice is inextricably tied to
the evolution of royal authority in primitive societies. Eventually,
a tribe begins to grant authority to

> someone who is designated as a future victim and who draws his
> power and prestige retroactively from the reconciling power of the
> original scapegoat. With the passage of time the substitute victim's
> authority becomes more durable, more stable; the factors opposing it
> lose their importance, and another victim, human or animal, is sub-
> stituted for the king. . . . The vestiges of ritual are discarded. Sacred
> royalty is transformed into royalty pure and simple, into political
> power. (*Violence* 303–4)

It is interesting to note that the Woman is given a female dog,
Flora, and that this gift could in the future evolve into the sacrifice of the dog as substitute.

Many critics have tried to explain, some in a way that patron-
izes Lawrence, the seemingly inconsistent attitudes of the Chilchui. Laurence Steven suggests that their portrayal violates the
symbolic structure of the story because Lawrence's personal hatred interferes with his creative process (215). Few critics can reconcile the Chilchui's solicitousness towards the Woman with the
looks of hatred and feelings of revenge she describes. Although
they consider her wicked, they clearly look to her for salvation.
There are two reasons for their attitude. The first is the nature of
the gods and their representatives. Only in comparatively recent
times have gods been seen as wholly beneficent. Historically,
across the spectrum of cultures, gods embody both good and evil.
The sacralized victim in particular is problematic since benefits
accrue after its death rather than before. The god/victim is dangerous while it is alive and has human form. The community
"fears and owes everything to the sacred. It assumes it has been
engendered by it; the act of generative violence that brought it
about is attributed not to men, but to [the sacred], thereby it
brings about its own expulsion—releasing the community from
direct contact" (Girard *Violence* 267). As the young cacique explains to the Woman, she is to look "at [the tribe] from a distance" and not to "come near [them]" (64). The sacrificial victim
has a "dual connotation. . . . [I]t is an object of scorn . . . sur-

rounded by a quasi-religious aura of veneration" (Girard *Violence* 95). Lawrence's complication of the Indians' attitudes demonstrates his understanding of the sacrificial mechanism.

Equally important, however, is the way Lawrence envisions the Chilchui as vacillating between religious sincerity, accompanied by cultural regeneration, and irreligious attitudes that accompany decadence, cruelty, and decline. These attitudes are continuously present in the Indians, as the Woman senses. She notes their absorption in "something that was beyond her" as she undergoes the last rituals of the ceremony. She also, however, recognizes their "fixity of revenge" (67) and claims that the young cacique likes her personally while hating what she represents (66). Evidently revenge or hate sometimes takes the upper hand since stories relate that the Chilchui "kill a missionary at sight" (41) and that there are rumors of "human sacrifices" (42). We can speculate that the missionaries are killed quickly, as criminal victims. This is very different from the way the Woman is to be killed, but there is tension in the story between pure religious impulses and less noble motives. As Girard notes, the practice of human sacrifice may move a group in the direction of malevolent persecution. He calls this the contrary evolution of sacrifice, when the lapse in time before death is foreshortened; privileges disappear and victims are offered only tokens of sympathy, like the rum and cigarette given to prisoners in the ritual of French capital punishment (*Things Hidden* 53). Since the story ends with the sacrifice suspended, we are to see that the culture may move in either of two directions: cultural regeneration or eventual extinction.

The reader never learns which direction the culture takes because that is not the point of the story. Lawrence's emphasis is on the Woman. It seems that if the story were really evidence of his murderous feelings toward women, he would glory in the last bloody details of the sacrifice: spilt blood and the human heart held in the hand of the cacique. But he doesn't. Clearly, this would sensationalize the story and take the emphasis away from the Woman herself. The title of the story is not "The Woman Who Was Killed" but "The Woman Who Rode Away." This emphasizes her agency, her central place in the story, and, as she lacks a name, her mythological status. In *The Escaped Cock* Christ will not ask the woman of Isis her name, "for a name would set her apart" (59). Likewise, the Woman's lack of a name places her above the merely personal kind of existence Lawrence so regularly maligns in his writings. The Woman has transcendent status—both on the literal, anthropological level of the story and in the symbolic structure of Lawrence's work.

Kingsley Widmer writes that the destructive rituals of "The Woman Who Rode Away" parallel the regenerative rituals in Lawrence's later work (191). It is more accurate to see the story as part of Lawrence's attempt to find a myth of cultural regeneration with a modern woman at the center. In considering the question of misogyny in "The Woman Who Rode Away," one is tempted to ask why it is that Lawrence chooses to kill a woman. No one ever seems to ask why it is necessary for Christianity to be founded on the murder of a man, yet critics of patriarchal religion are aware that part of the power traditionally offered to men in its structure corresponds to the male figure's preeminence in the religious myth. As Sheila MacLeod explains, in the short story "male salvation is dependent on a prior female salvation" (126). Lawrence realizes that the Woman's sacrifice may allow the Chilchui culture to transcend its crisis, thus profoundly affecting the role and status of women. Meanwhile women themselves have the power to turn away from the models Lawrence sees as so destructive in modern Western culture.

Looking back over Lawrence's earlier bacchantes, priestesses, and victims that he rhetorically links with primitive religion and sacrifice, the contrast between them and the Woman is striking. The guilty immolation of the doll Mrs. Arabella and Miriam's sexual self-sacrifice in *Sons and Lovers* bring only deathly feelings to Paul. Bernard in "The Witch à la Mode" risks immolating himself and the "Goddess" Winifred, who reminds him of "Euripides' 'Bacchae'" before running away (66, 67), while Aaron chooses isolation over his sexual relationship with the "priestess" Marchesa and his own role as "God and victim" in *Aaron's Rod* (273). The Woman is much more like Brunnhilde in Wagner's Ring Cycle, which Lawrence so admired. Brunnhilde first sacrifices her godhead to save Siegmund, then, in *Die Götterdämmerung*, immolates herself on Siegfried's funeral pyre. This act returns the cursed ring to its origin, thereby restoring cultural order. No male, either human or god, can perform this feat. "The Woman Who Rode Away," with its realistic emphasis on ritual, may lack the drama and flair of the Wagner opera, but the parallels are there.

Lawrence's last work, *Apocalypse*, offers a final window into his aims in the short story. There his explanation of the modern malaise replicates the language of the Chilchui, as he writes that "half dead" (142) modern men and women "have lost the sun. . . . And we have lost the moon . . . the moon is black to us, and the sun is as sackcloth" (77–78). Lawrence wants to see the great cosmic mother given her due reverence. He writes with regret about her loss:

> Gone is the grand pagan calm which can see the woman of the cosmos wrapped in her warm gleam like the sun, and having her feet upon the moon. . . . For the great Woman of the pagan cosmos was driven into the wilderness at the end of the old epoch, and she has never been called back. (121)

Lawrence bemoans the loss of woman's centrality in Western culture. "The Woman Who Rode Away" is his first full-fledged attempt, however problematic, to restore her to her former position. His attempt to regenerate a representative of the modern woman he liked least shows his desire for reconciliation and belief in change. The trope of sacrifice in "The Woman Who Rode Away" clearly aligns the story with the regenerative rituals of Lawrence's later work.

## WORKS CITED

Balbert, Peter. "Snake's Eye and Obsidian Knife: Art, Ideology, and 'The Woman Who Rode Away.'" In *D. H. Lawrence and the Phallic Imagination: Essays on Sexual Identity and Feminist Misreading*. New York: St. Martin's, 1989.

Contreras, Sheila. "'These Were Just Natives to Her': Chilchui Indians and 'The Woman Who Rode Away.'" *DHLR* 25 (1993–94): 91–103.

Cowan, James C. *D. H. Lawrence's American Journey: A Study in Literature and Myth*. Cleveland: Case Western Reserve University Press, 1970.

Ellis, David. *D. H. Lawrence, Dying Game 1922–1930*. Cambridge: Cambridge University Press, 1998.

Frazer, Sir James George. *The Golden Bough: A Study in Magic and Religion*. 1890. Reprint, New York: Touchstone, 1996.

Girard, René. *The Scapegoat*. Translated by Yvonne Freccero. Baltimore: Johns Hopkins University Press, 1984.

———. *Things Hidden Since the Foundation of the World*. Translated by Stephen Bann and Michael Metteer. Stanford: Stanford University Press, 1987.

———. *Violence and the Sacred*. Translated by Patrick Gregory. Baltimore: Johns Hopkins University Press, 1977.

Kinkead-Weekes, Mark. "The Gringo Señora Who Rode Away."*DHLR* 22 (1990): 251–65.

MacLeod, Sheila. *Lawrence's Men and Women*. London: Heinemann, 1985.

Marcus, Phillip L. "'A Healed Whole Man': Frazer, Lawrence and Blood-Consciousness." In *Sir James Frazer and the Literary Imagination: Essays in Affinity and Influence*, edited by Robert Fraser. New York: St. Martin's, 1991.

Millett, Kate. *Sexual Politics*. Garden City, N.Y.: Doubleday, 1970.

Parsons, Elsie. *Taos Pueblo*. General Series in Anthropology. Vol. 2. 1936. Reprint, New York: Johnson Reprint Corporation, 1970.

Rudnick, Lois P. "D. H. Lawrence's New World Heroine: Mabel Dodge Luhan." *DHLR* 14 (1981): 85–109.

Steven, Laurence. "'The Woman Who Rode Away': D. H. Lawrence's Cul-de-Sac." *English Studies in Canada* 10 (1984): 209–20.

Widmer, Kingsley. *The Art of Perversity: D. H. Lawrence's Shorter Fictions*. Seattle: University of Washington Press, 1962.

# Lawrence's Theater of the Southwest

John Worthen

## I

THE FACT THAT WE ALL *KNOW* THAT NEW MEXICO WAS THE GREATEST experience from the outside world which Lawrence ever had, and that "the moment I saw the brilliant, proud morning shine high up over the deserts of Santa Fé, something stood still in my soul, and I started to attend" (*P* 142)—this knowledge dazzles us to the fact that it actually took Lawrence some time to find out what kind of an experience he was having. Those famous remarks about New Mexico were made more than six years after he arrived. This is what he wrote, just days after arriving:

> And here am I, a lone lorn Englishman, tumbled out of the known world of the British Empire onto this stage: for it persists in seeming like a stage to me, and not like the proper world. (*P* 192)

In that essay, "Indians and an Englishman," Lawrence makes the Southwest a stage, a circus, a farce, and a comic opera. After a week in Taos he would tell Robert Mountsier (in the first hint of difficulties): "If it doesn't *suit* me here, I shan't stay more than a month" (*L* iv. 300). Three days later he wrote to Earl Brewster in a very determined way about leaving:

> I don't know how long I shall stick it: probably, as a sort of lesson to myself, until the spring. Then I shall come away. But if I dislike it *too* much, I shall leave as soon as I decide that it is too much. (*L* iv. 305)

What he was up against in Taos, of course, was Mabel Ganson Evans Dodge Sterne Luhan. I shall be looking at his version of her in *Altitude*. The letter to Brewster (an American) makes it clear how Mabel was the problem:

What you dislike in America seems to me really dislikeable: everybody seems to be trying to enforce his, or her, *will*, and trying to see
how much the other person or persons will let themselves be overcome. . . . I dislike that: and I despise it. (*L* iv. 305)

Consider, therefore, the likelihood of Lawrence being back in
Italy by early in November 1922, after (doubtless) a passing visit
to England. No *Quetzalcoatl*, no *Plumed Serpent*, no "Woman
Who Rode Away," no *St. Mawr*, no "Princess," no *Mornings in
Mexico*. No *Altitude*, no *David*. His next book would probably
have been a very sour and very European rewriting of *Studies in
Classic American Literature*; Taos having been (as Gudrun and
Ursula fear marriage will be) an experience, but certainly unde-
sirable, and likely to be the end of experience. And Lawrence
would never have had that "greatest experience of the outside
world" at all.

Mabel's extraordinary, theatrical self-obsession—her writing
about Lawrence reminds me of a very young child in the way she
acknowledges nothing in the world except her own desires—is
perfectly described in Lawrence's letter to Brewster after his first
few days here: "People must be very insufficient and weak, wanting, inside themselves, if they find it necessary to stress themselves on every occasion" (*L* iv. 305). He may have come to
America for a new experience of the "outside world"; what he
*found* was the white world at its most theatrically impossible.
Tony Luhan's house, in which he and Frieda lived during those
first weeks, was a mere satellite of the big house, caught in the
unending orbit of its drama. However, with the mountains also
fully in view, away beyond Mabel's house, the Lawrences' escape
route was also clear.

The fact that together Frieda and he *did* manage to live their
own lives near Taos in the winter of 1922 (up at Del Monte with
Knud Merrild and Kai Götzsche), and then during 1924, up at
Kiowa to rebuild it and make it habitable (Kiowa originally of
course Mabel's ranch, so that she remained possessive of it even
after giving it to Frieda): they lived their own lives without either
compromising with Mabel, or finally quarreling with her. Just
riding away from it all would have been so tempting, and at different times both were tempted. But the Lawrences did what they
wanted, without ever being so ungrateful as to reject the person
who was (after all) responsible for bringing them there, and who

had enriched their lives in so many ways. How to enact gratitude to someone so self-willed, so bullying, without getting caught up in the whirling circles of her needs and fantasies? But they managed it.

## II

It was not, however, an accident that Lawrence wrote so much theater in the Southwest, for in one sense, he had found himself thrown on to the stage constantly in the play into which Mabel insisted on writing him (as she wrote all the guests encircled in her compound, eating at her table). Her dedication of her book *Lorenzo in Taos* to Robinson Jeffers very appropriately declares that she wanted to show in it "how we felt and acted" (Luhan ix).

But if life with Mabel was at times tragi-comedy, farce, and comic opera, what of Lawrence's experience of the Indians to whom she so ruthlessly directed him? Barely had he arrived before he was sent off with Tony to the Apache festival in Arizona. And then, of course, he wrote it up. He did not write what Mabel wanted, however, and she declared his account "not very good" (Luhan 52). For not only did he declare Taos a stage, and by implication all its inhabitants merely players; he also argued that his experience as a contemporary Anglo did not touch Indian experience at any point: "The voice out of the far-off time was not for my ears." He ends up convinced that he didn't "want to go back to them, ah never. . . . I can't cluster at the drum any more" (*P* 99). What he had thus started to attend to, in September 1922, was not (as the essay on New Mexico suggests) Indian religion; it was a certainty that his life, and Indian religion, did not meet or touch at any point that mattered.

This, of course, was heresy in Mabeltown, and it is worth stopping a moment to realize just how deeply it went against what people in Mabel's circle believed, people like the writer Mary Austin and the Indian rights campaigner John Collier. And above all, Mabel was living with Tony Luhan, and would shortly be marrying him—thus demonstrating in her own way the relationship of the races. It had been to help promote that relationship that she had persuaded Lawrence to come to Taos in the first place; she had told him "all I could about Taos and the Indians—and about Tony and me" (Luhan 4). Accompanying that letter she sent "an

Indian necklace to Frieda that I thought carried some Indian magic in it. . . . In the letter I put a few leaves of *desachey*, the perfume the Indians say makes the heart light, along with a little *osha*, the root that is a strong medicine" (Luhan 5). She was appealing, with Indian magic and medicine, to Lawrence the writer who would write about the Indians. It says, again, a good deal for Lawrence's self-possession that, instead, he wrote exactly what he wanted. It took him more than a year, perhaps as long as eighteen months, to escape the certainty that his life and Indian life had nothing to do with each other. And even then, he was capable of the deepest cynicism about the ways in which Indian life *could* be viewed by whites: the white gaze made even the most extraordinary Indian ceremonies (like the Hopi Snake Dance) nothing but a kind of circus, here in what he called "[t]he great Southwest, the national circusground" (*New Mexico* 64).

## III

His two Taos plays record, in quite different ways, how his experience changed. The two-scene fragment *Altitude*, from June 1924, demonstrates his comic realization that white people's reverence for (and belief in) the Indians is both hypocritical and unreal. This dramatic fragment is an oddly comic version of what he was simultaneously writing in "The Woman Who Rode Away." In *David*, a year later, however, he would write one of his first deeply sympathetic imaginative accounts of Indian experience, the experience which in 1928 he would celebrate in his essay on New Mexico.

Most readers of Lawrence think of his plays as "*black* with miners" (Kinkead-Weekes 479). I saw *A Collier's Friday Night* on at the Royal Court Theater in London in 1968—my first Lawrence play—and still do not forget the number of times men took off their boots, and put them on again, in the course of the evening, to say nothing of the moments when they were going round the stage with their lace-ends flapping. That's social realism.

It probably comes as a shock, then, to realize that three of Lawrence's ten plays not only had nothing to do with miners but were either conceived—or actually written—near Taos, New Mexico; they were, in the second of the senses in which I am using the phrase, his theater of the Southwest.

Lawrence had last written a play in 1918: *Touch and Go*. That was the end of his English theater. But when he, Frieda, and Dorothy Brett got back to New Mexico in March 1924, significantly the one-time actress Ida Rauh arrived too to stay with Mabel. Ida and Lawrence talked about theater immediately after they met (he had met very few actors, even retired ones, in the course of his career); and it was with her, her son Daniel Eastman, and partner Andrew Dasburg that the Lawrences took part in games of acting and charades at various times during the spring and summer of 1924. She was the first actress with whom he had a chance of doing this. Brett remembered:

> [Y]ou [Lawrence] and Ida are the stars. . . . you and Ida are in bed together, lying side by side under a blanket on the floor, and quarrelling as to who should get up, as you think you hear a burglar in the house. The quarrel is an exact replica of yours and Frieda's famous quarrels, and we are all helpless . . . with laughter. (Brett 52, 125)

Mabel Luhan also had happy memories of charades: Lawrence "was so gay and witty when he was playing! He could imitate anything or anybody" (Luhan 68). One evening, according to Mabel,

> we acted a scene that represented me taking Tony to Buffalo to introduce him to my mother! Lawrence was my mother, Ida was I, and Tony was Tony! Spud was my step-father, Monty; and Frieda was "a guest." That was so funny we couldn't finish the act! (Luhan 190)

It sounds a highly dangerous subject, concentrating as it did on the gap between the Anglo and the Indian. Humiliating Tony in public was never wise, either, and this scene was potentially explosive. Brett's account of the same evening records the explosion:

> We have a hilarious evening of charades. You are eager, alive, and full of fun. Even Tony is roped in: solemn, bewildered, he re-enacts with Mabel their marriage.
>     "I have married an Indian Chief," announces Mabel [presumably Ida].
>     "No," says Tony, with offended dignity, "not a chief." And he turns and walks solemnly out of the room, which brings the charade to an abrupt finish. (Brett 125)

The same danger of offense was, however, true of a good deal that they performed: Mabel remembered Lawrence and Frieda "being Tony and me in the front seat of the car" (Luhan 190), again a potentially explosive subject, with Frieda (I suspect) being Tony Luhan (she had the figure for it) and Lawrence being Mabel. Mabel simply commented that "We used to laugh until we were tired" (Luhan 190); the theatricality of her own life could accommodate such ups and downs, although Tony could not.

## IV

The matter of Tony and Mabel, of the Indians and the Anglos, was something to which Lawrence returned. On 19 June 1924, he, Frieda, and Brett came down from Kiowa for a visit to Taos, and met a number of Mabel's guests, including Clarence Thompson and Alice Sprague. The writer Mary Austin was either there at the time or had been there very recently. According to Mabel, the play's starting point had been Lawrence's annoyance with the word "fine": " 'Fine—fine—fine! That's all Americans have to say about themselves!' Lorenzo had scolded one day. 'I'll show them' " (Luhan 177). Brett, writing a few months after Mabel, told an elaborated version of the same story: how, one morning, "there is no Amelia [in fact Emilia: Mabel's cook], so you and I [Lawrence and Brett], finding ourselves the first up, cook the breakfast. The others come in one by one, and each one, to your polite amused inquiry as to how they feel, say: 'Fine—oh, fine!' On this theme you start, later, to write a play" (Brett 108). Spud Johnson, a friend who was a regular visitor but not actually there in mid-June, offered a very different version of the play's origin: a group production. This would have been characteristic of Lawrence. He had done exactly the same while living with Frieda, Philip Heseltine, and Dikran Kouyoumdjian in Cornwall, back in 1916: "At night we write a play, which is rather fun . . . all of us together, a comedy for the stage, about Heseltine and his Puma and so on" (*L* ii. 508, 501). Nothing exists of that comedy, although I suspect that Halliday and the Pussum in *Women in Love* are its survivors. Spud believed that, for *Altitude*,

[Lawrence] scribbled the opening lines on the back of a candy box one evening in Mabel Luhan's living room, with several friends present offering suggestions as to who the characters should be and what they should do and say. (*Plays* lxii)

The joke about Americans saying "fine" occupies only a few moments of the first scene. It is secondary to the individual self-images of the various characters, and in particular to the conflict between the white idealizing of the Indians, and to their actual treatment of the Indians. The Mabel character unthinkingly and habitually tells the Indian Joe to do things: "Fetch a pail of water, Joe" (*Plays* 543). When he brings the water, he is told, "You can go and chop some wood if you like." The stage direction runs: "(JOE *grunts, and doesn't like*)" (544)—but as soon as he reappears with the wood, Mabel says to him: "Can you stay help [*sic*] wash dishes? Put some water in the kettle" (546). Shortly afterwards, her husband Tony enters. She asks him if he wants a fried egg—and when he says he does, she responds: "Well get up and fry it then" (548). All the time, she and Mary Austin are insisting upon the Indians' natural superiority to the whites, and Mabel is given this devastatingly simple speech:

> The Indians *do* feel fine. They always feel fine. That's because they live right. They've got something that white people haven't got. We've got to get it. That's what we're here for. That's what I married Tony for. (548)

The parody of Mabel is here shading into simple truth; she herself might not have objected to this account. That's Mabel; this is Mary:

> I think the Indians are almost *always* right. . . . Mabel, when you say the Indians have that wonderful thing that white people haven't got, I think *I* have it.—Joe, more wood on the fire.—The Indians have the rhythm of the earth. (547, 548)

She and Mabel thus collaborate in fantasies of Indian superiority, while continuing to treat them as servants. Mabel insists:

> [T]he Indians have *life*. They have *life*, where we have *nerves*. Haven't you noticed, Mary, at an Indian dance, where the Indians all sit banked up on one side, and the white people on the other, how *all* the life is on the Indian side, and the white people seem so dead. The

Indians are like glowing coals, and the white people are like ashes.
(543–44)

Ida slyly asks her which side *she* feels herself on, to which Mabel
*"snorts"* and replies, "The Indian." There are various protests—
Spud saying "I don't know that I feel so *ashy* at an Indian dance,"
and Clarence campily complaining, "I *certainly* don't get any
glow from the Indians"—but Mabel rounds on them as betrayers:
"Well, you all know what I mean. And you do *all feel* it. Anyway
you *look* it" (544).

This Mabel is the target of some of Lawrence's wickedest im-
personations of behavior and point of view, the Mabel he himself
portrayed in charades. She rushes at things: the stove, the bacon,
the coffee. She is full of energy for the Indian, for non-Anglo life,
but when Clarence proposes going down to Taos Plaza in rose-
colored trousers, she vehemently opposes it: "Think how the people will *jeer*—and then talk. Another sign of vice from over here"
(545). But even that point is not quite as clear as she would like
it. In the debate over rose-colored trousers, she proposes: "Let's
ask Tony. He sees both sides. Tony! Tony! Clarence is going down
to the Plaza in those trousers. What you think of it." Tony's reply
is characteristic: "Make a guy of himself, sure" (547)—good, old-
fashioned, solid, rounded prejudice. The other Indian, Joe, the
servant, then makes things even more confusing for the poor Anglos. What does he think of the trousers? He answers: "They're
fine for a dance, for an Indian" (547). For a lesser race, fine; fine
for the silly things which Indians get up to, like dancing, but they
are not right for a *white* man!

Tony's status as Indian seer is also compromised by his choice
of breakfast food when he finds there is no cook and no breakfast
egg: "Well, I guess I eat a can of sardines." Mabel is outraged by
this cowardly act of submission to the tin-can culture of the white
man: "Tony, you don' want a can of sardines for breakfast." Tony
knows his own mind, however: "Guess I do!" (548). Mabel however finally gets him to "explain how the Indians feel when they
feel good" (550), and we may well anticipate something impres-
sive: the whole scene has led up to this moment. This is what
Tony says (stage direction: *chewing a sardine*):

Well—the Indians—they feel the sun. They feel the sun inside them,
and they feel good. Like what the sun shine inside them, and they
love everybody. (550)

Ida's sarcastic question—"Sunshine, Tony, or moonshine inside them?" (550)—is interrupted by Mary Austin, who is determined to explain the mystery of the Indians, which Tony has failed to articulate. But the scene instead ends in chaos. Spud enters with a bunch of poppies, Mabel shouts orders, Elizabeth argues, and Ida on the phone is quite unable to hear. So much for the rooted wisdom of the Indian about the sun, to which Lawrence had started to attend.[1]

*Altitude* is strictly a *jeu d'esprit*, belonging wholly to the time and circumstance of its composition. I am sorry that Lawrence did not write more in this vein; he could write drawing-room comedy effortlessly. And, in particular, the way even such a slight piece continually revolves around the subject of how the Indians are different, whether they are superior, how they might be superior, what might be wrong with the Anglos—this is characteristic. The play reminds me of Lawrence's comment on E. M. Forster's *A Passage to India*, which he read within a couple of weeks of writing *Altitude*:

> At least the repudiation of our white bunk is genuine, sincere, and pretty thorough, it seems to me. Negative, yes. But King Charles *must* have his head off. Homage to the headsman. (*L* v. 143)

The bunk *he* was writing about in *Altitude*, however, was not only white bunk about themselves but also white bunk about the Indians, as well as Indian bunk about sunshine.

# V

The larger question of what the North American Indian meant to Lawrence remained unanswered. In his essays "The Dance of the Sprouting Corn" and in particular "Indians and Entertainment," dating from April 1924, he constantly used comparisons with theater to describe his sense of the difference between white consciousness and Indian. However, first the essay on "Pan in America," which he wrote in May 1924, and then the long essay on the Hopi Snake Dance, which he wrote in August 1924, represented a breakthrough in the ways they find of writing about animism. He could not resist partnering the latter with the little essay "Just back from the Snake Dance—Tired Out," which he gave to the *Laughing Horse* and which they printed in September 1924 (no. 11, 26–29). Mabel Luhan reacted violently against that piece: "I had not taken him to the Snake Dance to have him describe it in this fashion" (Luhan 268). But the short essay acts as a kind of lightning conductor, leading away all the negative reactions which Lawrence knew were part of his own honest reaction to Indians in America—the fact that, to the Anglo, Indians *are* often theatrical, *are* easily seen as just part of a show. The long essay, however, was Lawrence's first attempt to describe what North American Indian animism might be like in practice.

His next attempt—worked out in ways that people actually talk and behave—is found in a most unexpected place: *David*, written in the spring of 1925. *David* has usually been regarded as an unreadable piece of Old Testament pastiche. I can only agree that it is *not* a good play. Yet it seems to me to be a crucial document in the history of Lawrence's writing about the Southwest.

When Lawrence and Frieda finally got back to the ranch on 5 April 1925, Lawrence was still too sick to do much, following his illness after finishing *The Plumed Serpent*. For a long time the only thing he wrote, apart from letters, was *David*. Frieda remembered that

> it was spring and he lay on a canvas bed on the small porch outside the cabin and slowly, day by day his strength came back, he could hardly believe it. It seemed a miracle. . . . The poignancy of "David" is partly a result of Lawrence's own escape from the valley of death. (Squires 173–74)

Writing in bed with his notebook propped up on his knees, using a pencil and not his customary fountain pen, at his usual speed Lawrence could have written the play in a week. But he was working slowly—Frieda said he was "sleeping quite a lot of the time" (*L* v. 233)—and it took him about a month. He finally finished it on 7 May. Within ten days, Ida Rauh had come up from Santa Fe to hear him read it aloud. She did not much like it, but did what she could to help him try to find a theater group which might take it. No one did, until a London society produced it in 1927.[2] I am interested in the fact of Lawrence writing this play, of all things, as he came back to life in the quietness—what quietness!—of the ranch during April 1925.

During that month, the Lawrences saw almost no one—just the

Hawk family, and Brett—but their constant companions were the Indian couple Trinidad and Rufina, who were actually living with them in the third cabin. Rufina helped in the house, and Trinidad outdoors. As soon as he was on his feet, Lawrence worked with Trinidad, as he recalled in the "New Mexico" essay:

> And the Indian, however objectionable he may be on occasion, has still some of the strange beauty and pathos of the religion that brought him forth and is now shedding him away into oblivion. When Trinidad, the Indian boy, and I planted corn at the ranch, my soul paused to see his brown hands softly moving the earth over the maize in pure ritual. He was back in his old religious self, and the ages stood still. (*P* 147)

The version of religion Lawrence had come to realize was one "which precedes the god-concept," and—he argued—"is therefore greater and deeper than any god-religion" (*P* 147). Carl Jung wrote an essay about the Taos Pueblo (written after his own visit in January 1925—he just missed Lawrence). It shows a sensitive European observing (on the one hand) the absolute secrecy with which the Pueblo Indians guarded their religion, and (on the other) the tremendous emotion which it involved. Jung sat on the roof of the pueblo with one of the chiefs, "the blazing sun rising higher and higher":

> [H]e said, pointing to the sun, "Is not he who moves there our father? How can anyone say differently? How can there be another god? Nothing can be without the sun." His excitement, which was already perceptible, mounted still higher; he struggled for words, and exclaimed at last, "What would a man do alone in the mountains? He cannot even build his fire without him." (Jung 250)

Lawrence had also reached exactly that awareness:

> For the whole life-effort of man was to get his life into direct contact with the elemental life of the cosmos, mountain-life, cloud-life, thunder-life, air-life, earth-life, sun-life. To come into immediate *felt* contact, and so derive energy, power, and a dark sort of joy. This effort into sheer naked contact, *without an intermediary or mediator*, is the root meaning of religion. (*P* 146–47).

But, the reader must be wondering, what has *that* got to do with a play which constantly addresses the Old Testament God?

## VI

It was actually Frieda who pointed out, about *David*: "The outer form of the life of these Old Testament people Lawrence believed to have been much like the near Taos Indians" (Squires 174). When you start to look, a great deal falls into place. The play may be Biblical Palestine, but it is actually set in Taos. The houses in the play are made not just of dried mud-brick but specifically of adobe; in front of them they have (a colonial word) a "compound": "the area in front of a native house." The houses have flat roofs, true of both Palestine and New Mexico, but the bread is also "flat"—he means tortillas. It is also a tented culture; outside the adobe houses, the tents are made of "worsted." Finally, in the village of Bethlehem in scene iii you find a "Plaza," like those in the Southwest. The "Great White Bird" of Saul's madness is probably a version of the Eagle or Thunderbird in North American Indian mythology; but the whole outer form of life—including costume—is Indian. When Saul, possessed by the chants of religion at the end of the play, strips his clothes off, he emerges *a dark-skinned man in a leathern loin-girdle*—in contrast with David, who is always described with the King James Bible word "ruddy"—pinko-white Anglo, as against Saul's Indian self.

But it was not just the outer life for upon which Lawrence drew upon his knowledge of the Indians. The play demonstrates an old religion, rule, and king being supplanted by a new, specifically more modern civilization, personal, individual, in a way that exactly parallels the cultural and religious change Lawrence saw destroying Indian culture. *David* was at last his work for "the strange beauty and pathos" (*P* 147) of Indian religion—the work which Mabel Luhan was so disappointed he had not done when he first came to Taos.

Having started by writing—of course—about "God" and "Lord," Lawrence gradually brought in another vocabulary altogether: "Deep," "Bolt," "One," "Might," "Fire," "Thunderer," "Strength," "Full," "Dawn," "Hope," "Morning Wind," "the bright horn," "Night," "Giver," "day," "Hill," "Name," "Kindler," "Wave," and "Sun." So that where, for example, Samuel had originally asked "Who knoweth the ways of the Lord?" Lawrence altered this to "Who knoweth the ways of the Deep?" And so on throughout. His printers, however, although conscientiously making all these changes from "Lord" to the animist language Lawrence continued to develop in proof, were determined to make all references to God which they could find start with capital letters, in the forms "his" and "him," "thee" and "thou," although Lawrence had not used capitals in his manuscript. As a result, the printed text has up to now looked and felt far more Biblical than it ever should have: "the Lord poured his power over thee," for example, acquired a capital letter on the "his" from the printer, which remained even when Lawrence changed "Lord" to "Deep."

The play's animism has hardly been noticed, as a result. Where it really counts, I think, is in the presentation of Saul. Saul, representative of the old animist belief, dies at the end of scene 15. But on two occasions he goes into religious ecstasies which are (to my mind) the most important things in the play; they represent Lawrence working his way deep into the consciousness of someone for whom animism was not a theory developed in an essay but a fact, developed in a fiction. David sings a psalm in scene 11, addressed of course to the "new" God of Israel: David's God. It drives Saul really wild, out of his mind, as he considers what David's new Anglo world will be like:

Hath Saul no sight into the unseen? Ha look! look down the deep well, how the black water is troubled. . . . And men shall inherit the earth! Yea, like locusts, and whirring on wings like locusts. To this the seed of David shall come, and this is their triumph, when the house of Saul has been swept up, long, long ago into the body of God.—Godless the world! Godless the men in myriads even like locusts.—No God in the air! No God on the mountains! Even out of the deeps of the sky they lured him, into their pit! So the world is empty of God, empty, empty, like a blown egg-shell bunged with wax and floating meaningless. (*Plays* 488–89)

That's just a taste of the ecstasy into which Saul works himself. Here he is, saner, in one of the fragments Lawrence cut from the play:

There is no commandment from God, save one, which is the commandment of the fire: *Oh, take my flame into the fuel of your life.*— There is but one sin, to deny the flame of God its rushing leap in my body. (*Plays*, 584)

Lawrence had always been good at writing out of extreme states, and this is some of the most extraordinary writing he ever did.

When at the end of the play Saul is overtaken by the rhythms of the chanting, he speaks the language of the tribal chief who believes in the sun as father:

> I will come up! Oh! I will come up! Dip me in the flame of brightness, thou Bright One, call up the sun in my heart, of the clouds of me. Lo! I have been darkened, and deadened with ashes! Blow a fierce flame on me, from the middle of thy glory, oh thou of the faceless flame! Oh dip me in the ceaseless flame! (*Plays* 519)

At this point he strips, and is seen as that *dark-skinned man*:

> Nay, I carry nought upon me, the long flame of my body leans to the flame of all glory!—I am no king, save in the Glory of God. I have no kingdom, save my body and soul. I have no name. But as a slow and dark flame leaneth to a great glory of flame, and is sipped up, naked and nameless lean I to the glory of the Lord. (*Plays* 519)

This kind of writing strikes me as right on the edge of the possible, and might easily turn into pretentious nonsense. But it sustains a tremendous charge of energy as religious utterance.


# VII

Having written those speeches, Lawrence took perhaps another eighteen months to develop a conscious understanding of what he meant. The essays he wrote for *Sketches of Etruscan Places* in 1927 would finally claim that

> The old idea of the vitality of the universe was evolved long before history begins, and elaborated into a vast religion. . . . [W]e see evidence of one underlying religious idea: the conception of the vitality of the cosmos. (*SEP* 57)

Confirming that he learned this from his play, Lawrence drew a direct comparison with David: "This was the idea at the back of all the great old civilisations. It was even, half-transmuted, at the back of David's mind, and voiced in the Psalms. But with David the living cosmos became merely a personal god" (*SEP* 58).

Such a distinction between an older, heroic, I would say Indian Saul, living instinctively the vitality of the cosmos, and a younger, cleverer, Anglo, self-conscious David, believing in a personal relationship with a personal God, was the culmination of a distinction which had been growing clear in Lawrence since 1922. Consequently, *David* became (paradoxically) the work of Lawrence's most steeped in the language of the Bible, and an attempt to get behind the Bible completely, to recreate the religion of the Southwest, to recreate a myth of the past, to make us feel what religious belief might, once, have been. And it was New Mexico, for sure, which gave him the first clue for this new, recreative theater; it *was* where he first began "to attend."

## NOTES

1. I would like to thank the six people who helped me with the original lecture version of this essay: Jill Franks (Mabel), Lois Ascherman (Ida), Nora Stovel (Mary), Lou Greiff (Tony), Bruce Clarke (Joe), Howard Booth (Spud).

2. See *Plays*, ed. Schwarze and Worthen, lxxi–lxxiii, lxxv–lxxvi, lxxix–lxxxix.

## WORKS CITED

Brett, Dorothy. *Lawrence and Brett; A Friendship*. Philadelphia: Lippincott, 1933.

Jung, C. J. *Memories, Dreams, Reflections*. Translated by Richard and Clara Winston. New York: Pantheon, 1963.

Kinkead-Weekes, Mark. *D. H. Lawrence: Triumph to Exile 1912–1922*. Cambridge: Cambridge University Press, 1995.

Luhan, Mabel Dodge. *Lorenzo in Taos*. New York: Knopf, 1932.

Squires, Michael, ed. *D. H. Lawrence's Manuscripts: The Correspondence of Frieda Lawrence, Jake Zeitlin, and Others*. New York: St. Martin's, 1991.

# Deconstructing Myth in
## *Lady Chatterley's Lover*
### Ginette Katz-Roy

> Once a book is fathomed, once it is *known*, and its meaning
> is fixed or established, it is dead.
>
> D. H. Lawrence, Apocalypse

> [W]hat I have tried to systematize a deconstructionist criti-
> cism against is precisely the authority of meaning, as *tran-*
> *scendental signified* or *telos*.
>
> Jacques Derrida, Positions

SINCE MOST CRITICS (AND EVEN DERRIDA HIMSELF) AGREE THAT DE-
construction does not offer a definite method for literary analysis,[1] this essay, although inspired by that theoretical approach,[2]
cannot lay claim to any particular orthodoxy. In very simple
terms, I am concerned with Lawrence's problematic use of myth
and with the resultant indeterminacy of meaning in *Lady Chatterley's Lover*.

Near the end of 1929, Lawrence wrote that "Myth is an attempt to narrate a whole experience, of which the purpose is too
deep, going too deep in the blood and soul, for mental explanation
or description" (*A* 49). Both Lawrence and Derrida obviously distrust "the authority of meaning" and absolute truths. Paradoxically, most readers think of Lawrence as a man with a message,
and of his last novel as the final expression—in near mythical
terms—of his unshakable faith in sexual emancipation, Constance and Mellors being one of the many versions of the ideal
couple in literature, if not a conventional model of virtue.

*Lady Chatterley's Lover* cannot be considered mythical in the
sense of, say, *Frankenstein* and *Dr. Jekyll and Mr. Hyde*, which,
though rooted in a historical context, evade history and convey a
clearly decipherable ethical message to generation after generation. But *Lady Chatterley* has engendered a sort of myth of the

Lawrentian myth. There has always been a wide gap between the complex contents of Lawrence's book and its reception by the general public (or even more informed readers). The story has become a "myth" in the banal understanding of this term, that is to say, that its bad reputation is largely based on a certain amount of misunderstanding or delusion. In fact, because of its explicit and "realistic" descriptions of sexual intercourse, this novel has always been more mythicized than a less heterogeneous and more obviously mythopoeic construct like *The Plumed Serpent*, for instance. The erotic theme has become an object of fascination, scandal, or caricatured representation, as if the mythical or the symbolic were reduced to the literal.

Yet, the message is not as evident as it seems. Here, as elsewhere in his work, Lawrence's way of undermining a number of oppositions (sex/mind, nature/culture, working-class/upper-class, realistic story/fable, philosophy/myth) is in itself a deconstructive practice which helps him convey a holistic outlook on life, denounce the tyranny of the logos,[3] and avoid univocity. The "poet-thinker" that he was would certainly have agreed with Derrida that in literature as well as in philosophy, "The opposition between intuition, concept and consciousness is totally irrelevant. . . . These three values belong to the order and the movement of meaning. So do metaphors"—and, we could add: so do all metaphorical forms of expression like symbols and myths.[4]

Jonathan Culler says that "To deconstruct a discourse is to show how it undermines the philosophy it asserts" and also that "What is deconstructed in deconstructive analyses . . . is not the text itself but the text as it is read" (86, 215). Now, *Lady Chatterley's Lover* is often seen as an unsatisfactory blend of realist novel and philosophical tale. John Middleton Murry already stressed this generic tension in his review of the novel in 1929 and found the "implicit philosophy" of the book unpalatable because, by underrating the importance of feelings, Lawrence had "chosen to be the prophet of a half truth":

> As a narrative it is perfectly convincing: the two people are real, and most real precisely where Mr Lawrence would have them appear most real, namely in their sexual mating. But in such a narrative a philosophy is implicit; and the philosophy makes us pause. (281)

Murry misses the point that Lawrence's writing strategy tends precisely to eliminate this doubleness. In order to reconcile more or less effectively the realistic story and the philosophy, Lawrence resorts to myth, in the form of mythological references and fabulistic elements. These elements participate in the building up of what Charles Mauron would have called the author's "personal myth." In the case of Lawrence, this "personal myth" entails a belief in salvation through the necessary reconciliation of body and mind, or nature and culture, thanks to a new approach to sex, a belief which includes a certain amount of doubt, like any belief.

André Malraux, who wrote the preface to the 1932 French edition of *Lady Chatterley's Lover*, was probably the first to analyze this novel in terms of "the creation of a new sexuality-myth." In his very perceptive reading of the book, he reveals mixed feelings and expresses a distrust of "pledges whose roots strike into the very depths of flesh and blood." He sees that Lawrence was trying to destroy our Western myth of sexuality and make a moral value of eroticism. But however attractive the theme of the reawakening of the body, the French novelist is unsure that it would really be the starting point of a new myth, since no one could predict whether Lawrence's work would speak to the collective imagination of his day or of times to come: "A myth admits of no discussion; either it lives or it does not live. . . . [M]yths do not develop in the way that they control emotions, but only in so far as they justify them" (Malraux 296–97).

As we have seen, *Lady Chatterley's Lover* did speak to the public's fantasies but not as its author had wished. Because of the scandal it caused, Lawrence's book is still vaguely associated with a notion of transgression both of sexual and social taboos, but many will either read it as outdated erotic literature or, at best, consider it a landmark in the history of sexual emancipation. The novel is constantly being reinstated in the historical context of the post-Victorian era instead of breaking free from it to acquire the dimension of a literary myth.

Roland Barthes says that, in our modern society, myth is a socially suggestive object (*Mythologies* 181–82). When in 1929 Lawrence realized that his book was suggestive in a way that was alien to his convictions, he wrote *A Propos of "Lady Chatterley's Lover,"* a defense of healthy sexuality and, unexpectedly, of the Christian marriage sacrament as a means of escaping the tyranny of the State and all forms of authoritarian regimes: "Do we then want to break marriage? If we do break it, it means we all fall to a far greater extent under the direct sway of the State. Do we want to fall under the direct sway of the State, any State? For my part, I don't" (*LCL* 321). This interpretation of his own venture, marked by his resentment against the state and his fear of censorship, sounds more clearly disingenuous than the "message" of the novel whose *aporias* do not appear at first sight.

The essay throws light on one of Lawrence's customary and disturbing narrative strategies: the frequent changes of focus from the general to the personal and back from the individual to the social being through references to the sacred, whether Judaeo-Christian or pagan. Recalling his main mythical sources, the story of Adam and Eve, the Apocalypse, and ancient cosmological myths, Lawrence claims that his book shows "the renewal of marriage: the true phallic marriage," the phallus being (in near Lacanian terms[5]) "the great old symbol of godly vitality in a man, and of immediate contact" (*LCL* 328). Here we have the expression of the author's intention, in the guise of an act of faith; but since "there is nothing outside the text," as Derrida says (*De la grammatologie* 227), we will now turn to the novel to see if it really has anything to say in its own defense as a cogent ethical project or if the reputation from which it suffers does not stem from a particularly misleading system of meaning.

In *D. H. Lawrence's "Lady": A New Look at "Lady Chatterley's Lover*," Lydia Blanchard, quoting Barthes, draws our attention to the problem of the treatment of sexuality in the novel:

> To understand a text, as Barthes has pointed out, "is not only to pass from one word to another, it is also to pass from one level to another"; to do so with *Lady Chatterley* is to experience *jouissance*, the "rapture of dislocation produced by ruptures or violations of intelligibility." . . . [*Lady Chatterley's Lover*] is in the tradition of realism but does not take realism too seriously—it cannot, after all, adequately convey the experience of sexuality, which underlies the rhythms of language itself. (32)

Blanchard points out a number of parodic passages and distancing devices which somehow destabilize the reader. It is clear that an analysis of Lawrence's narrative strategy can only emphasize the play of unifying and disruptive narrative devices at all levels, even that of the mythical project—a play which undermines any authoritative interpretation of the text.

Many thinkers have noted that myth aims at the symbolic res-

toration of primordial unity and tries to answer questionings
about the meaning of life by offering the prospect of an escape out
of linear time. I won't dwell on the well-known patterns of mythic
regeneration and cyclical time which underlie the novel and indicate its symbolic meaning without too much ambiguity. Like
many myths, including that of Genesis, *Lady Chatterley's Lover*
is the story of a new beginning after a period of loss, frustration,
and dereliction. Here is how Connie perceives what is happening
to her during one of the many scenes of sexual intercourse described in the book: "it came with a strange slow thrust of peace,
the dark thrust of peace and a ponderous, primordial tenderness,
such as made the world in the beginning" (174). The cosmic and
universal dimensions of this experience are reinforced by the
image of the Flood: "She dared to let go everything, all herself,
and be gone in the flood" and by the theme of the fall into nothingness: "the consummation was upon her, and she was gone, she
was not, and she was born: a woman" (174). She is reborn after
feeling totally destroyed. Let us note that Mellors's first name,
Oliver, recalls the olive branch brought by the dove after the
Flood as a token of peace.

Lawrence presents the sexual encounters as ordeals punctuat-
ing Connie's initiation into a new life of the body, here and now.
Mellors is the incarnation of the sacred with all the violence that
is attached to this notion in primitive cultures (as René Girard
has shown in *Violence and the Sacred*). The place where he lives
is "a sort of little sanctuary" (88); the first time Connie sees him
washing half-naked near the hut, it is "a visionary experience"
(66); to her he is a god: "And now she touched him, and it was
the sons of god with the daughters of men" (174). Connie approaches him with religious awe. There is something impersonal
about him. He is the "nameless man, moving on beautiful feet,
beautiful in the phallic mystery" (138). During their lovemaking,
she feels the "anguish of terror" (174) and is "afraid of the violent muscles" (171); elsewhere she realizes that she is "a little
afraid of him, as if he were not quite human" (227). The exorciz-
ing of death through lovemaking involves a sacrifice: "she
moaned with a sort of bliss, as a sacrifice, and a new-born thing"
(174). Ritual death redeems one from actual death,[6] ritual impurity from actual impurity. After having experienced anal intercourse with her lover, Connie thinks: "what one supremely
wanted was this piercing, consuming, rather awful sensuality"

(247). Mellors, another version of "the man who died," is a dying god who requires a sacrifice to be revived. His function of gamekeeper leads him to kill in order to protect those who threaten the living. This is exemplified at the beginning of the book by his killing a cat he considers a poacher. After two allusions to Héloïse and Abelard in the novel, Mellors's apology for chastity at the end refers us back to the natural cycle of organic life and the Persephone myth: "I love being chaste now. I love it as snowdrops love the snow. I love this chastity, which is the pause and peace of our fucking, between us like a snowdrop of forked white fire" (301).

Lawrence constantly departs from realism through a rich (even internal) intertextuality in the evocation of his new edenic couple. The "snowdrop of forked white fire" points toward the "blue, forked torch" of "Bavarian Gentians" with the additional reference to Lawrence's own idiosyncratic use of white as symbolic of death. Connie's discourse is so fraught with intertextual references that it almost sounds like a guide for deciphering her symbolic function or an author's comment within her stream of consciousness:

> She wanted to forget, to forget the world and all the dreadful carrion-bodied people. "Ye must be born again!—I believe in the resurrection of the body!—Except a grain of wheat fall into the earth and die, it shall by no means bring forth.—When the crocus cometh forth I too will emerge and see the sun !" In the wind of March, *endless phrases swept through her consciousness.* (85; my emphasis)

Derrida believes that writing is made of "grafts" or that it only consists of "traces of traces." Lawrence constantly stresses the inscription of discourse within discourse that constitutes the very nature of literature. All the literary and biblical allusions, all the references to Adam and Eve, Persephone and Pluto, Vulcan and Venus, Héloïse and Abélard turn the lady and her gamekeeper into an archetypal couple that often seems overconscious of the role they are playing at a diegetic level. Lawrence's practice undermines both the mimetic illusion characteristic of novelistic literature and the sense of the supernatural found in myth. His characters are more than human and less supernatural than the creatures (whether gods or monsters) of myths, legends, and tales.

*Lady Chatterley* echoes popular tales like Sleeping Beauty or the archetypal tale of a prince who marries a shepherdess (in reverse). The description of Mellors's hut at the beginning is very much like that of a pretty little cottage in a fairy-tale. "Till she came to the clearing on the far end of the wood, and saw the green-stained cottage looking almost rosy, like the flesh underneath a mushroom, its stone warmed in a burst of sun" (86). The lovers seem to meet in the magic circle of a clearing in the legendary Sherwood Forest. But what an unlikely Prince Charming Mellors is!

And meanwhile, romance is debunked from the start in the passage in which Clifford in his wheelchair admires the landscape as an intellectual who always perceives nature through the lens of culture: "He sat looking at the greenish sweep of the riding downwards, a clear way through the bracken and oaks. It swerved at the bottom of the hill, and disappeared. But it had such a lovely easy curve, of knights riding and ladies on palfreys" (42). Later, Connie mocks her husband's relationship with Miss Bentley in these terms: "But Clifford, do you realise you are the *Roman de la Rose* of Miss Bentley and lots like her?" (160). The association of Clifford with "romance" in both its meanings (legendary medieval tale and sentimental story) is not devoid of irony, particularly when we also note that, in a conversation with Connie, he declares: "What we need is classic control" (139)—a classic control which is of course alien to Lawrence's conception of literature.

There is also a satire of the type of modernist psychological novels Clifford writes, a criticism of neo-platonic metaphysics by Tommy Dukes in chapter 4, and mythology itself sometimes loses some of its aura according to the variations of the narrative perspective. I don't know what to make of the passage in which Connie becomes rhapsodic about her lover's penis in terms which may either be taken seriously as an author's comment or ironically as a token of female self-delusion. She wants to "call on Iacchos, the bright phallos that had no independent personality behind it, but was pure god-servant to the woman" (136). I have the same doubts about the description of Hilda as "a ruddy, rich-coloured Athena" (238). Mellors's display of classical culture when he is at Duncan Forbes's shows very well the ambiguity created by the dissemination of the author's voice through different characters: "'Better do us in a group, Vulcan and Venus under the net of art.—I used to be a blacksmith, before I was a gamekeeper'" (287), he says to the painter, almost like a ventrilo-quist's dummy handled by Lawrence, even if the author's knowledge of mythology proves to be slightly inaccurate.[7] We may also wonder if the fact that Mellors's daughter, who is described as a little monkey, bears the same nickname as Constance Chat-terley is an ironical pseudo-coincidence or a possible reference to the birth of Eve from one of Adam's ribs (Mellors having given birth literally to his daughter Connie and figuratively to Con-stance).

The often critical *mise en abyme* (embedding) of various types of literature and various images and voices of the writer within the text creates a flickering of meaning which weakens the coher-ence of the surface mythopoeic project. As we have seen, quota-tions and textual references circulate through the characters' speech in such a way that the omniscient narrator as author, crit-ical reader, and interpreter of his own text is insistently present, even when at the end he makes believe that he has vanished to let several characters communicate directly through letters. The book ends with a written monologue within a text largely devoted to dialogues. The direct speech in the letters permits a return to a unified point of view, if not a totally convincing one, given the confusing narrative strategy employed up to that point in the novel. Mellors's letter is of course acceptable within the frame-work of a realist novel since he is far from Connie, but its style is heterogeneous and at times surprisingly literary. The reader perceives that it has both a diegetic and a hermeneutic function. Mellors has the last word in a very didactic peroration conflating an apocalyptic vision of human society and a religious belief in the redemptive value of physical love—in short, the Gospel ac-cording to Lawrence, such as it is presented in *A Propos* and else-where. Blending Christian imagery and references to the natural cycle of life, his letter underlines the mythical pattern of rebirth after a temporary death but also the mythical aspect of the myth insofar as it remains a piece of fiction, a promise. At the end there is no paradise regained, no restoration of a primordial unity, just separation, hope, and doubt: "But we have to be separate for a while, and I suppose it is really the wiser way. If only one were sure" (301).

A series of unflattering portraits of writers—Clifford, Michael-is, and Hammond—reveals the self-reflexivity of the text in a sa-tirical mode. Connie's capacity for detachment and involvement is the measure of Lawrence's own. Just as he makes her capable of seeing the grotesque side of the sexual act, he ridicules the figure of the writer and also, anticipating the public's reaction to his book through a vapid remark of Hammond's, he reveals a humorous clear-sightedness: "The whole point about the sexual problem . . . is that there is no point to it. Strictly, there is no problem. We don't want to follow a man into the W.C. So why should we want to follow him into bed with a woman?" (32).

In fact, Lawrence inhabits his text through many characters, especially the writers, first through Tommy Dukes whom Connie considers with remarkable lucidity as her "oracle." This man's speech—note that he is a brigadier-general—offers a grandiloquent parody of Lawrence's style and themes: "[O]ur civilisation is going to fall. It's going down the bottomless pit, down the chasm. And believe me, the only bridge across the chasm will be the phallus! . . . Give me the resurrection of the body !" (75). This recalls the very first line of the novel with its prophetic tone and surprising assertion: "Ours is essentially a tragic age, so we refuse to take it tragically" (5). Interestingly, Connie establishes an explicit link between Tommy Dukes and Mellors, who, in the end, will take up the same themes in a slightly less bombastic style: "[Mellors] looked like a free soldier rather than a servant. And something about him reminded Connie of Tommy Dukes" (47). The gamekeeper's letter contains another reminder of the author's original warning to his readers in the first line of the novel: "There's a bad time coming" (300), a sentence which contrasts strikingly in tone and content with the facetious open ending: "John Thomas says good-night to lady Jane, a little droopingly, but with a hopeful heart—" (302).

The mixture of tragedy, romance, and comedy, of precious and vulgar language, of flippant and very serious tone is certainly the most baffling characteristic of this novel. Michael Bell, who compares it in this respect to *Mr Noon*, insists that "*Lady Chatterley's Lover* is no less serious a book than its predecessors but it takes a humorous awareness as part of its central subject-matter and this is inseparably registered in its narrative tone" (Bell *Language* 223).[8] Connie and Mellors's experience is somehow sacralized by the mythical pattern superimposed on the realistic story, but myth itself is constantly desacralized.

If this novel represents the last development of what I have referred to as the author's "personal myth," the latter is largely desacralized too. It is true that in the end is the beginning. The couple Connie-Mellors is the last variation on the central theme of the problematic balance already present in *Sons and Lovers* between the man of instinct and the lady. The theme is also developed in two other early works, *The White Peacock* and "The Shades of Spring," which feature gamekeepers who are the prototypes of Parkin and Mellors. The evolution of Mellors from version one to versions two and three, which to a certain extent erases the social and cultural differences between the gamekeeper and the lady, may be interpreted at once as an effort to reach greater verisimilitude and a desire to lessen the gap between the mythical pattern and the social realism. But even then, the open end of the novel, Mellors's gloomy predictions as well as his jokes, his withdrawal, and the lack of certainty about the future cast doubt on the credibility of the myth and Lawrence's apparent act of faith.

I would like to offer one last example of Lawrence's wavering between affirmation and skepticism, which makes for the complexity of the novel and the fascinating instability of its meaning.[9] *Lady Chatterley* contains a famous didactic statement about the function of the novel included rather artificially within Connie's stream of consciousness as a warning to the reader: "here lies the vast importance of the novel, properly handled. It can inform and lead into new places the flow of our sympathetic consciousness, and it can lead our sympathy away in recoil from things gone dead" (101). But Connie has just railed against Clifford's habit of quoting from his favorite authors, angrily expressing her distrust of literature: "How she hated words, always coming between her and life . . . : ready-made words and phrases sucking all the life-sap out of living things" (93). The ethical project which might have been the foundation of a modern myth is somewhat shattered by this tragic questioning of the validity of a lifetime devotion to words—words that suck "all the life-sap out of living things," words that come ready-made and are so hard to fill with new meanings.[10]

Lawrence had already asserted in *The Boy in the Bush*: "Vision is no good. It is no good seeing anymore. And words are no good. It is useless to talk. We must communicate with the arrows of sightless, wordless knowledge, as Jack communicated with his horse, by a pressure of the thighs and knees" (*BB* 341–42). Even if it contains a lot of chatter,[11] *Lady Chatterley's Lover* conveys some sort of "sightless, wordless knowledge"—a potential supplement of meaning[12]—through a tale which tries to reconcile utopian dreams with down-to-earth realism, and the myth of a pagan paradise regained with the story of the irretrievable loss of mythical vision in our modern world.

## NOTES

1. See Jonathan D. Culler, *On Deconstruction: Theory and Criticism after Structuralism*: "The implications of deconstruction for literary study must be inferred, but it is not clear how such inferences are to be made" (180). See also Jacques Derrida, *Positions*: "Reading is a transformation process. . . . But this transformation does not operate at random. It requires reading protocols. And why shouldn't I confess it frankly: I have not yet found any which satisfy me" (86; my translation).

2. Deconstruction, as originally conceived by Derrida, is basically a philosophical strategy built on a critique of Western metaphysics and of the belief in truth, reason, or any transcendental signified.

3. At once God's word (see his poem "St John"), our Western metaphysics, and reason. There is also a violent criticism of Western metaphysics (the metaphysics of presence) and logocentrism in Derrida.

4. See Introduction to *The Dragon of the Apocalypse*: "And the images of myth are symbols. They don't 'mean something.' They stand for units of human *feeling*, human experience" (*A* 49).

5. Let us recall that for Lacan, the phallus is not to be taken literally as the name of an organ, it is the signifier of desire.

6. Cf. "It would take many years for the living blood of the generations to dissolve the vast black clot of bruised blood, deep inside their souls and bodies" (*LCL* 50).

7. The blacksmith, Vulcan—Venus's husband, not her lover—caught his wife with Mars.

8. This awareness of Lawrence's humor is a relatively recent critical trend. See John Bayley, "Lawrence's Comedy, and the War of Superiorities," in *Rethinking Lawrence*, ed. Keith Brown (Milton Keynes, England: Open University Press, 1990); Humour et satire." *Etudes lawrenciennes* 6 (1991); *Lawrence and Comedy*, ed. Paul Eggert and John Worthen (Cambridge University Press, 1996).

9. Michael Bell emphasizes that this is a typical feature of modernist mythopeia which "combines the life-enabling, unifying aspects of archaic myth with radical scepticism." *Literature, Modernism and Myth: Belief and Responsibility in the Twentieth Century*, 83.

10. In Greek, *mythos* is synonymous with *logos*, speech or narrative.

11. Joyce called it *Lady Chatterbox's Lover*.

12. See Derrida, *L'Ecriture et la différence*, 314: "Everything begins with reproduction. Always, already: that is to say, repositories of a meaning which was never present, whose presence is always reconstituted by deferral, *nachträglich*, belatedly, supplementarily" (314; my translation).

## WORKS CITED

Barthes, Roland. *Mythologies*. Paris: Éditions du Seuil, 1957.

Bell, Michael. *D. H. Lawrence: Language and Being*. Cambridge: Cambridge University Press, 1992.

———. *Literature, Modernism and Myth: Belief and Responsibility in the Twentieth Century*. Cambridge: Cambridge University Press, 1997.

Culler, Jonathan D. *On Deconstruction: Theory and Criticism after Structuralism*. London:Routledge, 1983.

Derrida, Jacques. *De la grammatologie*. Paris: Les Éditions de Minuit, 1967.

———. *L'Écriture et la différence*. Paris: Seuil, 1967.

———. "La Mythologie blanche." In *Marges de la philosophie*. Paris: Les Éditions de Minuit, 1972.

———. *Positions*. Paris: Les Éditions de Minuit, 1972.

Girard, René. *Violence and the Sacred*. Translated by Patrick Gregory. Baltimore: Johns Hopkins University Press, 1977.

Malraux, André. Preface to *L'Amant de Lady Chatterley*. Translated by Charles K. Colhoun. In *D. H. Lawrence: The Critical Heritage*, edited by R. P. Draper. London: Routledge, 1970.

Murry, John Middleton. Review of *Lady Chatterley's Lover* in the *Adelphi*, June 1929. In *D. H. Lawrence: The Critical Heritage*, edited by R. P. Draper. London: Routledge, 1970.

Squires, Michael and Dennis Jackson, eds. *D. H. Lawrence's Lady: A New Look at "Lady Chatterley's Lover."* Athens: University of Georgia Press, 1985.

# Contributors

KEITH CUSHMAN (Professor of English, University of North Carolina at Greensboro). Author or editor of five previous books about Lawrence, including *D. H. Lawrence at Work* and an edition of Lawrence's *Memoir of Maurice Magnus*. Past President of the D. H. Lawrence Society of North America. Associate Editor of the *D. H. Lawrence Review*. Recipient of the Harry T. Moore Award for Lifetime Contributions to Lawrence Studies.

VIRGINIA HYDE (Professor of English, Washington State University). Author of *The Risen Adam: D. H. Lawrence's Revisionist Typology*. At work on the Cambridge Edition of Lawrence's *Mornings in Mexico*.

EARL INGERSOLL (Distinguished Teaching Professor Emeritus and Distinguished Professor of English Emeritus, SUNY, College at Brockport). Author of *D. H. Lawrence, Desire, and Narrative* and *Engendered Trope in Joyce's "Dubliners."* Editor of collections of interviews with Margaret Atwood, Lawrence Durrell, Doris Lessing, May Sarton, and Rita Dove.

GINETTE KATZ-ROY (Professor of English, University of Paris-X). Editor of *Etudes lawrenciennes*. Recipient of the Harry T. Moore Award for Lifetime Contributions to Lawrence Studies. Co-editor of the L'Herne volume devoted to Lawrence and author of a book on *Women in Love* and many essays on Lawrence and other modern writers. At work on a new French translation of *The Plumed Serpent*.

KYOKO KAY KONDO (Professor of English, Chiba University of Commerce). Author of *The Development of Form in D. H. Lawrence's Novelistic Art* (one of the first English-language studies of Lawrence by a Japanese scholar), four other books, and twenty essays about Lawrence.

HOLLY LAIRD (Chair and Professor of English, University of Tulsa). Author of *Self and Sequence: The Poetry of D. H. Lawrence* and *Women Coauthors*. Editor of *Tulsa Studies in Women's Literature*.

LAURIE McCOLLUM (Doctoral Candidate, University of North Carolina at Greensboro). Completing a study that reads Lawrence from the perspective of René Girard's anthropological theories.

PETER PRESTON (Joint Director of the D. H. Lawrence Centre, University of Nottingham). Author of *A D. H. Lawrence Chronology* and co-editor of *D. H. Lawrence in the Modern World*.

GAVRIEL REISNER (formerly Gavriel Ben-Ephraim) (Senior Lecturer in Interdisciplinary Studies at Tel Aviv University, Senior Lecturer in English at Michlalah, the Jerusalem College for Women). Author of *The Moon's Dominion: Narrative Dichotomy and Female Dominance in Lawrence's Earlier Novels* and many essays. His new book, *The Death-Ego and the Vital Self: Romances of Desire in Literature and Psychoanalysis*, is forthcoming from Fairleigh Dickinson University Press.

NEIL ROBERTS (Professor of English Literature, University of Sheffield). Author of books on George Eliot, George Meredith, Peter Redgrove, Ted Hughes, and narrative in contemporary poetry. Many essays on nineteenth- and twentieth-century literature, including Lawrence. He is currently working on a study of Lawrence, travel, and cultural difference.

CARRIE ROHMAN has completed a doctorate at Indiana University with a dissertation entitled, *Stalking the Subject: Modernism, Alterity, and the Question of the Animal*.

JUDITH RUDERMAN (Vice Provost for Academic and Administrative Services and Adjunct Professor of English, Duke University). Author of *D. H. Lawrence and the Devouring Mother*. Past President of the D. H. Lawrence Society of North America. Author of books on William Styron and Joseph Heller.

MICHAEL SQUIRES (Professor Emeritus of English, Virginia Tech). Author of *The Pastoral Novel, The Creation of "Lady Chatterley's*

*Lover,"* and *The Manuscripts of D. H. Lawrence.* Co-author of *Living on the Edge: A Biography of D. H. Lawrence and Frieda von Richthoften.* Editor of the Cambridge Edition of *Lady Chatterley's Lover* and co-editor of *D. H. Lawrence's"Lady"* and *The Challenge of D. H. Lawrence.* Past President of the D. H. Lawrence Society of North America. Recipient of the Harry T. Moore Award for Lifetime Contributions to Lawrence Studies.

JACK STEWART (Professor Emeritus of English, University of British Columbia). President of the D. H. Lawrence Society of North America and a member of the editorial board of the *D. H. Lawrence Review.* Author of *The Vital Art of D. H. Lawrence: Vision and Expression* (1999) and numerous essays on Lawrence.

JOHN WORTHEN (Professor of D. H. Lawrence Studies, University of Nottingham). Author of *D. H. Lawrence: The Early Years 1885–1912, D. H. Lawrence and the Idea of the Novel, D. H. Lawrence: A Literary Life.* Author of *The Gang: Coleridge, the Wordsworths and Hutchinsons in 1802* (Yale, 2001). Member of the Editorial Board of the Cambridge University Press Edition of Lawrence. *The Prussian Officer and Other Stories, The First "Women in Love," The Plays, Women in Love,* and *The Lost Girl* are among the books he has edited for Cambridge. Advisory Editor of the Lawrence titles in Penguin Twentieth-Century Classics. Recipient of the Harry T. Moore Award for Lifetime Contributions to Lawrence Studies.

# Index

273